MOBILIZATIONS, PROTESTS & ENGAGEMENTS

Canadian Perspectives on Social Movements

EDITED BY
MARIE HAMMOND CALLAGHAN & MATTHEW HAYDAY

ALTERNATIVES SERIES
Series editors Andrew Nurse & Robert Summerby-Murray

FERNWOOD PUBLISHING · HALIFAX & WINNIPEG

Editing: Brenda Conroy
Cover photo: Erin George
Cover Design: John van der Woude
Printed and bound in Canada by Hignell Book Printing

Published in Canada by Fernwood Publishing
Site 2A, Box 5, 32 Oceanvista Lane
Black Point, Nova Scotia, B0J 1B0
and #8 - 222 Osborne Street, Winnipeg, Manitoba, R3L 1Z3
www.fernwoodpublishing.ca

Fernwood Publishing Company Limited gratefully acknowledges the financial support
of the Government of Canada through the Book Publishing Industry Development
Program (BPDIP), the Canada Council for the Arts and the Nova Scotia
Department of Tourism and Culture for our publishing program.

Library and Archives Canada Cataloguing in Publication

Hammond-Callaghan, Marie
 Mobilizations, protests and engagements : Canadian perspectives
on social movements / Marie Hammond-Callaghan and Matthew Hayday.

(Alternatives series)
Includes bibliographical references.
ISBN 978-1-55266-263-2

1. Social movements--Canada--History. 2. Protest movements--
Canada--History. I. Hayday, Matthew, 1977- II. Title. III. Series.

HM881.H35 2008   303.48'40971   C2007-907024-8

CONTENTS

ACKNOWLEDGEMENTS

An edited collection is by definition the product of a collaborative effort by a group of people, and a great many people worked very diligently to make this book come together. This process started with the organization of the March 2007 conference on social movements held at Mount Allison University to kick off the Alternatives project. This conference could not have happened without the organizational and planning efforts of Andrew Nurse, the director of the Centre for Canadian Studies at Mount Allison. It certainly would not have been such a success without the invaluable efforts of Joanne Goodrich, who handled all of the administrative and on-the-ground organizational tasks to make sure that everything went off without a hitch. We would also like to thank the students who helped coordinate events during the conference itself: Devin Ashley, Katherine Austin-Evelyn, Harry Borlase and Angela Hersey. The conference benefitted from the participation of delegates from across Canada, including a large number of graduate students. This would never have been possible without the generous grant provided to the conference series by the Harold Crabtree Foundation.

This collection contains a dozen papers that were presented by participants at the conference. However, the final articles that are included here have been revised with the benefit of feedback of the other delegates and presenters at the conference. With that in mind, we would like to acknowledge the contributions of all of the individuals who presented papers — Laurie Arron, Sarah Beardmore, Michael Boudreau, Donna Chovanec, Dominique Clément, Angela di Nello, Marc Doucet, Lee Ellis, David Frank, Kyle Franz, Elizabeth Lange, Roberta Lexier, Ian McKay, Amie McLean, Ajamu Nangwaya, Richard Nimijean, Ryan O'Connor, Geneviève Pagé, Pauline Rankin, Judy Rebick, Larry Sanders, Nick Scott, Michael Temelini, Brook Thorndycraft, Hubert Villeneuve — as well as all of the individuals who chaired sessions and attended the conference as interested observers. Finally, we would like to thank Errol Sharpe and the editorial team at Fernwood Publishing for their hard work in turning this manuscript into the book that you are holding in your hands.

CONTRIBUTORS

Laurie Arron has served as director of advocacy for Egale Canada and national coordinator of Canadians for Equal Marriage. He is currently the executive director of the Green Party of Canada.

Matt Baglole is a PhD candidate at the University of New Brunswick. His dissertation centres on the means by which social movement activists in Halifax, Nova Scotia, launched campaigns for greater equality between 1960 and 1982. He has presented his work at numerous conferences and has taught in the Distance Education Department at Mount Saint Vincent University, the Human Rights Program at Saint Thomas University and the History Department at the University of New Brunswick.

Donna Chovanec is an assistant professor in Educational Policy Studies at the University of Alberta. She is most interested in research, education and learning for progressive social change. Her area of specialization is adult education. In her research, she explores the learning dimension of social movements. Her interests also include qualitative research, feminist and critical pedagogy and women's issues.

Marc G. Doucet is an associate professor in the Department of Political Science at Saint Mary's University, Halifax. He earned his PhD from the University of Ottawa in 2000. His research interests include international relations theory, democratic theory and global social movements. He has published articles in *Millennium: Journal of International Studies*; *Global Society*; *Contemporary Journal of Political Theory*; *Alternatives: Global, Local, Political*; and *Theory & Event*.

Lee Ellis (1949–2007) was a doctoral candidate in Educational Policy Studies at the University of Alberta, where he was conducting a critical analysis of human rights education. He was a long-time social and environmental activist committed to his work in numerous global justice organizations and he is sadly missed.

David Frank teaches Canadian history at the University of New Brunswick, where he is director of the New Brunswick Labour History Project (www. lhtnb.ca). He edited and introduced George Vair's book, *The Struggle against Wage Controls: The Saint John Story, 1975–1976* (Canadian Committee on Labour History, 2006) and is the author of *J.B. McLachlan: A Biography* (James Lorimer and Company, 1999).

Kyle R. Franz completed his BA (Hon) at Simon Fraser University and his MA at the University of Lethbridge, and is now working on his PhD at Queen's University under the guidance of Ian McKay. His current areas of research interest include the Communist Party of Canada and radical local movements during the Great Depression, particularly among the coal miners of southwestern Alberta and southeastern British Columbia.

Marie Hammond-Callaghan is an assistant professor in the Women's Studies Program and the History Department at Mount Allison University. She received her PhD from the National University of Ireland, Dublin, in 2004. Her research focuses on contemporary women's peace groups in Ireland and Canada.

Matthew Hayday is an assistant professor in the Department of History at the University of Guelph. His main areas of research deal with issues of public policy, English-French relations, federalism and identity politics in Canada. He is the author of *Bilingual Today, United Tomorrow: Official Languages in Education and Canadian Federalism* (McGill-Queen's University Press, 2005) and a number of articles on language policy, commemoration and Canadian political history.

Elizabeth Lange is an assistant professor in Educational Policy Studies at the University of Alberta. She teaches in the area of adult education and sociology of education. Her research interests encompass the theory and practice of transformative learning, sustainability education, citizenship learning and participatory democracy, and social responsibility in small business.

Roberta Lexier is a PhD candidate in the Department of History and Classics at the University of Alberta. Her dissertation focuses on the emergence, evolution and disintegration of the student movements at University of Toronto, University of Saskatchewan Regina Campus (now University of Regina) and Simon Fraser University, contributing to the literature on the sixties and to an understanding of resistance and rebellion in society more generally.

Amie McLean is a sama7 (non-Indigenous, Caucasian) woman raised in the un-ceded territory of the Lil'wat Nation. Witnessing firsthand the prevalent discrimination against Aboriginal peoples from a young age, particularly in the education system, made her highly aware of the vast race-based privileges she enjoys and eventually led to scholarship in Indigenous studies. This article is drawn from her master's research examining the dissonance between prevalent whitestream conceptualizations of Indigenous peoples' "special treatment" regarding post-secondary education and the realities that First Nations and Aboriginal students negotiate in their attempts to access and allocate education funds.

Richard Nimijean teaches in the School of Canadian Studies at Carleton University in Ottawa. His research focuses on the politics of branding Canada. His most recent article is "The Politics of Branding Canada: The International-Domestic Nexus and the Rethinking of Canada's Place in the World," *Mexican Journal of Canadian Studies*, vol. 11 (2006): 67–85.

L. Pauline Rankin is an associate professor of Canadian Studies and associate dean of research in the Faculty of Arts and Social Sciences at Carleton University. Her work focuses on the relationship between gender and politics, specifically on issues related to gender mainstreaming, state feminism and women's movements.

Nick Scott is a PhD student in sociology at Carleton University in Ottawa. He completed his master's degree in the same department.

Michael Temelini is an assistant professor in the Department of Political Science and lectures in the Humanities M.Phil Program at Memorial University of Newfoundland in St. John's. He teaches social and political theory and Canadian politics, and his research focuses on multiculturalism, federalism and Canadian social movements. He is also a frequent guest commentator for CBC radio news.

THE ALTERNATIVES SERIES

Canada is both a complex and contradictory society. In terms of values, Canadians set high standards for themselves. In practice, their aspirations often occasion fierce and intensely political debates. The Centre for Canadian Studies Alternatives Series is guided by the belief that ongoing debate on important matters of public policy enhances democracy and provides a basis for reconsidering Canada's aspirations as a political community. This series of edited volumes, part of the Centre's commitment to publicly engage matters of national import and promote public education, is intended to address key considerations in Canadian public life. The series promotes a re-evaluation of Canada's evolution as a political community and the factors that guided this process. It also reflects on the current status of Canadian society, economics and culture, and considers how Canadians might re-construct their nation-state to address their problems, meet their objectives and reflect their values. By promoting dialogue on, study of and consideration of alternative conceptions of Canada, this series contributes to a re-thinking of the diverse experiences and potential futures of Canadians. Among key issues this series addresses are social movements and alternative conceptions of Canadian political and public life, Canada's position in the changing matrix of North America, the cultural dynamics of Canada, and the scope and nature of Canadian national life. We invite readers to continue the dialogue needed to realize an alternative and better Canadian community.

Andrew Nurse,
Centre for Canadian Studies, Mount Allison University
Robert Summerby-Murray,
Department of Geography, Mount Allison University
Alternatives Series General Editors

INTRODUCTION

Marie Hammond Callaghan and Matthew Hayday

In the final decade of the twentieth century, protest activity and social movement engagement seemed to have undergone a rebirth, displaying levels of energy and vitality that had not been evident since the 1960s. Rallying around causes ranging from environmentalism to gay and lesbian rights to alter-globalization, a new generation of protestors took up the torch passed to them by their baby-boomer parents. Their massive rallies dominated media coverage, far outstripping the formal outcomes of world leaders' international conferences including the 1997 Asia-Pacific Economic Cooperation (APEC) conference in Vancouver, the 1999 World Trade Organization (WTO) meetings in Seattle and the 2001 Free Trade Area of the Americas (FTAA) summit in Quebec City. The advent of new communication technologies centred around the Internet created new forums for protest organization, as terms such as "flash mob" entered the jargon of social mobilization.

Some commentators, including Neil Nevitte, have argued that this new wave of protests was qualitatively different from those of a prior generation (Nevitte 1996: 84–85). While earlier protests centred around issues related to the distribution of wealth in the industrial West, and participants tended to be those excluded from the benefits of this system, newer protests centred on quality-of-life issues and post-materialist concerns. Others have disagreed with this typology of "old" versus "new" social movements (Tully 2000), contending that "old social movements" continue to display vitality and that the economic questions they raise continue to inform the "new" quality-of-life movements. In certain respects, the new culture of political engagement that emerged towards the end of the millennium was cut short by the events of September 11, 2001, which prompted governments to adopt radical security measures that restricted the freedom of action afforded to non-governmental actors. Nevertheless, social engagement on a wide array of fronts continues to proliferate, challenging the manner in which elected officials govern our societies.

But are these forms of mobilization, whether old, new or a hybrid of the two, having their desired impact on their societies? What lessons can we learn from protest movements and social mobilizations of the past? Do newer movements differ from those of the past in either process or outcomes?

How have globalization and international events changed and shaped the way that Canadian social movements operate? How effective are (and have been) social movements as agents of change? How does the Canadian state engage with and respond to social movements and civil society activism? Are there particular features of state-civil society interactions that are distinctive to the Canadian experience? Is there validity to the critique that social movement actors somehow lack legitimacy as the self-appointed "voices" of communities they claim to represent? Are the stated democratic values espoused by these movements borne out in their internal processes and practices? It was to consider these and other questions relating to social movement activity that a group of scholars and activists from across Canada met at Mount Allison University in March 2007.

The chapters in this book reflect some of the main lines of inquiry pursued at that conference. Organized by the Centre for Canadian Studies, the conference participants offered their perspectives on social movements, past and present, in Canada. This collection includes the voices of activists and scholars working in the fields of history, political science, education, sociology and women's studies, covering over eighty years of social movement activism in Canada. Despite the wide range of time periods, geographical locations and disciplinary approaches, a surprising number of themes repeat between the chapters, suggesting that we can learn much about how social movements have shaped society and about how these movements operate in Canada.

The first section of this collection looks at theoretical and structural dimensions of social movement activity. Marc Doucet examines the concept of democracy as it applies to the trans-national alter-globalization movement and asks us to consider how social movements acquire their legitimacy as social actors. Doucet engages with the complex chicken-and-egg dilemma of how social movements that stress the virtues of the democratic process can advocate on behalf of an alternative social order whose *demōs* has yet to be established. His chapter speaks to broader theoretical questions about representation and legitimacy of social movement actors who claim to speak not only for themselves but for others whose voices are unrepresented in the current liberal order.

The questions of who these social activists are and what factors facilitate their social engagement are addressed by Nick Scott. Using the Canadian data from the World Values Survey, Scott identifies a number of key factors that correlate to social movement engagement in Canada, including post-secondary education and left-wing political identification. His conclusions suggest that our understanding of the "typical" protest movement actor needs to be revised to reflect changing trends in Canadian political activism. Indeed, other authors in this collection also indicate that certain social movement protest activities tend to be the province of the political left, whereas political actors on the right end of the political spectrum have privileged other forms of engagement.

The question of whether new communication technologies have helped to spur social movement engagement is the subject of Richard Nimijean and L. Pauline Rankin's chapter. Using the Canadian women's movement as a case study, Rankin and Nimijean question whether new Internet-based technologies (IT) such as email and online discussion forums have revolutionized social movements as much as initial proponents predicted that they would. The authors offer a pessimistic conclusion, arguing that in the case of the Canadian women's movement, the Canadian state has remained resistant to social change. While communication with movement members has become easier, the less personal forms of interaction facilitated by IT may be disconnecting would-be activists from more traditional action-oriented approaches to social movement engagement.

Indeed, the liberal order in which Canadian social movements operate is a difficult one to challenge. Examining how Canada's Aboriginal communities have fought not only to gain access to post-secondary education but also to control the scholarship programs established by the federal government. Amie McLean demonstrates how the liberal order has constrained their freedom of action. McLean argues that as the government downloaded administrative responsibilities to First Nations, it simultaneously applied strict accountability provisions on how these programs were to operate. Paradoxically, this limited the possibilities to change how these programs operate, while at the same time removing the federal as the primary target for grievances. Concessions were made, but as Antonio Gramsci might argue, the hegemony of the liberal order largely maintains the status quo.

The second section of this collection contains a series of case studies that examine individual Canadian social movements in a number of different historical contexts. In the first of these articles, Kyle Franz examines a communist municipal government elected to office in Depression-era Alberta. Although Communist Party activity was illegal in the 1930s in Canada, Franz demonstrates how socialist activists were able to accomplish their goals by working through established political structures, putting the municipal government at the service of the workers of Blairmore rather than the industrial elite, and stymieing a provincial government opposed to their movement. His chapter highlights the potential for using the state to accomplish social movement objectives.

Questions of collaboration and confrontation between groups working for social change are central to Roberta Lexier's analysis of student movements in English-speaking Canada in the late 1960s and early 1970s. She explores how university professors and student leaders, both of whom sought to alter the entrenched governance structures of Canadian universities to make them more democratic, worked together to accomplish their aims. As she notes, there were limits to how far the professors were willing to fully support the democratization sought by the students, given the professors' greater power and attachment to the institutional structures. Her chapter echoes other studies of social movements that have shown that agents of the state and other institutions are often willing to collaborate with social movement activists to a point, yet resist a full-scale overhaul of their institution, which might threaten their own power and influence.

The state assumes a central role in Matthew Hayday's case study of how one social movement organization exploited Canada's system of federalism to accomplish its objectives. Hayday demonstrates how a group of parents lobbied three levels of government to obtain French immersion education for their children. His study highlights one of the key peculiarities of the context in which Canadian social movements operate — the availability of government funding to support the activities of lobby groups. In the case of the Sackville French immersion parents, support from the federal government helped the parents to convince the New Brunswick government to accede to their demands, overruling the local school board. This divided governance in Canada, as Hayday, Franz and Arron all note, means that social movements may accomplish their objectives by obtaining success with one branch of the state even as they fail to convince another.

In his examination of the English Speakers' Association and the Confederation of Regions Party in New Brunswick, Matt Baglole contrasts how social movement activity and direct political party activism were used to support the agenda of a right-wing, anti-bilingualism movement in New Brunswick. He argues that traditional social movement mobilization in support of the English Speakers' Association's objectives proved difficult for the organizers because of a political climate that constructed its viewpoints as bigotry. However, these same individuals believed, rightly so in Baglole's assessment, that it would be possible for voters to quietly support the movement's objectives in the privacy of the ballot box by voting for CoR-NB. His conclusions support Nick Scott's assessment that left-wing objectives were more likely to be the focus of Canadian social movement organizations, while right-wing activists have had greater success with other tactics.

The internal processes of social movements are the focus of Donna Chovanec, Elizabeth Lange and Lee Ellis. Specialists in the field of adult education, their chapter includes multiple case studies of how social movements — ranging from the Chilean women's movement to the global justice movement to Canadian environmental movements — can also be sites of learning and adult education. Indeed, they contend that the more successful movements deliberately include these processes of self-reflection and education into their work, not only to learn from their experiences but also to help train a new generation of activists. Influenced strongly by the work of Brazilian theorist and educator Paolo Friere, this chapter not only examines the internal workings of social movements but also highlights the transnational commonalities of the mobilization and learning processes experienced by activists.

In the third and final section of this collection, activists themselves relate their experiences of engagement with social movements. The first account was adapted from Laurie Arron's keynote address to the conference. Arron, who served on the board of Egale Canada and as the executive director of the Coalition for Equal Marriage, provides us with an insider's perspective on the struggle to revise Canada's marriage laws to include gay and lesbian couples. In particular, he highlights key strategic issues such as the importance of language, the need to comprehend and be respectful of the fears of one's opponents, and above all, "not letting the perfect be the enemy of the good." The debate over equal marriage also serves to highlight some of the institutional structures that shape Canadian social movements, including the courts and Parliament, and how rights discourse can be used to accomplish certain forms of social change using those institutions.

Writing about social mobilization activities which took place a generation ago, historian David Frank collaborates with activist George Vair to understand the dynamics of the New Brunswick labour movement. Examining protests against the price and wage controls imposed by the government of Pierre Trudeau, Frank and Vair chronicle efforts to organize a day of action in New Brunswick's largest city. This account of Vair's labour activism nicely complements the case studies of Chovanec, Lange and Ellis, since it is itself an effort to use labour activism as a site of social movement learning, a process Vair notes has characterized his life as an activist.

The final chapter in this collection provides political scientist Michael Temelini with the opportunity to analyze a social movement in which he directly participated. As an organizer with the Canadian Federation of Students, Temelini played a key role in organizing simultaneous coast-to-coast demonstrations against cutbacks to post-secondary education and the income-contingent loan repayment program proposed by Lloyd Axworthy, human resources minister in Jean Chrétien's government in the mid-1990s. With the benefit of a decade's hindsight, Temelini argues that this was ultimately a successful movement that managed to attract massive amounts of media coverage, forcing Axworthy to abandon his reforms. The success, he notes, came as the result of extensive planning, a disciplined message and efforts to collaborate with Quebec-based francophone student associations and labour unions.

Taken together, chapters in this collection suggest that there is remarkable continuity to the experience of social movement activism in Canada, even as values have shifted and technologies evolved. Underlying many chapters is the common thread of the hegemony of the liberal order (some in Canada would capitalize the "L"). In spite of a degree of support furnished by the Canadian state in response to demands from social movement actors, governmental structures and processes have remained remarkably resilient in the face of social change. Indeed, even as different branches and levels of the Canadian government have provided funding to social movement actors to enable them to lobby state representatives, they have shaped the types of demands made by these groups. The state is a key actor in each of the social movement case studies presented in this collection, and thus a thorough understanding of how it responds to pressures for social change is crucial to an understanding of why social movement organizations both succeed and fail in Canada.

Another critical area highlighted, explicitly and implicitly, in many of these chapters is the formative and interactive roles played by gender, race and class as well as national, ethnic and sexual identities within social movements. Feminist theorists in this field view social movements as "simultaneously political and gendered" both in terms of their "external contexts," reflecting how the dominant institutions of state and culture "influence the emergence and course of social protest," and their "internal dynamics," reflecting "how organizational structures, tactics and strategies" are fundamentally gendered and socially stratified (Taylor and Whittier 1999). While civil society resistances, protests and challenges to hegemonic social orders have received some serious examination over the last decade or so, there is still much to illuminate.

In spite of evident limitations, we should not discount the prospect for change resulting from social movement activism. Many, although not all, of the movements discussed in this collection had at least some of their demands met. In so doing, they helped to open the processes of governance and democracy to groups whose voices had hitherto been excluded. To succeed, they also had to deal with conflicts internal to their movements, wrestling with questions of process, ideology, identity legitimacy and strategy. Not all movements managed to resolve these internal tensions, and many crumbled as both internal and external forces mitigated against their ideals. Others opted to pursue alternative tactics when their social movement efforts failed. And yet each social movement, whether old or new, left or right, must tackle the challenge of mobilizing supporters around its objectives and determine how to engage with the state and society at large. We invite our readers to consider how these actors approached their task, the challenges they faced and how they have shaped Canadian society both over the past century and in the present day.

SECTION I – THEORETICAL AND STRUCTURAL PERSPECTIVES

CHAPTER ONE

WORLD POLITICS, THE ALTER-GLOBALIZATION MOVEMENT AND THE QUESTION OF DEMOCRACY

Marc G. Doucet

"This is what democracy looks like" was one of the most recognized chants heard at anti-globalization protest events during the last half of the 1990s. Captured in cinematic form through the famous documentary of the same name, the chant, made synonymous with the 1999 Seattle protest, illustrates the centrality of the democratic imaginary in the critiques and demands of the then emerging alter-globalization movement.[1] As the movement began to supplement protest events with social forums, this centrality was carried forward in the slogan "Another world is possible," introduced at the first World Social Forum (WSF) held in Porto Alegre, Brazil, in January 2001.[2] If one can identify a common thread capable of knitting the diverse and eclectic ways in which the political form of these "other worlds" are envisioned by the "movement of movements," as some have called it (Mertes 2004), it is undoubtedly democracy. Most of the subsequent social forums and protest events held around the world have carried the slogan forward, making it the signature statement for the movement. What both the chant and the slogan bring to light is how centrally the democratic imaginary operates within the alter-globalization movement and how this operation occurs at multiple levels. It not only informs the critiques and demands expressed initially through protest events, but it also widely populates the movement's internal organizational principles and the imaginaries that seek to envision the other possible worlds articulated at the social forums.

My argument is that in making democracy a nodal point of its politics, the alter-globalization movement actually finds itself entering the foundational ground of much of modern political thought as it relates to efforts to theorize democracy. In so doing, it raises anew, and perhaps also in new ways, many of the same questions that modern political theorists often sought to resolve through the image of a *dēmos*[3] centred on the imagined community of the nation-state. At issue is the resolution of the fundamental theoretical problem of founding political legitimacy, which surfaces most dramatically whenever there is an attempt to inaugurate a new political order that claims to ground its authority in the image of "the people." The nature of the problem can be stated as this: in order to abide by the democratic principle of consent, and thus be democratic, any new order (e.g., "other possible worlds") would first have to be sanctioned by the people the order is meant to govern. But this consent cannot be given in formal or practical terms because the order that creates the new *dēmos* has not yet been created. In other words, how do we render democratically the shape of this new *dēmos* if we require the legitimacy of its authority *before* it comes into being? The new *dēmos* can only come as the result of a process that it cannot authorize and legitimate, because it does not yet exist. The crux of the discourse of democracy — that power must find its formal moorings in the image of a *dēmos* in order to be legitimate — leads the alter-globalization movement into the irresolvable problem, or *aporia*, of the democratic political form. The "other possible worlds" cannot be inaugurated without undermining the very democratic principles upon which such "worlds" are to be founded. In using the discourse of democracy as a central nodal point, the alter-globalization movement is thus caught in a fundamental disjuncture between itself and its narrative of the legitimate source of political power and authority.

The objective of this chapter is to explore how democracy's irresolvable problem of foundation relates to the alter-globalization movement. However, my intent is not to critique the movement's democratic claims in order to provide ammunition for those who would argue that the movement fails the test of democratic legitimacy because it operates without consent. To be clear, the irresolvable problem of democracy is not limited to the alter-globalization movement. As I have shown elsewhere, it lies with the particular symbolic order that democracy's political form seeks to render (i.e., power and authority grounded within an image of "the people"), and it is a problem that becomes most apparent whenever efforts to theorize the inauguration of new forms of democracy are ventured (Doucet 2005a). Nor is my intent limited to merely highlighting how this problem relates to the alter-globalization movement. Rather, the second but related layer of the argument I advance here is that the irresolvable problem of democracy offers a vantage point from which we can theorize the relationship between the political contestation social movements are meant to embody and potential transformations of the established political order that is the object of their contestation. A key element of this relationship is how the alter-globalization movement targets the global and international political orders rather than other levels of politics. Past social movements have certainly appropriated elements of the democratic imaginary to contest established political, social and cultural arrangements, but none have done so within the imagined space of international and global politics as directly as the alter-globalization movement. In doing so, the movement can be seen as producing its most significant political effect by opening the irresolvable problem of democracy within new political terrain in ways that past social movements have not.

The first section of this chapter seeks to flesh out the centrality of the democratic imaginary as it relates to the alter-globalization movement by examining how it operates at multiple levels. Second, I explore in greater detail the *aporia* of democracy's political form. Finally, I briefly outline how this *aporia* may be understood as creating a theoretical opening through which the appropriation of the democratic imaginary by the alter-globalization movement within the imagined space of world politics may lead to new possibilities. The issue here is the possibility of opening the way for housing the democratic imaginary within the imagined space of international and global politics.

DEMOCRACY AND THE ALTER-GLOBALIZATION MOVEMENT

A first key area in which the democratic imaginary appears in the alter-globalization movement is as part of its general critique of the contemporary world order. This critique charges that existing patterns and sites of economic, technological, cultural and political globalization are not only undemocratic but that they also contribute to undermining existing institutions of democracy wherever these are found. This position coincides with what many observers have labelled in broader terms the "democratic deficit" of globalization (Scholte 2002a, 2004; McGrew 1997: 12). This deficit is most often said to be the a result of globalizing processes that tend to restructure power transnationally and globally in ways that can undercut late modern democratic arrangements confined to the territorial boundaries of the nation-state. As has been laid out by the vast literature on globalization, patterns of formal and informal power have undergone a process of deterritorialization and reterritorialization that at times follow and reinvigorate old nodes of power (e.g., state and state agencies, international organizations) while also circulating through more recently formed networks (e.g., multinationals, non-governmental organizations, the Internet, global media). As with the alter-globalization movement, most scholars, ranging from reformist liberal and republican positions (e.g., David Held, Daniele Archibugi, Richard Falk and Jan Aart Scholte) to more radical post-Marxist and post-modern perspectives (e.g., Michael Hardt and Antonio Negri, Chantal Mouffe and Ernesto Laclau), agree that such transformations have the effect of circumventing established democratic formations. Most critics also go on to add that the democratic form is the only available political counter-solution to these developments.

From this initial critical assessment, greater democracy, often understood as stronger and more authentic forms of self-governance and direct citizen participation, then goes on to inform many of the proposals and demands articulated within the alter-globalization movement's discourse as part of its effort to map alternative worlds. For instance, in 2004 the eminent group of alter-globalization scholar-activists known as the International Forum on Globalization (IFG) published its second edition of *Alternatives to Economic Globalization*, which listed democracy as the first principle among the ten core principles they identified as central to any alternative to current patterns of economic and political globalization (Cavanagh and Mander 2004: 79). Members of the IFG wanted to answer the question levelled at them by proponents of the status quo: "if you are not for globalization, then what are you for?" (Cavanagh and Mander 2004: xii). Any answer, they argued, would necessarily start from the political principles of democracy since such answers could only come about as a result of "citizen movements [...] becoming more proactive in creating the world that can be" (IFG 2002: 1). Another notable example is the Hemispheric Social Alliance (HSA), a broad coalition of civil society groups, non-governmental organizations (NGOs) and organized labour, which came together in 1998 to mobilize and coordinate opposition to the negotiations of the now suspended Free Trade Area of the Americas (FTAA). In addition to participating in protest events, members of the alliance drafted a document outlining not only their critique of the FTAA but also the alternative world they envisioned in its place (on the HSA see Doucet 2005b; Massicotte 2004; Cavanagh, Anderson and Hansen-Kuhn 2001; Brunelle and Deblock 2000). The document — *Alternatives for the Americas* — was explicit. Critiques of the FTAA needed to move beyond protest by providing a relatively detailed account of the principles and actions that would guide what they understood to be a more just, democratic and sustainable process of economic development for the Western continent (HSA 2002). In addition to highlighting how the sectors of negotiations within the FTAA would merely continue to defend and enhance the narrow economic interest of large transnational corporations to the detriment of the vast majority of the Hemisphere's peoples, *Alternatives for the Americas* contained other sections that explored the central themes of the alternative world that was being championed, among which elements of the democratic imaginary figured prominently. As exemplified through the above cases, reinvigorating and reimagining the principles, practices and even institutions of democracy are offered by the movement as the necessary initial foundational ground to any alternative to current patterns of world order.

The discourse of democracy also informs the key organizational principles and methodologies of the internal decision-making of the movement itself. The master principle of self-governance, and its corollaries of self-organization and participatory decision-making, largely trumps all other formal models of organization within the meetings, discussion groups, debates and seminars held at alter-globalization events. This "democracy as a process" in addition to "democracy as an end" is perhaps most clearly articulated within the social forums. While there has been no shortage of critical commentaries written by the movement's activists (e.g., Sen, Anaud, Escobar and Whitaker 2004) on how individual forums or specific dimensions of the forum process have failed the democratic principles of openness, diversity, representation, transparency and accountability, others point out that if such problems emerge *as* problems it is precisely because of the centrality of democratic principles within the organizational makeup of the movement. Some of the activist-academic observers within the movement have argued that at the heart of the learning process which has marked the social forums has been the dominant objective of learning to be more democratic (de Sousa Santos 2006: 47-84; Teivainen 2002; and Teivainen forthcoming). Following this line of argument, de Sousa Santos has highlighted how the succession of world social forums has been marked by a strong internal labour of self-reflection that is guided by a desire to remedy structural and organizational deficiencies in view of rendering more faithfully democratic principles in practice (2006: 47–84). From this perspective, even the critiques articulated within the movement can be seen as part of a broad learning process of self-reflection and auto-evaluation that ultimately seeks to make the practices and processes of the social forums more open, participative, representative and hence democratic. In other words, while it is clear that internal decision-making and organizing can often be critiqued as undemocratic, for many observers, "learning to be more democratic" has been a key dimension of the movement's methodology and organizational structure. Because past social movements acting in the realm of international politics were most often guided by other discourses or objectives, notably the further expansion of human rights, the concern with the democratic credentials of internal decision-making processes was often less urgent, or at least could be deferred in favour of other political goals such as recognition of claims.

For some, the prevalence of democracy at multiple levels within the alter-globalization discourse highlights an important element of distinction with past social movements (della Porta, Andretta, Mosca and Reiter 2006: 241; and Smith 2002: 209). In addition to combining elements of what can be seen as the demands of "old" social movements around specific measures to address social and economic inequality for particular classes, and the claims of "new" social movements surrounding the legitimacy of plural and diverse forms of social identity/difference (Guigni, Bandler and Eggart 2006: 5), the turn towards the discourse of democracy within the alter-globalization movement can be seen as marking a return to politics. There is a clear sense that in mounting its challenge, the alter-globalization movement not only opposes specific and general globalized economic and cultural processes, but also envisions these processes and the world order they figure as "a constructed narrative, 'a political project which can be responded to politically'" (Shiva quoted in Bleiker 2002: 195). In this sense, the alter-globalization movement has arguably targeted the shape of the political sphere more so than past social movements, which have tended to be understood as focusing more squarely on the material demands or the identity claims of particular social groups.[4]

Since a significant dimension of the discourse of the alter-globalization movement maps its battleground as specifically global, this return to politics *via* the democratic imaginary may also be seen as part of a broader moment of politicizing the form of territorialized politics that has accompanied the modern nation-state model. One can identify here as part of the contestation a problematization of the inside/outside hinge through which modern statecraft has configured and legitimized its political order. This configuration has meant not only sequestering the democratic experience and forms of social and political contestation within the imagined community of the nation-state; it has also meant maintaining the imagined space of the international as one largely uncontaminated by the principles of the democratic imaginary (Connolly 1995: chapter five). The fact that alter-globalization protests and street demonstrations organized in parallel to the meetings of key institutions of economic global governance have often entailed a clash with the security fences and barricades lining the perimeter of official meeting venues serves to highlight in more dramatic and physical terms the manner in which part of what is being contested is the inside/outside line segregating modern politics. Attempts to pull down fences or confrontations with police lines may be part of the spontaneous dynamics unleashed by street protests, but they also challenge and contest the ability of the state to use disproportionate public order measures in service of securitizing zones for foreign officials (see della Porta 2006: 150–95). In many ways, the fences and perimeters outlining official meetings are authorized and sustained by the discursive imaginary of inter-state politics. These zones appear as miniature enclaves of the international, which then authorize an array of security measures and police actions within state borders that would be likely untenable otherwise.[5] One can identify then a borderland effect with these zones where elements of the law are suspended in the name of security. In challenging their perimeters, the alter-globalization movement is not only challenging directly the authority of the police acting in the name of the state, but also symbolically contesting the form of state territorial politics through which the zones are authorized.

Aside from contesting the security perimeter of international events, there are other obvious facets of this broad challenge to territorialized politics. While the role that new communication technologies can play in fostering the organization and mobilization of civil society groups across borders has been largely recognized (Bleiker 2005; Tarrow 2005b;

Warkentin 2001), it also underscores the multifaceted dimension that the contestation of borders has taken. Although the range and depth of its roots in most parts of world can easily be questioned, for some the Internet, as a vast and growing multipolar medium, fosters the material conditions that have been instrumental in generating transborder "horizontality" as a significant feature of the movement's politics (see the critical assessment offered by Nunes 2005: 301). From this vantage point, the virtual world of cyberspace has become instrumental in claiming real-world spaces within nation-states as connected to a global web of public spaces of contestation and protest. This web of public spaces can appear in the form of shadowing the meetings of the key institutions of global governance wherever they happen to meet — whether in fenced-in zones such as Genoa, Italy, in July 2001 during the G8 summit, or heavily securitized environments such as the World Economic Forum meeting in New York in January 2002 a few months after the events of September 11, 2001. It has also come in the form of the numerous internationally coordinated "global days of action" (see archives of Peoples' Global Action <www.agp.org> and Protest.Net <www.protest.net>), and it is reflected in the decision taken by the International Council of the WSF to internationalize the forums by shuttling its annual gathering to cities other than the first host city, Porto Alegre (de Sousa Santos 2006: 49). Following the analogy used by Chico Whitaker, the image that emerges is that of transversally connected public squares (Whitaker 2004: 113). Although concentrated in specific areas of the globe, they can nonetheless be envisioned as "nomad points" or "transitive spaces" in which the movement temporarily breaks to the surface in its labour of claiming the globe as a public space (Hardt and Negri 2003: xvii). In claiming these spaces, and organizing and acting within them, the alter-globalization movement's return to politics can be seen as further problematizing the territorialized political order of the state and inter-state system.

It is by triangulating its return to politics through the democratic imaginary and *via* a global web of public squares that the alter-globalization movement enters the grounds of the *aporia* of the democratic political form. As noted at the onset, this problem is brought to light most clearly whenever the foundation of a new democratic order is ventured. To recap the nature of this *aporia*, in seeking to inaugurate its "other worlds" how can the alter-globalization movement claim to be acting on behalf of democracy if the dilemma of this other world has yet to be brought into being and therefore can not possibly grant authority and consent to the world that is said to be created on its behalf? The following section seeks to examine in greater detail the nature of the *aporia* revealed by democracy's discourse on legitimate power and authority in order to isolate the opening it creates within the democratic political form. It is through this opening that we can understand, in theoretical terms, the manner in which the appropriation of the democratic imaginary by alter-globalization movement in its contestation of current patterns of world order may lead to new political configurations.

THE *APORIA* OF THE DEMOCRATIC FORM

The lack of democratic legitimacy of would-be democratic orders is obviously not new.[6] In historical terms, the process of creating modern democratic regimes was hardly democratic since they required "non- or even anti-democratic forces" acting "within and against undemocratic social structures" (Anderson 2002: 25; see also Näsström 2003). For modern democratic theory, this produced the uncomfortable reality that democracy's political order and founding political legitimacy could never be provided democratically. Early modern liberal and republican theories of democracy found a way of glossing over this problem most often by deploying the notion of an already existing bounded political space in which pre-established political communities could be theorized. Metaphors and fables of already existing sovereign nations or peoples could draw from a border effect in order to set the parameters of the *dēmos* while avoiding the problem that the people who counted as members of these communities had not themselves decided on the status of their membership. Neither did those excluded from the communities decide on their exclusion. By taking the boundaries of the political community as already given, modern democratic theory could then proceed with the business of theorizing a political regime where power and authority are grounded on the principle of consent of those the order is meant to govern while avoiding the issue that the origins of such a regime could not themselves be said to have emerged from any democratic process.

There are at least two reasons why such a sleight of hand would likely be untenable today. First, the inauguration of any new democratic order would have to theorize its transition from the old to the new order within the democratic imaginary. Contrary to the inauguration of modern democratic regimes that emerged from the *ancien régime*, the question of democratic legitimacy and consent are made all the more salient by the fact that the existing political order is marked by the dominance of the democratic imaginary over those of contending political models. Even though the current political order under patterns of globalization may suffer from a democratic deficit this does not obviate the fact that the transition towards new democratic arrangements would be faced with the need to comply with democratic principles. Indeed, the centrality of the democratic imaginary within the alter-globalization movement necessarily entails that any theorization of the transition towards other possible worlds would have to take place within the confines of such principles. As we saw previously, the alter-globalization movement has made the democratic form not only an end but also a means.

Second, as Sofia Näsström has nicely illustrated, assuming that the space of political communities is already given, which once served to side step the problem, is no longer possible (2003). Within the context of globalization, the inauguration of any new democratic order most often means starting from a position in which the parameters of community cannot be taken as pre-established. Indeed, one of the main consequences of globalization is to problematize in multiple ways the social, political and cultural foundations of such parameters. The question that unavoidably surfaces then is how we are to decide democratically where the boundaries of the community of any new democratic order will now stand? As Näsström shows in regards to how this same problem surfaces within theories of cosmopolitan democracy,

> before we can decide on a cosmopolitan understanding of political community, we have to face the prior question of who should count as the relevant citizens to decide this question. Yet this decision — being necessarily prior to the former — cannot be resolved by democratic process. It is itself presupposed by the democratic process. (2003: 824)

It would seem then that we are indeed at an impasse. In order to be legitimate, the inauguration of any new democratic order must summon a political authority figured as a *dēmos* that can only come into being after the new order has been created.

As William Connolly (following Paul Ricoeur) has argued, this problem illustrates the troubled relationship between the democratic form and the political act as such. He writes:

> A political act is legitimate if it reflects the previous consent (or will, or decision, or tacit agreement, or rational consensus, etc.) of a sovereign authority (a people, an elected assembly, a ruler following a constitution, etc). But, Ricoeur persuasively argues, no political *act* ever conforms perfectly to such a standard. If it did it would not be a *political* act, but one of administration or execution; because it does not, a political act always lacks full legitimacy at the moment of its enactment. It always invokes in its retrospective justification of the act, presumptions, standards, and judgements incompletely thematized and consented to at its inception. (1995: 139)

Within established democratic regimes, political decisions will appear legitimate because they can be seen as administered from existing institutions, practices and principles that have already gained the status of legitimacy through retroactive naming. But in the case of inaugurating a new political order the scenario is no longer the same. There is a temporal disjuncture between the political act of inaugurating a new political order and the standards of legitimacy that the order will rely upon because such an act projects into the future rather than the past.

Connolly's understanding of the political act points towards the earlier work on the foundation of democracy's political order by French political theorist Claude Lefort. For Lefort, the political act operates at the level of what he calls the "institution of the social" (Lefort 1989: 11; see also Doucet 1999; Howard 2002: 78; and Edkins 1999: 1–6). Lefort sought to define the specificity of the political as the very labour that institutes the social order in its particular form and renders it distinct from other possibilities. Thus, while the realm of politics in a given society is defined by a constituted or already established order, the political operates at the level of the constitutive, or generative, principle of the social order as such (Prozorov 2005: 81). In this sense, the political entails a return to foundational ground and to a virtual moment of an "originary decision" in regards to the manner in which the social order is configured in relation to what is necessarily left out by its configuration (Lefort and Gauchet 1971; and Labelle 2003). As Connolly noted, such a moment can never be legitimized using the standards of legitimacy set out in the political order being created because such standards can only come as a result of the order's inauguration.

Most importantly for the purposes of the analysis presented here, the institution of the social entails a general "*mise en forme*," or shaping of power, that is discernable through the political order's symbolic order. One can distinguish regimes by the form the shaping of power takes in the latter's symbolic order. Lefort's work is well known for having defined the particularity of democracy's symbolic order as one in which, contrary to the *ancien régime* which came before it, the figuration of power appears as an empty place, meaning that power can not be consubstantiated or made one with the image of a unified social agency. Although the image of "the people" appears to provide the basis for just such a social agency, when called upon as a guarantor of political legitimacy the lack of any positive or settled determinants capable of defining the precise content of the *dēmos* without simultaneously excluding certain social groups risks highlighting the degree to which the democratic imaginary rests upon the disincorporation (rather than the unity) of the social body (Lefort 1999: 189). Even though claims to power in modern societies invoke its name incessantly to justify all manner of political decisions, and quite often with great effect, the point is that the *dēmos* remains incapable of offering unconditional ground for political legitimacy precisely because it always remains open to a logic of counting that will unavoidably highlight plurality and division over unity. This central feature of the democratic political form is brought to light by the fact that periodic voting and endless polling, which are meant to translate the common voice of the "will of the people" can only take place through the atomization of the social body. Voting and polling illustrate in formal and institutional terms the deeper institution of the social inaugurated by the democratic adventure in which power must remain unfigurable as a unity. Rather, the image upon which claims to legitimate power are grounded will always risk appearing divided because the *dēmos* cannot render itself as "One."

This constitutive principle of the democratic form then goes on to institute a unique logic at the heart of the social order with regards to the manner in which claims to power are articulated (Laclau 2001: 10; Browne 2006: 43–44). Given that no unified or unconditional social agency can consubstantiate itself with power or make itself one with it, democracy's symbolic order ensures that the place of power ultimately remains unoccupied. In turn, this ensures that claims to power are never capable of securing with certainty the gap between themselves and the place of power. The institution of the social that is rendered by the democratic symbolic order installs therefore a radical interdeterminacy at the very centre of the political and social order in regards to the ground upon which claims to power are made (Mouffe 2000: 2; Rosanvallon 2000: 10). Rather than seeing this symbolic transformation as merely formal and unsubstantial, Lefort argued that it must be understood as the originary constitutive political principle that demarcates the democratic adventure from all other regimes (see Howard 2002: 78–80). Indeed, as its generative principle, the empty place of power is to be understood as the very condition of possibility of democracy's political form.

Democratic theory has often seen the *aporia* of democracy as a problem in need of resolution in order to safeguard the foundation of a political order in which a "we" is said to hold legitimate power and authority. In other words, the *aporia* is particularly problematic when the issue of concern as we explored above is finding a way of solidly grounding the political legitimacy of a new community in which its members, as a *dēmos*, appear to hold collectively the final source of legitimate power. There is, however, another side to the way in which this *aporia* relates to democracy's story.

The counterpart to the radical inderterminacy unveiled by democracy's symbolic answer to the question of power is that it brings to light the necessary relationship the democratic political form institutes with the possibility of contesting claims to power. In rendering the place of power unoccupable, democracy's symbolic order, through its own generative principle, holds itself open to contestation precisely because claims to power are incapable of making themselves one with a place of power that is necessarily rendered as empty. In this sense, democracy is unique in that it is the only political form that holds itself open to "otherness" as a built-in feature of its own order. Democracy's radical indeterminacy reveals a political order that always already contains the potential to transcend its own constitution. This is a constitutive feature of its own symbolic ordering of power. It is in this sense that we can see how, following Jacques Rancière, democracy's political form creates the "grounds for a claim" for those who have no status or voice within the established order, and does so as a necessary feature of its own shaping of power (1995: 47; see also Rancière 2006). It is this other dimension of democracy's story that allows us not only to understand the nature of the alter-globalization movement's political challenge but also why the democratic imaginary carries such potential vis-à-vis opening other grounds of contestation.

THE ALTER-GLOBALIZATION MOVEMENT AND DEMOCRACY'S *APORIA*

How can we use this reading of democracy's political form in our analysis of the alter-globalization movement? We saw earlier that in contesting globalization, the alter-globalization movement can be seen as having triangulated its return to politics via the democratic imaginary and through a global web of public squares. In doing so, it has contributed to bringing this imaginary into the space of the "international" and the "global," that is, into the space in between nation-states and the imagined space of a global community.[7] As this was taking place, what we saw emerging during the late 1990s and early 2000s was a counteroffensive — most often as a response to protest events shadowing official summit meetings — from some of the various nodes that network the globalization of power. Interspersed throughout the discourse of this counteroffensive, one can find attempts to marshal elements of the democratic imaginary in an effort to recapture the ground of political legitimacy made tenuous by the critique emanating from the alter-globalization movement.

Within the Western Hemisphere, perhaps the clearest instance of this effort came in the form of the Democracy Clause added by state representatives to the negotiations of the FTAA during the 2001 Summit of the Americas in Québec City. Formally, the clause meant that only democratic governments would be allowed to participate in the negotiation process. From the perspective of most of the activists and protesters gathered at the Second Peoples Summit of the Americas, held on the outskirts of the official summit, the Democracy Clause did little to address the substance of the democratic deficit of the FTAA negotiations. However, in broader terms, it symbolized at the time the battle being waged on the terrain of political legitimacy between the alter-globalization movement and state representatives. By introducing the clause, state representatives conceded that the battle of legitimacy for negotiating an international trade and investment agreement could no longer be fought in the language of neoliberal economic imperatives alone. Rather, there was a tacit acknowledgement not only that would the legitimacy of such an agreement have to be won on the field chosen by the alter-globalization movement, but also that the space of the international, in which the agreement was being negotiated, could not be excluded from democracy's discourse.

There are numerous other moments, chronicled through press briefings, official summit documents and leaders' declarations, when the democratic imaginary became an important feature of the discursive battleground between the alter-globalization movement and representatives of world order. State and other officials have often mounted their counteroffensives by claiming to be the true representatives of democracy if merely by virtue of their status as members, or representatives, of elected governments. These counteroffensives were often meant to appeal to national public opinion. At the same time however, one can also isolate in these strategies an attempted appeal to a *dēmos* that is ostensibly global, or at least one that is meant to figure a "we" that does not coincide with any single territorial space. It would be difficult to argue for instance that the appropriation of the issue of development aid for Africa by the G8, or the so-called Development Round initiated by the World Trade Organisation in November 2001, or even the poverty reduction strategies packaged by the International Monetary Fund and the World Bank were not initiated as attempts to formulate policy responses in issue areas first raised by the boisterous and growing protest of the alter-globalization movement during the 1990s. From an institutional perspective, such policies were likely motivated by attempts to shore up support among nervous member governments shaken by mass protest, but they were also public relations efforts targeting other constituencies. In effect, they were seeking to recapture some element of legitimacy in the eyes of a global (Western) audience.[8]

Along a similar tack, each of the Bretton Woods institutions have, to varying degrees, responded to the alter-globalization movement by further developing consultation mechanisms in an effort to integrate elements of civil society within their broad policymaking process (see for instance O'Brien, Goetz, Scholte and Williams 2000; Fox and Brown 2000; Scholte 2002b). Most assessments of these mechanisms have tended to conclude that this process has been marked more by window dressing than by substantial changes to institutional practices. Indeed, there is little evidence that such steps towards "democratization" have moved beyond the innocuous "stakeholder" and "partnership" approaches; nor have they remedied the domination of Western power within the institutions. That said, the salient feature of these developments for my analysis is that they were often meant to counter a crisis of legitimacy through solutions meant to be more "democratic." What can be seen as emerging from these responses as they relate to the protests mounted by the alter-globalization movement is, again, a concession that the democratic imaginary is part of the political battleground upon which the fight for the legitimacy of the global governance of globalizing processes would be waged.[9] Drawing from the reading of democracy's political order developed above, one of the potential lingering effects of this concession might very well be the sedimentation of the democratic *aporia* within what historically has been the autocratic structure of world politics. As we learned from mainstream international relations scholarship (e.g., Hans Morgenthau, Kenneth Waltz, John Mearsheimer), this structure has meant that political decisions were most often legitimated through a mix of *raison d'état*, real-politik and national interest that left little room for mounting contestation beyond opposing specific foreign policy decisions on moral and humanist grounds, as was the case for the anti-nuclear and the international peace movement. By deploying the democratic imaginary a potentially different political dynamic is released. In bringing the democratic imaginary to the terrain of world politics and in eliciting a response that accepts, at some level, the grounds of the debate, the alter-globalization movement has engendered its most significant political effect. If the democratic imaginary were to take hold in the space of the international/ global, then the *aporia* might bring to bear on world politics a structure of contestation described in the previous section. To concede that the democratic imaginary is relevant to issues of global governance is to introduce within the dynamics of its politics a symbolic order in which power is rendered empty. Such conditions open the space of the international and the global to a logic of contestation that was absent prior to the emergence of the alter-globalization movement. In this scenario the alter-globalization movement can be seen as laying claim to ground in a political space in which, from the standpoint of the established order, it has no legitimacy to do so. It is this illegitimate "squatting" within the virtual space of world politics, *via* the democratic imaginary, that may in fact signal the movement's most significant political act.

CONCLUSION: THE *INTERREGNUM*

This chapter develops an analysis of the relationship between the age old question of democracy and the alter-globalization movement. I argue that the *aporia* that lies at the heart of democracy's discourse on legitimate power points towards a particular symbolic order that offers a way to theorize the relationship between the forms of contestations social movements are meant to embody and democracy's symbolic order of power. The unique logic unleashed by this symbolic order brings to light the constitutive relationship to otherness that democracy must hold as a feature of its condition of possibility. Bringing this reading of democracy into an analysis of how the alter-globalization movement has articulated its contestation of world order through a global web of public spaces offers a way of understanding the movement's political significance as it relates to transformation in world politics.

Where these transformations initiated during the 1990s stand in regards to more recent developments in world politics remains uncertain. As was made clear with the invasion of Iraq, it would be premature to overstate the potential political effect of the alter-globalization movement on the "hard core" of international politics. That the invasion went ahead despite the massive internationally coordinated anti-war protest in February 2003 serves to remind us of the nature of the *interregnum* marking contemporary world politics. While attempts by the United States and Great Britain to justify the invasion in fora such as the U.N. Security Council may speak of the need to gain a measure of international legitimacy, the fact that no U.N. resolution was passed condemning the invasion after the Council's approval was denied highlights the current disjuncture between the continued effects of the formal international system of states and the potential transformations in regards to the ground of political legitimacy for international politics put in motion by the alter-globalization movement.

Moreover, there is little doubt that the visible shift initiated by the "global war on terror" in the post 9/11 era towards disqualifying the political standing of forms of social and political contestation in the name of security has renewed the state's licence on reserving the space of the international/ global as off limits to expressions of dissent and protest. While the security measures and the dramatic show of force that marked the international summits in Gothenburg, Québec City and Genoa during 2001 had already signalled the start of this shift, it was certainly consolidated after the events of 9/11. At the same time that this retrenching was occurring, the contemporary moment has also been marked by a widespread triumph of the rhetorical purchase of the democratic imaginary, which has often served to banally justify, within and outside state borders, all forms of political decisions with little concern for democratic principles. As Pierre Manent has argued, this has meant paradoxically that democracy's victory has coincided with a profound depoliticization of political life that threatens to reduce to mere surface effect the very contribution that democracy makes to providing as a constitutive dimension of its own order grounds for social and political contestation (Gauchet, Manent and Finkielkraut 2003: 12–13). What these more recent developments bring to the surface in dramatic terms is that, while democracy's symbolic ordering of power invites contestation, it also tends to allow counter efforts by claims to power to seal over the opening it provides, ironically in the very name of protecting "democracy." As Lefort cautioned in his analysis of the democratic adventure written with an eye turned towards the world events of the first half of the twentieth century, one would be wrong to conclude that more democracy is *ipso facto* the result of a symbolic order which renders power as empty. He argued in particular how the totalitarian regime can be seen as one possible outcome. One can interpret this regime as inaugurating a symbolic order that sought to arrest democracy's radical indeterminacy through the phantasm of the image of the people as One with the party and the state. Given recent developments in Western democracies it would be difficult to argue that this desire to reconstitute the social body as One as a key dynamic of the political logics unleashed by the democratic form has disappeared.

NOTES

This chapter stems from ongoing research on the relationship between the political foundation of democracy and the alter-globalization movement. The main analysis presented here draws from published and unpublished articles. I would like to acknowledge the generous support of the School of Political Studies at the University of Ottawa, which granted me a position as visiting professor during the time that this chapter was written. I would also like to thank Andrew Nurse, Matthew Hayday and Marie Hammond-Callaghan as well as the other organizers and participants of the Mobilizations and Engagements conference held at Mount Allison University, Sackville, New Brunswick, March 8-10, 2007. Finally, I am indebted to Marie-Josée Massicotte and Michael Orsini for their insightful comments and suggestions on an earlier draft. As always, any errors or omissions remain the sole responsibility of the author.

1. During much of the 1990s, "the anti-globalization movement" was the preferred term used to label the mass of protesters that gathered outside the official meetings of the world's key multilateral economic institutions. More recently, and with the emergences of the world social forums, we tend to find more commonly among activists and academics the terms "global justice movement" or "alter-globalization movement," the latter translating the French language term "*les alter-mondialistes.*" The change reflects the recognition that in addition to organizing protest events, many of the activities of those associated with the movement have had as an objective the formulation of alternatives to current patterns of globalization. On the anti/alter-globalization movement see de Sousa Santos (2006); della Porta, Andretta, Mosca and Reiter (2006); Eschle and Maiguashca (2005); and Starr (2005).

2. The slogan is said to have originated from an article written by Ignacio Ramonet titled "There is another, better world: A need for a utopia" published in *Le monde diplomatique* in May 1998 (Teivainen forthcoming: 75). Within the context of the social forums initiated in Porto Alegre, "Another world is possible" quickly became a dominant theme and central nodal point in the discourse of the movement and was taken up by many of its leading activists.

3. As inherited from the Greeks, the word democracy combines *dēmos*, meaning "people" and *kratos*, meaning "rule." How we have come to understand the spatial delimitation of "the people" within modern democratic theory is overwhelmingly framed by the nation-state model. Given that this chapter examines the ways in which the alter-globalization movement may in fact be challenging this understanding of democracy, I have chosen use the term *dēmos* rather than "the people" as a way of disaggregating the democratic form from its conventional frame of meaning.

4. Of course, this is not to suggest that past social movements were somehow non or apolitical. Rather, the point I want to make here is that their politics were often articulated through other discourses such as human rights and did not target directly the form of the political sphere itself.

5. Consider for instance the financial costs of holding these summits, which have exploded since the alter-globalization movement started shadowing the key institutions of global governance. The expenditures for the G8 meeting in Kananaskis, Alberta, in 2002 was estimated to have cost $300 million Canadian. The 2000 G8 meeting in Okinawa, Japan, was estimated at $750 million U.S. In comparison, the 1995 G8 meeting in Halifax, Nova Scotia, was a paltry $25 million Canadian (see

G8 Information Centre, University of Toronto <www.g7.utoronto.ca> accessed November 17, 2006). The international character of these enclaves has authorized other exceptional arrangements beyond increased government expenditures on security measures. The November 2002 NATO meeting in Prague for instance, saw the Czech government hand over significant aspects of security operations to the Pentagon for the duration of the summit. Other measures such as "beautification" operations designed to remove homeless people, increased border measures, mass arrests and detentions, states of emergency and imposition of identity cards have also been used.

6. Elements of the following analysis draw from the argumentation in Doucet 2005a.

7. There are similarities between the analysis presented here and John Dryzek's work on "transnational discursive democracy" (2006). However, whereas Dryzek's approach draws from Habermasian critical theory, the theoretical orientation developed in this chapter is informed by a broadly defined post-Marxist and post-structuralist position, which seeks to pay greater attention to the relationship between democracy and power.

8. A measure of these changes is also reflected in the emergence of global public opinion polling, suggesting that accounting for such an opinion is becoming necessary for political decisions at national and international levels. Two notable examples are the Pew Global Attitudes Project and World Public Opinion.Org.

9. On the question of legitimacy as it relates to global governance see Clark 2003.

CHAPTER TWO

THE SOCIAL DYNAMICS OF CANADIAN PROTEST PARTICIPATION

Nick Scott

The irreducible act that lies at the base of all social movements, protests, and revolutions is contentious collective action... not because movements are always violent or extreme, but because it is the main and often only recourse that ordinary people possess against better-equipped opponents or powerful states.

Collective action becomes contentious when it is used by people who lack regular access to institutions, who act in the name of new or unaccepted claims, and who behave in ways that fundamentally challenge others or authorities. (Tarrow 2005a: 3)

If new social movements are fundamentally reorienting Canada's political process in progressive and democratic directions, we should see protestors not only articulating claims, mobilizing resources and creating identities, but also overcoming socioeconomic and political exclusion. To test the capacity of contemporary protest politics as an agent of political change and social justice is partly to ask: Are "ordinary" people finding political recourse in protest? Does the repertoire offer a political access point for the less powerful groups of society, or merely another method for articulating claims in the civic toolkit of the well-off? To address these questions, this chapter analyzes Canadian data collected in 2000 as part of the World Values Survey (wvs), which, along with sociodemography, attitudes and other practices, ascertains information on the protest behaviours of a nationally representative sample. I use regression analysis to identify the variables that help explain individual protest participation and to measure the relative usefulness of recent theoretical models in predicting its occurrence among Canadians. The results depict a complex social dynamic underlying multiple forms of Canadian protest that reflects similar inequalities to those observed in other contemporary forms of political and civic engagement; typical participants capitalize on high levels of different kinds of resources such as education and social capital. The chapter concludes, however, that a general pattern of secular and liberal values distinguishes protestors from other kinds of civic actors, which may associate the repertoire with the pursuit of progressive goals.

THE DECLINE OF DEPRIVATION THEORY

As late as the mid-1970s the dominant explanation for Western protest activity was deprivation theory. Articulated over a century ago in the pioneering collective action studies of French psychologist Gustave Le Bon, it attributes protest to the dangerous confluence of lower-class frustrations with the primal and dysfunctional urgings of the anonymous crowd (1895). Classic breakdown models built on this premise characterize protest participation as deviant manifestations of shared grievances (Van Aelst and Walgrave 2001: 461). Drawing on the work of Le Bon and American sociologist Robert Park, Herbert Blumer developed an influential lexicon within his crowd transformation hypothesis (1939), which suggested that "social contagions" infecting "milling" crowds in "circular reactions" and "spirals of stimulation" convert gatherings into dangerous mobs. Chair of the Illinois Division of Correction Joseph Lohman, for example, drew on Blumer's ideas when instructing Chicago and Louisville police forces on crowd management (Schweingruber 2000). Lohman, in turn, heavily influenced Ray Momboisse, a California deputy attorney general, member of the Riot Advisory Committee of the President's Commission on Law Enforcement and prolific disseminator of late 1960s/early 1970s mob sociology. Momboisse urged preemptive thinking: "A crowd is not a mob, but it can become one! Each crowd constitutes a police problem, and each, even the most casual, has latent potential for widespread civil disobedience"[1] (in Schweingruber 2000: 373).

The modern standard for deprivation theory emerges in the work of Ted Gurr. In *Why Men Rebel*, he argues that the "primary causal sequence in political violence is first the development of discontent, second the politicization of that discontent, and finally its actualization in violent action against political objects and actors. Discontent arising from relative deprivation is the basic, instigating condition for participants in collective violence" (1970: 12–13). Crozier, Huntington and Watanuki extend his account to its logical conclusion: the rise of uninstitutionalized, discontent-driven political action produces nothing less than a crisis of democracy (1975). By the late-1970s, however, characterizing all political protest as deprivation-fuelled threats to political stability became untenable. Critical shifts in the nature of contemporary protest observed in the mass social movements of the civil rights era, as well as widespread skepticism over elitist conceptions of democracy that denounced unconventional forms of participation, called for new modes of thinking. Barnes, Kaase et al.'s seminal *Political Action: Mass Participation in Five Western Democracies* (1979) was one of the first studies to systematically examine contentious public engagement hitherto lumped into categories of political violence or socially dysfunctional mob behaviour. Emphasizing the critical, expressive and participatory nature of modern protest, their account responds to five significant transformations within the repertoire.

First, postwar protest activity diversified beyond its traditional focus on revolution and undercutting the legitimacy of entire political systems and institutions. Historically manifested in the fraught last resort of repressed social groups staging tax revolts, attacks on symbolic buildings and officials, urban insurrections, food riots or worker uprisings, protests began to attract many reform-minded participants with little incentive to overthrow established systems from which they garner many benefits (Dalton 2005: 63). In an era of protracted socioeconomic security, protest issues broadened beyond material or bread-and-butter issues of survival to include objectives hitherto seen as frivolous or elitist. "Postmaterial" value priorities, such as self-actualization and quality of life, provided the impetus for a range of new political movements, from identity and lifestyle politics to environmental protection, altering, argues Inglehart, "the criteria by which people evaluate their subjective sense of well-being" (Inglehart 1990: 66). Postmaterial issues challenged older class conflicts for centre stage, contributing to, for example, the decline of social class-based voting (Inglehart and Welzel 2005: 104). Such issues did not replace socioeconomic concerns, however, so much as supplement them, resulting "in a general increase in issues generating protest" (Van Aelst and Walgrave 2001).

Second, protest has become institutionalized. Its expanded use within a wide array of reform-oriented campaigns entailed the standardization of civil demonstrations, petitions and boycotts into a transposable and legible range of legitimate tactics. "Protest marches that once outraged authorities in scores of local communities became so routine," as Putnam puts it, "that police and demonstrators became joint choreographers" (2001: 152). Institutionalization entails the professionalization and potential cooptation of mass movements once pitted against the "establishment," but also reflects the creation of citizen lobbies, advocacy networks and non-governmental agencies (NGOs) fuelling "a general increase in small demonstrations over highways, schools, neighborhood issues, and other specific concerns" (Dalton 2005: 67). Third, a set of response procedures for protest control have become similarly institutionalized. A violent "escalated force" style of protest policing made infamous at the 1968 U.S. Democratic Convention gave way to "negotiated-management," which sought to arbitrate protest permits under public forum law irrespective of speech content, formalize open communication channels between police and demonstrators, and employ arrests and physical force as last resorts (Schweingruber 2000: 380). Although the new model has by no means heralded the end of repressive police tactics — as Ericson and Doyle (1999), for example, detail in the case of Vancouver's APEC summit — by and large it has lowered the costs of participation (Della Porta 1999).

The fourth key shift in modern protest across the West has been its increasing prevalence. Recent population-based studies with longitudinal scope portray a far-reaching phenomenon: since the 1960s and 1970s, protest behaviours have become increasingly frequent in nearly all liberal, postindustrial societies, and rising proportions of citizenries are engaging in them (Verba, Schlozman and Brady 1995; Putnam 2001; Norris 2002; Dalton 2005; Gidengil et al. 2004; Nevitte 1996). Canada generally fits into this pattern, showing a net increase between 1981 and 2000 of 11 percent in the number of citizens who have signed a petition, 5.5 in those who have joined a boycott and 6 percent in those who have attended a lawful demonstration (see Figure 1). The slight dip in protest activity recorded by the wvs between 1990 and 2000, moreover, is contested by other surveys. The 2000 Canadian Election Study, for example, reports that 84 percent of Canadians have signed a petition on at least one occasion, 25 percent have joined a boycott, and 22 percent have attended a lawful demonstration (Gidengil et al. 2004: 135–36).

Finally, the fifth significant shift has been the normalization of the protestor. Scholars largely take it for granted that more kinds of people protest than ever before. Far less consensus exists, however, over whether protest has actually become more democratic or representative, or whether profiles of demonstrators significantly differ from the average person (Van Aelst and Walgrave 2001). Issues of "differential recruitment" have consequently become a central preoccupation in a body of scholarship "devoted to understanding the types of people who join social movements, the characteristics or circumstances that predispose them to become activists, the mechanisms that mobilize some, and the barriers that deter others from

Figure 1: Protest Participation by Cohort

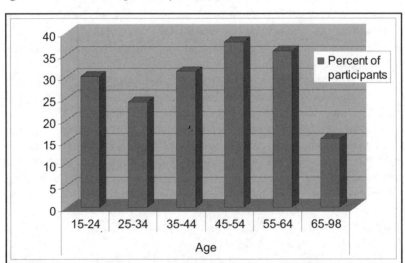

Source: wvs 2006, N=1918, Missing=7

participation" (Nepstad and Smith 1999: 26). Generally associated with the "resource mobilization" paradigm prominent in North America (see Jenkins 1983), differential recruitment is part of a larger research focus on processes of mobilization and the recruitment of individuals into movement organizations. This approach can be contrasted, for example, with perspectives that emphasize the role of political opportunity structures (Kriesi et al. 1995) or cultural processes of framing injustices and building collective identities (Snow et al. 1986). Discussions of differential recruitment and the normalization of the protestor (e.g., Gidengil et al. 2004) also resonate with the "contentious politics" approach, which views social movements as series of sustained interactions between power holders and their opponents (Tilly 2004); these approaches share the assumption that protest is largely manifested in visible forms of political action such as demonstrations and boycotts.

CONTEMPORARY MODELS OF PROTEST PARTICIPATION

Although differential recruitment has been the object of steady examination in the United States since the onset of the resource mobilization paradigm (McAdam 1992), very little attention has been paid to the same phenomenon in Canada. My analysis applies this approach with Canadian data, testing three theories of protest participation developed in the U.S. literature: biographical availability, strategic resources and structural availability. In addition to these models I measure the direct and moderating effects of other variables relevant to protest involvement, specifically political and religious values, ethnicity and gender.

Biographical Availability

One of the first post-deprivation models of protest participation, biographical availability, seeks to explain protest activity through the personal life-cycle constraints that affect people's availability to participate. The presence of such constraints increases the financial and temporal costs and physical, social and legal risks associated with activism (McAdam 1986: 67). Biographical availability is typically operationalized along four dimensions — marital status, parenthood, employment status and age. Citizens who have the responsibilities of a marital relationship, a full-time job, raising children or who are of an age where these responsibilities are more likely to be expected of them, are thought to be biographically unavailable. In other words, they face larger costs and risks and thus are less likely to engage in protest. Imprisonment or injury, for example, would deprive people of valuable time to care for partners and children, and potential activists may face negative sanctions from loved ones if their participation jeopardized family life and stability. Individuals who work full-time may have less time to devote to activism and stand to lose more financially if they do; employment may also raise the costs if co-workers or employers disapprove of participation in collective action, especially for people in sectors that oppose the goals of their protest (Beyerlein and Hipp 2006: 301). Age may curvilinearly relate to protest because of biographical availability (McAdam 1986). Younger and older people, free in youth or retirement from family and professional obligations and sanctions, are thought to have more time to engage and fewer alternative responsibilities than middle-aged citizens. The effects of these variables, finally, may significantly differ for men and women because of a gendered division of both paid and domestic labour, a point I address below in the section on gender.

In practice the biographical availability model has produced mixed results. In some cases protestors appear to be predominately unmarried students or individuals without children in flexible employment arrangements, such as the anti-nuclear activists interviewed by Jasper (1997). Schussman and Soule also provide survey-based evidence of the negative effects of parental status while controlling for other relevant factors (2005: 1089). The effects of marital and employment status, on the other hand, typically emerge as insignificant, with unemployment serving in some cases to depress participation (Schussman and Soule 2005; Van Aelst and Walgrave 2001). This likely reflects the trend that formerly contentious acts that ran the risk of arrest and/or jeopardizing careers and fulfillment of familial duties have become more innocuous (Della Porta 1999). Case study evidence on full-time employees in some inflexible occupations, in fact, has demonstrated that these individuals are more, rather than less, likely to participate in social movements (Nepstad and Smith 1999). Similarly, environmental sociologists identify a positive influence of parenthood on stimulating forms of environmental awareness that can lead to activism (Davidson and Freudenberg 1996). Student status continues in some cases to increase the odds of participation, but this may reflect access to concentrations of movement organizations, leaders and ideas on university campuses as much as biographical availability (Petrie 2004; Beyerlein and Hipp 2006). The effects of age, lastly, have been shown to contradict biographical availability. While some studies locate protesters disproportionately among younger cohorts (Dalton 2005: 71; Schussman and Soule 2005: 1089; Verba at al. 1995), most posit a curvilinear drop-off among both the youngest and oldest cohorts (Norris 2002: 202; Gidengil et al. 2004: 138–39; Putnam 2001: 164–65; Nepstad and Smith 1999: 33).

Strategic Resources
A more recently formulated theory of protest participation emphasizes not the life-cycle constraints that allegedly render people more or less available to protest, but rather the shares of human and political capital on which they are able to trade. According to the strategic resources perspective, the high levels of education, political knowledge and political interest presup-

posed by other forms of civic and political involvement, from voting to associational activity, also apply to protest. It predicts that unemployment, for example, will depress participation because the loss of resources that make involvement both feasible and desirable outweighs the gain in time or social freedom to protest (Verba et al. 1995). Similarly, it suggests university students disproportionately engage in protest not because of a dearth of professional or familial obligations but because their status reflects the attainment of cognitive skills and interests generally required of public engagement. The strategic resources model assumes that a principal consequence of normalization has been a shift of protest from the hands of socially disadvantaged groups to those wielding more power. Building on a growing body of evidence that suggests it is frequently the same people engaging in protest who participate in more formal activities such as political-party or interest-group work (Norris 2002: 200–02, Gidengil et al. 2004: 139–40), it positions socioeconomic status as an important explanatory factor.

Socioeconomic status, however, must be separated into its constituent elements. While income appears to have little direct influence after controlling for other resources (Beyerlein and Hipp 2006: 309; Schussman and Soule 2005: 1091), education has been shown to be pivotal. The robust, positive effects of formal educational attainment on not only protest but public engagement of *any* sort took shape in Verba et al.'s American Citizen Participation Study (1990), with subsequent scholarship adding support (Verba et al. 1995; Norris 2002; Gidengil et al. 2004; Dalton 2005; Inglehart and Welzel 2005; Beyerlein and Hipp 2006; Putnam 2001). By cognitively preparing and motivating citizens to identify and pursue their political interests in civil ways, in addition to opening up the networks through which they can do so (Nie, Junn and Stehlik-Barry 1996), education may comprise the foundation of protest participation; by some accounts, "education proves by far the best predictor of experience of protest politics" (Norris 2002: 201). Political interest in and political knowledge about public affairs, closely related to education, have been identified as further "critical preconditions for more active forms of involvement" (Putnam 2001: 35). Without the motivation to follow public affairs and an ability to retain a working knowledge of the key players and issues, citizens may be as unlikely to become protestors as they are to become voters, party activists or interest-group workers (Schussman and Soule 2005: 1091; Verba et al. 1995).

Structural Availability

A third prominent model of protest participation, structural availability (Schussman and Soule 2005), shifts the explanatory focus from the conditions rendering people biographically available and resources facilitating participation to the presence of interpersonal networks enabling recruitment into activism. Operationally speaking, structural availability encompasses organizational affiliation and participation. It builds on the robust finding that citizens rarely engage in protest unless first asked to do so by other engaged individuals and that such invitations are uniquely facilitated through organizational membership (McAdam 1986; Verba et al. 1995). What appears to be salient is not necessarily the *kind* of association involved so much as the baseline *affinity* that organizations create and, in an important sense, consist of. Members of the same mosque or church or temple, for example, sometimes rally behind issues not directly related to organizational goals; their ties constitute a potent and sometimes unpredictable avenue for mobilization (Schussman and Soule 2005: 1087). In this light one can, again, recast unemployment: rather than lacking strategic resources demanded of participants, economic disengagement may minimize the social ties reticulating people into mobilizable networks. "Isolation," Van Aelst and Walgrave argue, "is the most obvious reason for the absence among protestors of persons not actively engaged in the economy, resulting from a lack of formal and informal networks and mobilizing organizations" (2001: 471). Unemployment does not always, however, negatively impact participation. Specific protests, such as class-cutting mobilizations in Belgium against governmental and judicial failures to protect vulnerable children (Van Aelst and Walgrave 2001) and the anti-poverty and anti-free trade activities of the Metro Network for Social Justice in Toronto (Conway 2004), have attracted significant numbers of economically marginalized participants. Broad-based evidence is also mixed, with some studies highlighting a significant negative relationship (e.g., Petrie 2004: 567–68) and others recording no connection (e.g., Schussman and Soule 2005: 1091).

Whether loose, affinitive social ties or stronger, more participatory bonds are more important for engagement, however, is subject to debate. Moving beyond nominal "mailing-list" membership to active involvement may enhance recruitment possibilities by exacting more commitment from members and increase the potential of organizations to impart civic skills (Putnam 2001; Verba et al. 1995). Intense participation in a single politically contentious group, moreover, "might have a greater influence than being a member of three unrelated groups such as a book club or a neighborhood crime watch group" (Nepstad and Smith 1999: 35). On the other hand, protests and social movements rarely perfectly line up with one organizational structure. "More often," observes Tarrow, "formal organizations only imperfectly reflect the informal connective tissue of a movement" (2005a: 124). Elite-challenging actions also seem to thrive upon loosely knit but far-reaching civic networks in ways that elite-directed engagements, such as party involvement and voting, do not (Inglehart and Welzel 2005: 118). I study, therefore, both affiliation and participation, along with religious activity.

Religious engagement refers to a substantive subcategory of organizational activity and is singled out here for several reasons. Religious organizations, for one, furnish an uncommon "incubator for civic skills, civic norms, community interests, and civic recruitment," providing, for instance, "the organizational and philosophical bases for a wide range of powerful social movements throughout American history, from abolition and temperance in the nineteenth century to civil rights and right-to-life in the twentieth century" (Putnam 2001: 66–68). Rivaling education as a powerful correlate of most forms of U.S. civic engagement, religious participation has been shown to stimulate heightened rates of volunteerism in Canada as well (Reed and Selbee 2000, 2002a). Religion may even compensate for a systemic lack of other strategic resources depressing mobilization. Morris and Braine argue, for example, that religious frames and resources, having fortified large-scale oppositional movements in the past, "can also work to sustain the practice of more everyday democratic politics for those whose objective material situation makes them individually less powerful than the average citizen and collectively a distinct minority" (2001: 61). Scholars, finally, have also observed conspicuous links between the dynamics of new religious and new social movements in Canada (Hannigan 1991).

Values, Gender and Ethnicity

Several other factors outside of the biographical availability, strategic resources and structural availability rubrics are thought to be relevant for protest participation, specifically political and religious values, gender and ethnicity. Conventional wisdom several decades ago suggested protestors were a highly homogeneous population. It was "suspected by many that protests are usually carried out by a stage-army of mostly left-wing students of hirsute appearance who represent no one but themselves" (Barnes, Kaase et al. 1979: 58). Notwithstanding the unprecedented political mobilization of many right-leaning evangelicals and social conservatives over the last couple of decades (Putnam 2001: 161–66; Stackhouse 1993), protest appears to remain the tactical domain of the left (Dalton 2005: 73; Schussman and Soule 2005: 1091). Inglehart and Welzel advance an extensive framework in this regard:

> Both the shift toward postmaterialism and the rise of elite-challenging political action are components of a broader shift toward self-expression values that is reshaping orientations toward authority, politics, gender roles, and sexual norms among the publics of postindustrial societies. Postmaterialists and the young are markedly more tolerant of homosexuality, abortion, divorce, extramarital affairs, and prostitution than are materialists and the old, and this is part of a pervasive pattern — the rise of humanistic norms that emphasize human emancipation and self-expression. (2005: 126)

Younger generations benefitting from expanded education systems and socioeconomic security in their formative years imbibe progressive norms far more readily than older cohorts more beholden to the traditional, two-heterosexual-parent survival paradigm of the family. With the social and economic capital that helped shape these values, they are also more apt to confidently pursue critical or defiant forms of political action rather than defer to rigid and dogmatic organizational authorities (Inglehart and Welzel 2005). Consequently, protestors may also differentiate from nonprotestors in the lack of importance they attribute to organized religion.

The dynamics of recruitment into and experience of protest participation may differ significantly for women and men. Men may be more likely to be pulled into activism, for example, through formal networks and organizational connections and to take on formal leadership roles; women may more frequently be recruited through informal friendship or familial ties and take on pivotal bridging leadership roles (Kuumba 2001). Feminist sociologists also highlight how socialization and a gendered division of labour perpetuate social and economic inequalities that influence mobilization. An unequal division of domestic work in which many women take on a "second-shift" of household labour, particularly childcare, may make biographical constraints on activism outside of the home much more relevant for women. On the other hand, "[d]emographic characteristics like motherhood status affect women's ability to participate in movements in contradictory ways." While differential familial obligations structure time and opportunities for protest participation, "women's socialization into caring and nurturing roles in which they prioritize the health of their families, particularly their children" make mothers particularly apt to act upon specific environmental threats to their children (Tindall, Davies and Mauboules 2003: 912; Davidson and Freudenberg 1996). The net effect of such contradictory outcomes of gendered biographical constraints may be that women and men, despite socioeconomic inequalities and differences in the ways they pursue and impute meaning to protest, are equally prone to participate. Indeed, recent survey evidence (Petrie 2004; Schussman and Soule 2005; Van Aelst and Walgrave 2001; Gidengil et al. 2004) shows that gender consistently fails to significantly relate to the likelihood of protest participation.

Influences of ethnicity and race on protest likelihood, by contrast, may wax and wane on a group-by-group basis. In the U.S., for example, after controlling for strategic resources and structural availability the likelihood of protest among African-Americans has been shown to be statistically indistinguishable from that of majority groups (Petrie 2004; Schussman and Soule 2005); on the other hand, Petrie (2004) measures a significantly lower likelihood among Latinos relative to white Americans. Turning to Canada, Gidengil et al. (2004) found protest to be the preserve of the Canadian born, in particular those of European ancestry: "Among those of non-European ancestry, fully one-third have not taken part in any form of protest activity. The same is true of more than a quarter of those born outside Canada" (2004: 140). They suggest this may partly result from the undemocratic background of many newcomers to Canada who emigrate from countries where protest activities are banned, but could not speak to the potentially influential intersection of ethnicity with the resources and values associated with protest participation. The Canadian literature on protest is also reticent about the intersection of ethnicity and gender, despite strong evidence that such resources and values, as well as attitudes about the roles women and men should play in politics, vary significantly across different ethnic communities (Inglehart and Norris 2003). The biographical and resource constraints facing women in ethnocultural minority groups that delimit narrow public roles for women may be stronger than those generally facing white women.

HYPOTHESES

These frameworks for protest participation offer a number of hypotheses, which can be summarized in the following manner:

Biographical Availability

- Having children at home will reduce, if only marginally, the likelihood of engaging in protest.

Employment status will not significantly influence the odds of participation, except in two cases.

- Unemployment will marginally decrease the odds of protest and student status will significantly increase the likelihood, if only before controlling for educational attainment and number of organizational ties for which these statuses may be proxy indicators.
- Married Canadians will prove statistically indistinguishable from unmarried Canadians in terms of protest likelihood.
- Age will contradict the expectations of the biographical availability model. It will curvilinearly relate to protest with younger and older respondents showing significantly lower odds of engagement than the middle-aged.

Strategic Resources

- Years of formal education will exert one of the strongest influences on whether or not Canadians engage in protest. Each additional year of formal education will substantially increase the odds of participation.
- Both political knowledge and interest in politics will significantly increase the odds of protest participation.

Structural Availability

- Each additional organization an individual belongs to (i.e., affiliates with) will significantly and substantially increase the likelihood of protest.

+ Each additional organization within which an individual participates (i.e., performs unpaid work for) will significantly increase the odds of participation.
+ Canadians who attend religious services/ceremonies infrequently will be significantly more likely to engage in protest than people who frequently participate in religious services/ceremonies.

Political Values, Gender and Ethnicity

+ Individuals who place themselves on the left side of the political spectrum and who place little to no importance on religion will display higher odds of protest participation than respondents who place themselves on the right side of the political spectrum and place a relatively high degree of importance on religion.
+ Gender will show no significant relationship with the odds of protest participation.
+ Members of visible ethnic minority groups will show significantly lower odds of engaging in protest than white Canadians.

DATA AND METHODS

The data analyzed here was collected in the fourth cycle of the World Values Survey (N=1925), a nationally representative sample of Canadians eighteen and older at the time of interviewing (2006). Information on protest is provided in five "political action" items asking respondents whether they have signed a petition, joined a boycott, attended a lawful demonstration, joined an unofficial strike or occupied a building or factory for political purposes (for specific coding of all dependent and independent variables see the appendix to this chapter). "Participation" is coded as having performed at least two of these acts, which defines 29 percent of Canadians as protestors in 2000. Although some studies operationalize protest as engaging in one protest event (e.g., Schussman and Soule 2005; Petrie 2004), they are typically dealing with questionnaires that specify a time range within which the behaviour must have occurred (such as in the last one or two years), whereas the wvs data does not.[2] Setting the bar at two forms of protest also makes the important qualitative leap from those only having typically engaged in the relatively undemanding act of signing a petition to those having engaged in at least one other, more demanding form. Finally, I use logistic regression to model protest participation because I aim to explain the categorical distinction between those who take up the tools of protest and those who do not; logistic regression accounts for the binary or discrete nature of the dependent variable.[3]

ANALYSIS AND RESULTS

The logistic regression results are presented in Table 1. To begin with, the statistically insignificant coefficient for gender suggests that in Canada women are no more or less likely to engage in acts of protest than men. The result reflects a broad Western trend towards gender parity observed of other forms of political and civic participation (Gidengil et al. 2004). It may also reflect, however, the emphasis my protest measure places on overt public action and protest events. Feminist scholars propose alternative conceptions of protest that include "less visible protests within institutions and discursive politics" as well as "consciousness-raising, self-help, performative, cultural, and discursive forms of resistance oriented to cultural and social change" (Staggenborg and Taylor 2005: 46). Staggenborg argues (2001: 508), for example, while political demonstrations become important when women's organizations face significant political opportunities or threats, during slow periods cultural forms of feminism "perform an abeyance function for the movement insofar as women's movement culture spreads feminist ideology and creates networks that lead some individuals to political action." In their analysis of environmental activism in British Columbia, Tindall, Davies and Mauboules distinguish between political movement-supporting activism and "environmentally friendly behaviours" people incorporate into their daily routines. They found that while women and men were equally likely to engage in the former, women displayed a greater propensity to not only pursue conservationist behaviours but consciously link them to the environmental movement (Tindall, Davies and Mauboules 2003). "Visible" political action remains a critical indicator of protest participation, particularly as social movements crest in contention with elites or authorities. But understanding the gendered nature of protest participation may require attention to involvement in unconventional forms of protest including cultural, discursive and "movement friendly" behaviours.

By contrast, visible minorities, comprising 10 percent of the sample, are significantly less likely to engage in protest relative to the majority. After controlling for relevant resources, values and organizational ties they remain a substantial 70 percent less likely than white Canadians to engage in protest. Most members of visible minority groups in Canada are immigrants or their offspring, and a dramatic shift away from European sources of immigration since the 1960s saw their share of the population climb to 13.4 percent by century's end. The finding of their suppressed protest participation corroborates research showing lower levels of protest among those of non-European ancestry (Gidengil et al. 2004: 140). It also resonates with work associating members of ethnocultural minority groups to lower rates of voting and volunteerism (Tossutti and Wang 2006; Reed and Selbee 2000), and may reflect their systemically lower incomes and higher rates of poverty (Reitz and Banerjee 2007). The intersection of ethnicity and gender can be

Table 1: Protest Participation

Independent Variable	Biographical Availability	Strategic Resources	Structural Availability
Minority	-0.98**	-1.04**	-1.19***
	(0.33)	(0.34)	(0.35)
Gender	0.13	0.17	0.18
	(0.12)	(0.13)	(0.13)
Gender X Minority	0.90*	0.70	0.85
	(0.41)	(0.42)	(0.44)
Employed Part-time	-0.02	0.08	0.05
	(0.20)	(0.21)	(0.21)
Self-Employed	0.43	0.29	0.29
	(0.23)	(0.24)	(0.24)
Retired	-0.18	-0.23	-0.25
	(0.25)	(0.27)	(0.27)
Housewife	-0.61*	-0.45	-0.42
	(0.26)	(0.27)	(0.27)
Student	0.16	0.03	0.02
	(0.31)	(0.32)	(0.33)
Unemployed	-0.48	-0.39	-0.28
	(0.26)	(0.27)	(0.27)
Generation Y	0.28	0.46*	0.49*
	(0.22)	(0.22)	(0.23)
Late Boomer	0.50**	0.51**	0.45*
	(0.18)	(0.18)	(0.18)
Early Boomer	0.76***	0.68***	0.68***
	(0.19)	(0.20)	(0.20)
Silent Generation	0.91***	0.88***	0.84***
	(0.23)	(0.25)	(0.25)
Dutiful Generation	-0.02	-0.06	-0.05
	(0.32)	(0.33)	(0.34)
Middle	-0.79***	-0.60***	-0.58***
	(0.14)	(0.15)	(0.15)
Right of Middle	-0.95***	-0.93***	-0.88***
	(0.17)	(0.17)	(0.18)

Don't Know	-1.51***	-1.23***	-1.24***
	(0.23)	(0.24)	(0.24)
Marital Status	0.07	0.11	0.13
	(0.14)	(0.14)	(0.15)
Children	-0.15	-0.06	-0.09
	(0.15)	(0.16)	(0.16)
Religion Important	-0.59***	-0.54***	-0.64***
	(0.13)	(0.13)	(0.14)
God Important	-0.06	-0.02	0.04
	(0.13)	(0.14)	(0.15)
Middle Income	0.34*	0.09	0.06
	(0.15)	(0.16)	(0.16)
High Income	0.41*	-0.02	-0.16
	(0.17)	(0.18)	(0.19)
Missing	-0.21	-0.45	-0.48*
	(0.23)	(0.24)	(0.24)
Years of Education		0.16***	0.12***
		(0.02)	(0.03)
Politics Important		0.33**	0.31*
		(0.12)	(0.12)
Discusses Politics		0.54**	0.45**
		(0.17)	(0.17)
Follows News		0.47***	0.38**
		(0.13)	(0.13)
Religious Attendance			-0.45**
			(0.17)
Number of Organizational Affiliations			0.18***
			(0.04)
Number of Organizations Participating In			0.11*
			(0.05)
Constant			-2.55
			(0.42)

*Note: Numbers in parentheses are standard errors *p<.05, **p<.01, ***p<.001*
Source: wvs 2006, N=1869, Missing=52

observed in the interaction term in Table 1. In the biographical availability model the term proves significant, suggesting net of other biographical availability variables, political values and income the odds that Canadian women of minority status will protest are significantly lower than that of male minorities. However, this effect becomes insignificant after controlling for educational attainment. Depressed participation among minority women, that is, appears to be better explained by their relatively lower access to key socioeconomic resources — specifically the human capital manifested in education — than the direct effects of either their ethnicity or gender.

Three of the four biographical availability variables — marital, parental and employment status — emerge as having very little to do with protest participation. In line with previous studies (Petrie 2004; Schussman and Soule 2005), the odds of married respondents engaging in protest do not significantly differ from those of unmarried respondents. It seems social obligations and commitments to partners bear little on the likelihood of participation and that the greater costs and negative sanctions thought to accrue with marriage are insufficient to countervail activism.[4] Departing from previous research that found parental status to negatively influence participation (Petrie 2004; Schussman and Soule 2005), however, no discernible effect emerges here. Parenthood appears to either exert no such effect on engagement or produces constraints that are outweighed by other factors. Unemployment also fails to depress protest participation, and, surprisingly, student status fails to increase the likelihood of such action. Both fail to reach statistical significance before controlling for education and organizational activity, suggesting they do not play a proxy role in spurring protest through their association with either strategic resources or structural availability, as has been suggested elsewhere (Van Aelst and Walgrave 2001). These findings are limited by the fact that the wvs asked Canadians whether they have ever engaged in certain acts of protest rather than whether they have recently participated; it is possible that some respondents were protestors before they became parents, married or changed their employment status. Nonetheless, that these factors all point in the same direction suggests that biographical availability may be irrelevant for protest participation.

Age influences the odds of protest participation in a significant but by no means straightforward manner. The variable is treated here categorically to compare cohorts that correspond to what are often viewed as distinctive generations, shaped by unique collective experiences, shared witness to historical events and technological, political and cultural shifts (Keeter et al. 2002). Substantially higher proportions of both baby boomers (35–54 year-olds in 2000) and their predecessors (born between 1935 and 1945) report participation. Thirty-one percent of late boomers, 38 percent of early boomers and 36 percent of the 55 to 64 cohort report having done so, compared to less than a quarter of Gen Xers (born between 1966–1975) (see Figure 1). Once we control for strategic resources and structural availability, the results tell a similar but more detailed story. Figure 2 presents the odds of protest participation broken down by age cohort after controlling for the other factors. (Gen X constitutes the omitted or comparison group, comprising the baseline odds or the line marked by a 1.) Here meaningful differentiation emerges among boomers: early boomers are 97 percent more likely to have protested than Xers, whereas late boomers are 57 percent more likely. The picture of the late WWII generation (55–64) becomes quite stark. Members of their cohort are two and a third times more likely to have engaged in protest relative to Xers. This gulf is substantial and comports with the (respectively) participatory and apathetic portraits generally drawn of these two generations (Keeter et al. 2002).

Little can be done, of course, to disentangle cross-cohort and life-cycle effects in cross-sectional analysis. The pronounced engagement among middle-aged cohorts, moreover, may be exaggerated given the open-ended questionnaire item on the timing of protest activity; older Canadians have had more time, for example, to accumulate the resources that may be important for involvement and may have only protested when they were younger. On the other hand, the age distribution illustrated here mirrors in many respects that of other forms of Canadian civic engagement such as volunteerism (Reed and Selbee 2002a), which Putnam (2001) has connected in the U.S. to inter-generational change. Inglehart and Welzel (2005) credit

Figure 2: Odds of Protest Participation Relative to Gen X

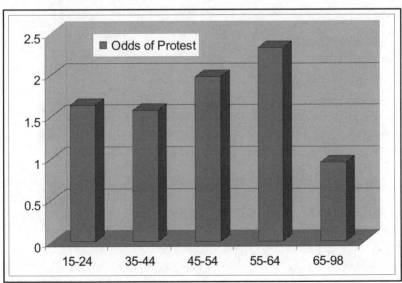

Source: wvs 2006, N=1869, Missing=52

similar cross-cohort effects for the recent spread of postmaterialism and self-expression values across many postindustrial societies, which closely relate to elite-challenging behaviours such as protest. Such an explanation may be plausible here. Precisely those lifecourse events referred to in lifecycle explanations — getting married, finding employment, having children — were entered as biographical availability indicators and proved insignificant. If this is the case, if some amount of inter-generational change is driving recent rises in Canadian protest, Generation Y (born between 1976–1985) may show some promise. Thirty percent report involvement, 6 more points than Gen Xers. Controlling for all other factors their odds of protesting are 63 percent higher than those of Gen X. This modest difference may be of more substantial importance given the cohort's disadvantage relative to other generations, who have had more time to amass the human, social and political capital demanded by participation. Indeed, this may explain why the cohort only becomes significantly different after controlling for these factors (see Table 1). As members of this young generation accumulate these resources over time we may witness the rise of a second wave in the age distribution of Canadian protest on the heels of a trough laid by Gen X.

Like ethnicity and age, political and religious values exert a significant influence on the likelihood of protest. They do so across the three separately entered models, suggesting effects independent of education and organizational participation. Looking to Figure 3, nearly half (48 percent) of Canadian

Figure 3: Protest Participation by Political Orientation

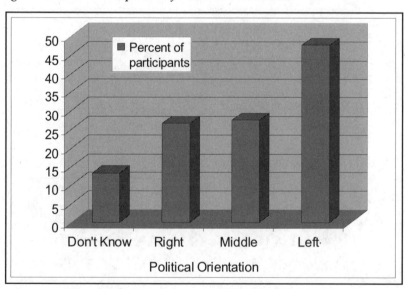

Source: WVS 2006, N=1925, Missing=0

adults who place themselves on the left side of the political spectrum report engagement, compared to 27 percent of those who identify with the middle and the same proportion of those who identify with the right. Interestingly, those who do not know where to place themselves constitute the group most disengaged from this repertoire, with little more than an eighth (13 percent) reporting participation. Once resources and structural availability are held constant, moreover, the pattern becomes even more linear. As Figure 4 illustrates, respondents in the middle and on the right remain quite distinct from those on the left, while differentiating from one another, proving, respectively, 44 percent and 58 percent less likely to engage in protest net of all other variables. Those who are unable to identify themselves, once again, comprise the most reticent of all the categories. Their relative odds of participation are .288, meaning they are 71 percent less likely to protest than those on the left.

As hypothesized, Canadians who place a high degree of importance on organized religion prove significantly less likely to engage in protest than their compatriots who place little to no importance on religion. Net of all other factors they are, in fact, about half (47 percent) as likely, suggesting a substantial negative influence of what could be said to constitute "social religiosity." This stands in contrast to the effects of the importance with which respondents hold God in their own life: those for whom God is of very high importance are statistically indistinguishable from those for whom God is unimportant. This variable was included to account for a more personal

Figure 4: Odds of Protest Participation by
Political Disposition Relative to Leftists

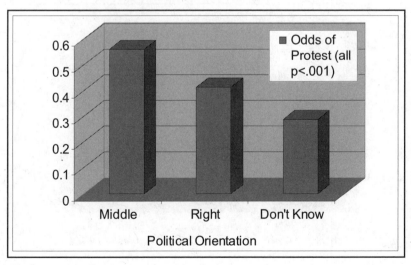

Source: wvs 2006, N=1869, Missing=52

and individualistic dimension of religiosity, and its insignificance is telling. Canadian protestors may disproportionately hail from the secular ranks of those who perceive religious institutions to have less political or social import than they once had — but this is not to suggest they are an atypically atheistic population. This subtle distinction resonates with the critical value system based on intellectual and emotional autonomy and skepticism of elites that Inglehart and Welzel (2005) argue motivates the actions of average protestors. The spread of elite-challenging political action such as protest, as aforementioned, arguably reflects a shift towards self-expression values that are both progressive and secular (126). Such values reduce the appeal of dogmatic and elite-directed organizations that militate against self-expression and critical thought, of which religious institutions may be prototypical.

In the first model presented in Table 1, we find that higher incomes marginally increase the likelihood of protest participation after controlling for gender, ethnicity and political values. After we introduce education, however, this effect disappears, affirming the importance of differentiating socioeconomic resources into its different components. When we parse protest by educational attainment (see Figure 5), we notice a clear, positive and linear pattern. While under a fifth (16.5 percent) of those who have attained less than high school and just over a fifth (21 percent) of those who have a high school education report engagement, the proportion moves up to 29 percent for both those who have partly or fully completed college. The spread then markedly grows for respondents with university-level training: 39 percent

Figure 5: Protest Participation by Educational Attainment

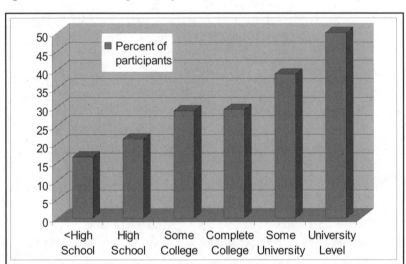

Source: wvs 2006, N=1913, Missing=12

of those with some university education and half of those who have completed their degree have protested. The ten point difference between college graduates and those who have started but have yet to finish at university, as well as the significant increase in odds attending university completion, suggests that university education plays a particularly important role in fostering the disposition to protest. Once we control for all other variables across the models, finally, we observe with some precision the strong and positive influence formal educational attainment independently exerts on protest participation: keeping biographical availability, structural availability and political consciousness indicators constant, for each additional year of education the odds of engaging in at least two forms of protest increase by 13 percent.

Political knowledge also positively influences participation. Before controlling for structural availability, respondents who discuss politics frequently are 72 percent more likely to protest than people who discuss politics occasionally or never, and respondents who follow politics in the news every day are 61 percent more likely than those who follow politics less often, although these relative likelihoods fall to 58 percent and 46 percent, respectively, upon controlling for organizational engagement. Political enthusiasm only marginally, if positively, influences participation, with those who feel politics are important 39 percent more likely to participate while keeping structural availability constant. That introducing organizational activity attenuates the influence of political knowledge and interest — a finding also reported for the U.S. by Schussman and Soule (2005: 1091) — suggests political consciousness, while retaining a direct, positive influence on protest participation, may be less critical than and, indeed, partially operate through, involvement in organizations. Ontologically speaking, organizations conducive to protest participation embody politically relevant discourse, or constitute in important respects a formalized or routinized way of consuming certain kinds of political news.

Finally, structural availability hypothesizes that by providing a baseline affinity for mobilization and facilitating recruitment to activism, organizational engagement will positively relate to protest participation. Regarding affiliation, this is exactly what we find. Keeping all other factors constant, including the extent to which people engage in any one organization, for every additional organization respondents were affiliated with their odds of protest increased by 19 percent. The influence of organizational participation, by contrast, is less pronounced. For each additional organization respondents performed unpaid work for their odds of protest increased by 12 percent, suggesting a weak, positive relationship. "Loose" affinitive ties, therefore, appear to play a relatively larger role than the "strong" ties of organizational participation, fitting Canadian protest into a larger "international pattern of social movement organization" based on "impersonal networklike connective structures" (Tarrow 2005a: 133). Putnam implicates the rise of such flexible structures over the routinized, face-to-face contact characteristic of old-style associations (e.g., Elks, the Boy Scouts/Girl Guides, the PTA) in the thinning or deterioration of social capital. Such affiliations, he argues, "provide neither connectedness among members nor direct engagement in civic give-and-take" and threaten to deplete our capacity for civil collective action (2001: 160). The rise in protest activities, however, does not necessarily indicate a degradation of social capital. Rather, some scholars argue uninstitutionalized, elite-challenging actions and the loose social ties of affiliation on which they typically subsist, although a qualitative departure from more intimate bonds, may nevertheless facilitate civil collective action. Inglehart and Welzel maintain, for example, that the decline of elite-directed forms of public engagement, such as voting and political party activity, and the dramatic rise of direct action across the West reflect "the changing nature of social capital: social capital has not eroded but has taken a new form, leading to changing types of collective action" (2005: 116).

The third dimension of structural availability provides an unexpected result. For several reasons one might try and positively connect religious participation in the form of regular attendance at religious services to heightened protest participation. Religious institutions have been deeply involved in many social movements (abolition, prohibition, pro-life, anti-poverty) and positively relate to other forms of civic engagement in which protestors are prone to engage in (e.g., volunteerism). Moreover, organizations such as the United and Anglican churches furnish resources and activists for all manner of progressive social activism and projects that resonate with the liberal values to which Canadian protestors typically subscribe. In a critique of contemporary "culture wars" arguments that define two internally consistent belief systems based on religious-conservative and secular-liberal values, Kniss and Burns point to the pluralist inevitability of cross-cutting cleavages: "Considerable sociological research... indicates that religion can [not only] provide a great deal of motivation, energy, and solidarity in social movements, but that the same religious tradition can have left-wing and right-wing manifestations" (2004: 707). Nonetheless, frequent religious ceremony attendance (weekly or more) *decreases* the odds of protest by a substantial 36 percent. In conjunction with the significant negative influence of social religiosity, the result is suggestive of a strong secular orientation among Canadian protestors.

CONCLUSION

The principal conclusion of this chapter speaks to the complexity of the social dynamics of Canadian protest behaviour. No one, or even two, models can adequately account for the diversity of significant factors that shape participation. Of four sets of explanatory variables — biographical availability, strategic resources, structural availability and values, gender and ethnicity — only biographical availability fails to play any kind of significant explanatory role.[5] Substantial support is given to the kind of resource-based model of political participation Verba, Schlozman and Brady posit (1995) and Nie, Junn and Stehlik-Barry's (1996) contention of a fundamental and robust link between formal education and the cognitive skills and networking opportunities necessary for democratic citizenship. Political consciousness and higher education consistently comprise the common denominators of a diverse range of public engagements. That they positively influence protest helps explain why it is typically "the *same* Canadians who are joining political parties, joining interest groups, and engaging in various forms of protest" (Gidengil et al. 2004: 139). Protest participation, therefore, presupposes much more than a mobilization of passions and lack of social constraints; it requires the critical capacity and will to identify and pursue one's interests in relatively democratic social structures whose accessibility, in turn, increases with high levels of human capital. One of the more interesting findings here supports such an interpretation: respondents who cannot locate themselves on the political spectrum are by a clear margin the least likely to engage in protest relative to those who identify with leftist politics. Simply by having the capacity to locate oneself *anywhere* within the general ideological scheme of things translates into greater odds of engagement relative to those who cannot. Education and political knowledge thus not only steer protestors towards critical engagement with postmaterial targets and issues, but, more germanely, help individuals constitute themselves as political actors with the power to produce concerted actions with public import.

Structural availability also receives strong support. Both organizational affiliations and participation positively influence protest involvement, with the former emerging as particularly significant. To better adjudicate between these two significant models and values and ethnicity, I calculated standardized logistic regression coefficients, presented in Table 2.[6] These coefficients reveal the *relative* influence of each variable by placing them on a common metric. A primary cluster of explanatory factors clearly emerges in education, organizational affiliations, secular-liberal values and ethnicity. A secondary cluster of variables with lesser but significant effects emerges in age, organizational participation, religious disengagement and political consciousness. Three salient details arise from this process of adjudication. First, strategic resources and structural availability are equally important in explaining Canadian protest participation, with indicators of both models figuring prominently in each cluster. Second, their combined influence is nevertheless insufficient: values and the ascriptive factor of ethnicity also play important roles. Third, that the primary cluster traverses sociodemography, values, and social capital speaks to, again, the marked complexity of Canadian protest participation.

Table 2: Standardized Coefficients

	b	Sx	Long (1997)		Menard (1995)	
			Sy	B	Sy	B
Education	0.122	3.012	2.183	0.169	5.800	0.063
Org. Affiliations	0.176	1.911	2.183	0.154	5.800	0.058
55–64	0.841	0.325	2.183	0.125	5.800	0.047
45–54	0.678	0.378	2.183	0.117	5.800	0.044
35–44	0.454	0.420	2.183	0.087	5.800	0.033
Follows News	0.380	0.474	2.183	0.082	5.800	0.031
Org. Participation	0.113	1.575	2.183	0.082	5.800	0.031
15–24	0.493	0.329	2.183	0.074	5.800	0.028
Politics Important	0.311	0.491	2.183	0.070	5.800	0.026
Discusses Politics	0.455	0.324	2.183	0.068	5.800	0.025
Gender	0.184	0.500	2.183	0.042	5.800	0.016
Self-employed	0.289	0.225	2.183	0.030	5.800	0.011
Married	0.126	0.475	2.183	0.027	5.800	0.010
Middle Income	0.063	0.484	2.183	0.014	5.800	0.005
God Important	0.042	0.483	2.183	0.009	5.800	0.003
Part-time	0.053	0.291	2.183	0.007	5.800	0.003
Student	0.018	0.195	2.183	0.002	5.800	0.001
65–98	-0.054	0.368	2.183	-0.009	5.800	-0.003
Parent	-0.091	0.444	2.183	-0.018	5.800	-0.007
Unemployed	-0.281	0.244	2.183	-0.031	5.800	-0.012
High Income	-0.164	0.425	2.183	-0.032	5.800	-0.012
Retired	-0.251	0.400	2.183	-0.046	5.800	-0.017
Housewife	-0.422	0.264	2.183	-0.051	5.800	-0.019
Missing (Income)	-0.478	0.320	2.183	-0.070	5.800	-0.026
Religious Attendance	-0.449	0.432	2.183	-0.089	5.800	-0.033
Middle of Spectrum	-0.579	0.499	2.183	-0.132	5.800	-0.050
Religion Important	-0.643	0.489	2.183	-0.144	5.800	-0.054
Ethnic Minority	-1.192	0.302	2.183	-0.165	5.800	-0.062
Right of Centre	-0.880	0.411	2.183	-0.166	5.800	-0.062
Don't Know	-1.245	0.344	2.183	-0.196	5.800	-0.074

Note: S denotes standard deviation; B denotes standardized coefficient (wvs 2006, N=1869, Missing=52)

The content of this social dynamic, however, mirrors that of other forms of public engagement in ways that present serious challenges to inclusive and responsive democratic governance in Canada. Specifically, as has been shown with civic and political behaviours from volunteerism and charitable-giving to associational involvement and party activism (Reed and Selbee 2001; Gidengil et al. 2004), protest presupposes high shares of human and social capital — on top of a peculiar social ethos borne of socioeconomic security. Taking stock of these wide-ranging social biases, Gidengil and her co-authors reiterate Schattschneider's classic observation: "the flaw in the pluralist heaven is that the heavenly chorus sings with a strong upper-class accent" (2004: 167). The close relationship between protest and associational activity further points to the polymorphic civic activism pursued by a cognitively mobile, middle-aged, well-educated and well-off class of disproportionately involved individuals. Rather than providing socioeconomically disadvantaged categories of citizens a channel to publicly express their interests, protest appears to provide more room in the repertoire of those already capitalizing on high levels of human and social capital with which they can make their voices heard. The intersection of socioeconomic status with ethnicity further challenges the representativeness of protest; minority groups are among those with the most acute need for multiple tactics with which to politically contest their relative deprivation but appear to lack such flexibility.

On the other hand, the general association between protest tactics and liberal values — a fascinating fusion of civic means and ends — presents uniquely progressive possibilities for Canadian protest. Contrary to "movement society" hypotheses that argue that normalization and institutionalization protest will pervade reactionary as much as liberal politics, the repertoire in Canada demonstrably remains the preserve of the secular left. Canadians who think abortion, homosexuality and prostitution are always or usually justifiable, for example, are all at least 15 percent more likely to protest than their compatriots who think they are always or usually unjustifiable, with the spread only dropping a few percentage points for divorce and euthanasia (wvs 2006). Canadian protestors are uniquely tolerant of deviations from the traditional, two-heterosexual-parent survival paradigm of the family, and draw attention to the uses of contemporary protest. "It is the *values* to which an activity is tied," observe Welzel, Inglehart and Daitsch, "not the activity as such, that makes a society civic. For it is the values that determine to which ends given actions are directed" (2005: 140). This is not to say that other modes of civic engagement are not motivated by specific patterns of pro-social values. Core volunteers and charitable-givers in Canada, for example, appear to be unusually apt to recognize a common good that they feel they have the responsibility to support (Reed and Selbee 2002b: 42). But insofar as Canadian protest connects elite-challenging tactics with the extension of tolerance and self-expression, it may provide an important counterweight to elite-directed and hierarchical modes of political participation that help perpetuate the established political order.

PRIMARY SOURCE

World Values Survey. 2006. "Four Wave Integrated Data File." *The World Values Survey Association* v.20060423. Available at <http://www.worldvaluessurvey.org/> (accessed August 15, 2007).

APPENDIX: DESCRIPTIONS OF VARIABLES FROM WORLD VALUES SURVEY 2006

Dependent Variable

1. *Protest Participation*: Coded 1 if respondents reporting having participated in at least two kinds of protest (29%, 0 cases missing).

Independent Variables

2. *Minority*: Coded 1 if non-white (10%, 0 missing).
3. *Gender*: Coded 1 if male (49%, 0 missing).
4. *Employment Status*: Coded as dummies (Student 4%, Full-time 47%, Part-time 10%, Self-employed 6%, Retired 20%, Housewife 8%, Unemployed 7%; 38 missing).
5. *Age*: Coded as dummies corresponding to 10-year cohorts (15–24, 12%; 25–34, 19%; 35–44, 23%; 45–54, 17%; 55–64, 12%; 65–98, 16%; 7 missing).
6. *Political Values*: Self-positioning on political scale converted to dummies (Don't Know 14%, Left 18%, Middle 47%, Right 22%; 2 missing).
7. *Marital Status*: Coded 1 if married or living together as married (35%, 2 missing).
8. *Children*: Coded 1 if reported having at least one child (73%, 5 missing).
9. *Religion Important*: Coded 1 if reported religion as important (61%, 5 missing).
10. *God Important*: Coded 1 if reported God as important in one's life (37%, 12 missing).
11. *Income*: Coded as dummies (Low/<$27500 31%, Middle/$27500-$62500 37%, High/>$62500, Missing 12%).
12. *Education*: Converted from categories to estimated years of education (12 missing).
13. *Political Interest*: Coded 1 if reported politics as very or rather important (41%, 6 missing).
14. *Political Knowledge*: Coded 1 if frequently discusses politics (12%, 7 missing).
15. *Political Knowledge 2*: Coded 1 if follows politics in news everyday (34%, 1 missing).
16. *Religious Attendance*: Coded 1 if attend weekly (25%, 7 missing).
17. *Number of Organizational Affiliations*: Coded as a scale of 14 kinds of organizations respondents were asked if they belonged to (0 missing).
18. *Number of Organizations Participating in*: Coded as a scale of 14 kinds of organizations respondents were asked if they conducted unpaid work for (0 missing).

NOTES

1. With scientific-sounding taxonomies and fearful depictions of a violent and voracious "crowd mind," Momboisse provided theoretical justification for the escalated force model of police protesting, which typically deemphasized First Amendment rights, minimized negotiation between police and demonstrators, and relied on police infiltration and massive arrests (McPhail, Schweingruber and McCarthy 1998).

2. The lack of a time parameter presents an important limitation when interpreting age and life cycle effects; the acts of protest participation to which respondents refer may have occurred much earlier in their lives when they, for example, were not parents or spouses. On the other hand, it bypasses other problems. Problems of recall are among the greatest challenges faced in survey administration. Even when respondents recall events in their life they often have trouble placing it in a specific time frame because of "forward telescoping," or the act of incorrectly recalling events as having occurred more recently than they did (Hall 2001: 519–20).

3. It does so by transforming probabilities into the natural logarithms of odds: the estimated coefficients reported in Table 1 denote the change in logged odds of protest participation effected by a one unit change in the explanatory variables. Because "logged odds" is not an intuitive metric, I refer to their values in exponentiated form as odds, which express the much more intuitive likelihood of an event occurring relative to the likelihood of an event not occurring.

4. An interaction term multiplying the effects of gender and marital status was included in a model not presented here, on grounds that women working a "second shift" or taking on the majority of the housework after performing a job outside the house might reasonably be expected to find less time and energy to protest than men. It proved insignificant, suggesting that this is not the case.

5. In contrast to findings from U.S. studies (Beyerlein and Hipp 2006), for example, married Canadians appear no more or less likely to protest than unmarried ones, and this pattern remains consistent across genders. To more closely examine the apparent insignificance of gender for protest participation, several interaction terms were included between gender and ethnicity, marital and employment status to test for multiplicative effects ill-captured in additive models, and they also proved insignificant.

6. Although no simple standard deviation exists in logistic regression for the estimated logged odds — "a transformation which represents a dependent variable without bounds and an arbitrarily defined variance" (Pampel 2000: 32) — a couple of options for meaningful measurement present themselves. Long (1997), for one, recommends calculating the standard deviation of the dependent by square rooting the sum of the variance of the predicted logged odds and the arbitrarily defined variance of the error term for logistic regression term ($\pi^2/3$). Menard (1995), for another, recommends calculating it by dividing the standard deviation of the predicted logits by the R^2 calculated by correlating the predicted probabilities with the dummy dependent. These techniques are not perfect; what matters more than the specific values of the standardized coefficients are their rank order, which remains consistent between Long and Menard's methods.

CHAPTER THREE

CAN MOVEMENTS "MOVE" ONLINE?
ONLINE ACTIVISM, CANADIAN WOMEN'S MOVEMENTS AND THE CASE OF PAR-L

Richard Nimijean and L. Pauline Rankin

In its thirteenth anniversary email on March 8, 2007,[1] the editors of the Canadian feminist listserv PAR-L (the Policy, Action, Research List) celebrated the listserv's important contribution to the Canadian women's movements by circulating information among women across the country. In particular, they highlighted PAR-L's key role in advancing a human rights complaint launched by feminist scholars against the federal government's Canada Research Chairs program.[2] Nevertheless, they also admitted to subscribers that it had been "a difficult year for women all across the country," due largely to the political agenda of Stephen Harper's Conservative government. In September 2006, the Conservatives cut $5 million from Status of Women Canada, the federal coordinating agency charged with promoting women's equality, and altered other programs that women's movements had historically relied upon to advance their claims, including cancelling the federal Court Challenges program. The following month, the Minister Responsible for the Status of Women, the Honourable Bev Oda, assured Canadians that "Canada's new Government fundamentally believes that women are equal." She justified the decision to no longer make funds from the Women's Program — the grants and contribution fund that had provided funding for women's organizations and equality-seeking groups since 1973 — eligible to women's groups that engaged in advocacy, lobbying or general research. Moreover, the mandate of the Women's Program would no longer concentrate on promoting equality but rather on "facilitat[ing] women's participation in Canadian society," a subtle but significant distinction.[3]

The PAR-L editors correctly noted that these and other developments reflected the "new" government's attitude towards women's rights. For example, the Conservatives temporarily removed the word "equality" from the mandate of Status of Women Canada.[4] Prime Minister Harper's 2006 and 2007 International Women's Day statements focused on the contributions of the government's "law and order" campaign to promoting the status of women. Not surprisingly, therefore, the current situation of women in Canada appears no better than in 1994, when PAR-L first appeared as a defensive measure in anticipation of further cuts to the "women's state."[5]

Perhaps unintentionally, the 2007 PAR-L anniversary message revealed the limitations of the new information and communications technologies (ICTS) as vehicles for social change, particularly when ICT usage replicates old tasks and orientations. In this case, a feminist listserv largely has replaced traditional phone and letter writing methods to share information and lodge protests. PAR-L can circulate information and news more effectively and rapidly; however, it also belies an ongoing orientation towards the state, characteristic of much of feminist activism in Canada. Thus, while we may have different politics because of these ICTS, we are not seeing transformed politics. Marginalized movements, such as women's movements, remain at the periphery of Canadian politics even with the advent of ICTS as activist tools, albeit in a slightly different form and context.

In this chapter, we use the case of PAR-L to examine the phenomenon of "listserv politics" and to analyze how these politics affect marginalized movements. Has this new tool, one of the many new electronic tools touted as a potential boon for social movement organizations, changed women's movements in Canada? Can the ICTS help the prospects of marginalized movements? We conclude that despite some benefits, particularly in the realm of information sharing, women's movements face barriers that transcend technology, namely the ongoing difficulties with mainstreaming a feminist message, promoting active engagement with mobilization tactics, and increasing resources, both financial and human, to advance women's interests.

First, we review the online activism literature and contemporary challenges confronting feminist mobilization in Canada. Then we examine the case of PAR-L, which demonstrates the value of linking studies of Internet activism to mobilization opportunities and outcomes for movements that already were facing profound challenges in the pre-Internet era. This case shows that we must revisit the early optimism expressed by Internet enthusiasts and cyber-feminists. A movement's ability to transcend significant changes in its operating environment (those produced by the new ICTS) can be affected by the state. The experience of Canadian women's movements reasserts the need for empirical studies when theorizing about crosscutting areas (in this case, women, politics, social change and technology), especially since much of the literature on the new ICTS, politics and social change ignores women.

ICTS AND THE CHANGING ENVIRONMENT FOR SOCIAL CHANGE

The widespread, rapid adoption of new ICTS in the 1990s reshaped the terrain for social change. Many activists believed that the Internet, the World Wide Web, cell phones and more powerful and affordable computing would help them articulate, organize and distribute counter-hegemonic messages and strategies, thus contributing to genuine social change.[6] Indeed, ICTs created new rules for protest and expanded possibilities for new strategies. Ayres (1999) speculated that a diminished role for geography could encourage longer-lasting transnational coalitions to emerge. Disruptive tactics for promoting change could become an accepted element of a social movement organization's "tactical repertoire," given their non-institutionalized nature. New technologies could encourage activism since activists would be able to circulate their messages in a timelier manner (Krause 1997). This would enhance internal group communication and democracy; as Kutner (2000) points out, the Internet allows activists to form a collective voice by connecting previously marginalized or isolated individuals.

The new ICTs significantly increased the repertoire of tactics available to activists, complementing traditional forms of organization, protest, lobbying and activism. Tools such as file sharing, email, listservs and flash movies allow activists to circulate a greater volume of information, in more varied formats, to wider audiences. Websites serve as clearing houses of information, publicize causes and provide fora for discussion. Consequently, new strategies of dissent emerged, including electronic forms of traditional lobbying campaigns (email and Web petitions), electronic civil disobedience, hacktivism[7] and culture jamming. Tactics include "virtual" sit-ins, cyber-graffiti, flash mobs, cracking, "hijacking" sites and denial of service campaigns.

The cost-efficient nature of these technologies has helped financially strapped groups. Public computing, open source software and free email and related services provided by Google, Yahoo! and Hotmail, make it easier to organize, circulate information and use the Web for research purposes. Free and accessible services like Yahoo! Groups offer resource-poor activist organizations many tools to pursue their advocacy, such as calendars, storage space, archives and discussion groups (Wright 2002: 244–45). The OAT collective, a Toronto-based group that attempts to use telecommunications to transform communications, provides a communications infrastructure for activist communities at <www.tao.ca>. The Ruckus Society conducts "technology toolbox action camps" to teach activists how to employ the new ICTs.

The use of these tools in high profile events — such as the Seattle protests against the World Trade Organization in 1999 — led to a belief that the new ICTs could rebalance power relations in the fight for social change.[8] Most notably, Wright (2002: 244) argued that activists would benefit from affordable access to the same technologies that allowed the international corporate community to "coordinate activities quickly and efficiently, and to avoid restrictions placed on them by governmental and non-governmental organizations. Activists around the world need to start connecting, communicating, and collaborating with the same tools that their adversaries have mastered."

In this vein, the Internet launched a "control revolution," embodying a shift in power away from public institutions towards private ones, resulting in increased individual power (Shapiro 1999). The change here is *who* is in control. Shapiro (1999: 50) argues that "use of the Net by activists shows how the ability to control information and experience means the ability to create new forms of social life and political power." He contends not only that activists can "play" with their identities, thus purportedly empowering them, but that individuals also can avoid messages they do not wish to hear.

Many observers predicted that radical transformations would accompany the emergence of the ICTs. At a systemic level, electronic communication and information dissemination would promote democratization, improve citizen engagement by increasing access to political elites, increase the flow of information between activists and governors and, generally, strengthen the citizenry. This was enhanced by the rise of an electronic alternative media (such as AlterNet, Rabble.ca and TomPaine.com) using email and the Web to distribute alternative analyses of current events and highlight issues ignored in the mainstream media. Surman and Wershler-Henry (2001: 2), for example, argued that the "commonspace" created by the widespread use of the Internet and the proliferation of ICTs could build a sense of community: "the real power of the Internet lies in the collective — the vital, thrilling interconnection of people and ideas that happens online." Indeed, they attributed great hope to the Internet's ability to change our world. Grassroots activists using the Internet believe that "they're creating a global equality movement that goes beyond tired ideas of left and right" (Surman and Wershler-Henry 2001: 3).

For many observers, the new ICTs continue to enhance and transform political life fundamentally. Today, the peace movement responding to the 2003 American invasion of Iraq attempts to get youth involved in politics. "Wiki politics" allow citizens to contribute to policy development by letting them offer ideas and debate policy options, increasing democratization through the creation and circulation of knowledge.[9] The *Washington Post* (Earl 2007) captured the changing environment for politics and social change when it noted that protests increasingly have become an online phenomenon, reflecting the fact that more people are using the Internet as a source of political news and information (Rainie and Horrigan 2007).

However, online protest may not embody transformed activism but rather signal a decline in engagement. This new arena of electronic communication and activism makes it easier for concerned citizens to become "passive activists": people who are concerned about change, but restrict their activist engagement to the comforts of home or office. Disembodied electronic communication may help people who are physically isolated to feel like they are part of a community; however, this does not translate necessarily into concrete social change. For example, Carty and Onyett (2006: 229) argue that the contemporary American peace movement, through its embrace of cyberactivism, may claim success not because it prevented war but because it has reshaped public opinion (among other factors): "success is not measured in terms of the achievement of absolute concrete goals or concessions from those in power, but rather a transformation of consciousness and a source of moral vision and voice." However, if the primary aims of a movement remain unrealized (they note that the peace movement "is rarely victorious in preventing war"), can it realistically claim success?

Indeed, it appears that the full democratic potential of the new ICTs is far from realized. The potential of the new ICTs is limited precisely because power relations remain heavily tilted in favour of political, economic and social elites. These technologies are also available to the powers being challenged (Kahn and Kellner 2004). The research and communication benefits of the Web are equally available to authorities, including intelligence agencies such as the Canadian Security and Intelligence Service, which tracks the activities of the anti-globalization movement, among others.[10]

Moreover, despite the new wave of Internet activism, the state retains significant powers that can curtail the work of activists (de Vaney 2000). Thus, while the Canadian state suggests that the new ICTs allow for a more inclusive relationship with its citizenry, it nevertheless appears less willing to engage with activists. As Barney (2005: 117–18, 184–85) observes, governments providing more information online is not the same thing as democratic engagement, and it remains difficult for Canadian activists to access the state. Probing beyond high-profile cases, the early hopes for online activism largely seem dashed. Political participation rates in Western democracies, including Canada, continue to decline, despite the goals of increasing connectivity (Barney 2005: 3–4).

In fact, access to the new ICTs remains uneven.[11] The most serious barrier to successful Internet activism is resource mobilization. While demands and expectations of activist groups are high, the lack of resources restricts the ability of groups (either activist or "independent media") to meet them, a situation compounded by the growing commercialization of the Internet and a concentration of ownership associated with convergence, such as Google's purchase of YouTube. As Barney (2005: 154) notes, unequal access to the new ICTs reflects differences not only in socioeconomic status and access to ICTs, but also in how they use them and the skills available to exploit them: "connectivity is only the most obvious way in which power surrounding these technologies is unequally distributed." Activists must find room in already stretched budgets to include these new expenses, while the cost of technical support, software, computing infrastructure, bandwidth, telephony, training and application development is often beyond the means of non-corporate users, affecting their ability to develop an online presence (see McChesney 1998; Surman and Wershler-Henry 2001).

The expansion of spaces for democratic communication has been positive for activists. Certainly, the Internet aided activists in the dissemination of information and to advance their agendas; however, this must be placed in perspective. Indeed, while Barney (2005: 143) states that "ICTs have been an indispensable instrument in the political activities of contemporary social movements and advocacy groups," he also acknowledges that their embrace and utilization do not lead necessarily to a more inclusive democracy. He writes: "the possibility of this outcome relies less on properties inherent in the technologies themselves than it does on the political will of those using them" (Barney 2005: 149).

Instead of altering politics, the political system may well normalize the Internet and other new ICTs, reinforcing existing patterns of political behaviour (Margolis and Resnick 2000: 18). Activists will use the new technologies, Margolis and Resnick argue, to disseminate information, communicate with sympathizers and lobby legislators. Moreover, activists adopt the technologies because it is now an expectation from others in the system: in other words, it is little more than a new medium for traditional political behaviour.

The targets of protest and activism also have agency; not only do they attempt to redefine a sense of political community and participation just like activists (Kahn and Kellner 2004: 185), but they also respond to new tactics by protesters (Ayres 2004: 25). One example is the increased attention to geographic location. Contrary to earlier arguments that the Internet would render geographic space irrelevant, capital and the political elite now respond to Internet activism by holding economic and political summits in isolated locations, making it more difficult both for activists to mount large-scale campaigns and for the mass media to provide comprehensive coverage. For example, the World Trade Organization held its 2001 meetings in Qatar and the Canadian government hosted the 2002 annual G-8 meetings in the Rocky Mountains.[12]

Digital communications and portable computing thus are potentially liberating and democratic insofar as they decentralize information and empower disenfranchised peoples. de Vaney and Gance (2000) remind us, however, that this potential is curbed by two important facts. First, the state still wields significant power and can curtail the work of activists. This is a growing concern in the post 9/11 world, as governments impose new legislation, such as the *Patriot Act* in the U.S., increasing their surveillance powers. Second, access to these technologies, especially (but not exclusively) in the developing world, is still very limited. Beyond low-cost mechanisms such as listservs, the lack of resources available to social movements functions as a critical barrier to achieving radical transformation of the political community. Information and its dissemination are neither necessarily free nor open. Agre (2002: 314) states that if the Internet is democratizing, "the political culture has to want it."

In fact, power relations are not altered by the new ICTs; they simply exist in a slightly altered (and mediated) form, particularly since, in the Canadian case, the rise of e-government coincided with the rise of neoliberalism and new public management, resulting in a state that now embraces more businesslike principles and practices (Barney 2005: 125–26). Consequently, we must situate the new ICTs within society's broader political struggles: "the social struggle needs to be conceived and carried out in the largest terms if it is to succeed. The struggle for non-commercial communications must be a core part of the battle waged by each social movement in a broader, radical alliance of social movements" (Dawson and Bellamy Foster 1998: 64).

In summary, the new ICTs, despite their potential, have not reshaped power relations in Canada dramatically. Indeed, in his comprehensive study of the relationship between politics, democracy and the new ICTs, Barney (2005: 176) concludes: "little evidence was found to support the claim that ICTs have been involved in a fundamental redistribution of power in Canada; considerably more was found to suggest that ICTs both reflect and reinforce the existing inequalities." This has serious repercussions, particularly for movements, such as women's movements, that struggled in the pre-Internet era to achieve their goals.

WOMEN AND INTERNET ACTIVISM

Our assessment that the new ICTs have not radically transformed politics and activism, even though they have altered how political actors act and contest power relations, also applies to women and women's movements. As Stewart-Miller (1998: 55–63) explains, feminist assessments of the impact of the online world on women's lives remain mixed. For example, liberal feminists, who promote gender equality through political reform, focus on the obstacles facing women on the Internet, arguing that with increasing participation, women will eventually overcome gender barriers. Cyber-feminists, who look at feminist issues through the lens of technology, optimistically see the new ICTs as tools for undermining traditional male dominance, viewing the Internet and the online world as a positive site for young women to explore feminism. Murdocca (2001) and Scott-Dixon (2001), for example, contend that e-zines furnish Internet spaces for feminists to critique existing power structures and propose alternative visions to those perpetuated in mainstream media. The fact that e-zines operate in the male-dominated arena of the Internet, they insist, only serves to show that they also serve as a form of resistance and thus constitute active political tools.

While offering a site for expression, communication and discussion, it nevertheless can be argued that e-zines may only connect tangentially to political activism. Stewart-Miller (1998: 62–63) questions cyber-feminism's optimism, noting that existing gender relations are replicated in the online world. Given cases of predatory behaviour on the Web (including harassment and stalking), the Internet is not always safe for women. Leslie Regan Shade (2004) warns us about the commercial interests at work that affect how women use the Web, how women are portrayed on the Web and how commercial interests target them as consumers. These realities can shift a woman's experience on the Web from one of potential collective consciousness and activism to a more individualistic and consumerist experience.

These shortcomings aside, the Internet increasingly serves as a critical tool for networking by feminists internationally. "Globalization from below" has been enhanced by the successful use of the Internet around issues and events as diverse as the 1995 U.N. Fourth World Conference on Women, public education about Zapatista women in Chiapas, Mexico, and the role of ICTs in mobilizing activism for social justice among women in transition societies across Central and Eastern Europe (Regan Shade 2002). Nevertheless, Regan Shade and Anne Scott (2001) both echo concerns raised by many feminist commentators that women's activism via ICTs is curtailed by "serious inequalities in economic, social and cultural power which restrict access to these technologies" (Scott 2001: 414). When adding gender to the barriers noted in the previous section, it is clear that some women face multiple layers of marginalization with respect to their online activism.

Canadian women's advocacy groups generally have followed international trends of employing ICTs as important media for political organizing. The websites of long-established women's groups like the National Action Committee on the Status of Women (www.nac-cca.ca) or the newer Feminist Alliance for International Action (www.fafia-afai.org) offer the usual, and now routinely expected, range of information including publications and data, links to government agencies and other activists, news and information, research links and, of course, membership information.

While important, these examples hardly constitute a radical reorientation of political activity and activism. Like their counterparts elsewhere, Canadian women's organizations report that their online organizing potentially enhances their capacity for equality work; yet, the barriers that impede such activism are many. In a consultation on women and ICTs prepared for the U.N. Commission on the Status of Women, Canadian women's groups cited lack of time and access, financial constraints, insufficient training and skill development, and lack of technical support as issues that negatively affected their capacity to fully exploit the Internet as an activist tool (Sutton, Pollock and Hauka 2002). In other words, the experiences of Canadian women's movements reflect the tensions of online activism globally. As Barney (2005: 156–57) notes, government emphasis on increasing connectivity ignores deeper structural issues that contribute to an ongoing "deeply gendered digital divide" rooted in structural relations to technology in the workplace, content on the Web, and other mediating factors such as education and income. While there remains hope that the new ICTs can contribute to transformed politics, the reality is that existing power relations remain intact.

ACTIVISM IN A CHILLY CLIMATE

Ayres (1999: 135) correctly notes that political conditions affect "Internet-inspired protest." Following this insight, we situate women's movements within the current Canadian political environment before assessing the opportunities and constraints associated with Internet activism for feminist organizing. The explosion of Internet usage among women's groups across Canada as an integral tool of political organizing paralleled, not coincidentally, the massive government restructuring initiative that dominated Canadian politics in the mid-1990s. These monumental shifts altered relationships between citizens and the state in Canada and recast long-standing traditions of interaction between women's movements and the federal government that date back more than a century. The rapid changes of recent years, in fact, resituated women's organizations back to the periphery of Canadian politics and precipitated much debate within the feminist community about the future course of women's activism in Canada.

To understand the magnitude of these shifts and assess the potential of the Internet as an effective tool for sustaining and advancing of women's equality struggles, it is important first to acknowledge that perhaps the defining feature of women's movements in Canada is their historical orientation towards the state (Sawer 1996; Phillips 1990). Feminist historians documenting the evolution of the relationship between the federal state and pan-Canadian women's groups note that turn-of-the-century feminists of the "first wave" were quick to understand that "[o]nly the power of the state could exert any influence" (Mitchinson 1987: 86, quoted in Bush 2001). They sought to establish strong, institutionalized links with the national government in order to maximize their access to decision-making by adopting organizational structures such as umbrella organizations to coordinate local and provincial women's groups (Griffith 1993). These efforts matured into the tradition of regular, state-focused lobbying that recognized women's groups as accepted actors in public policy development.

Feminist activists of the 1960s and 1970s capitalized on this continuity of interaction between women's movements and government most effectively. The Canadian federal state responded to women's equality demands by expanding existing political space for women and helping to develop new ones. Former Prime Minister Pierre Trudeau's vision of a "just society" fostering participatory democracy translated into the establishment of a complex of bureaucratic structures known as the "women's state" and a set of practices to facilitate citizen participation (Pal 1993; Vickers, Rankin and Appelle 1993).

One former feminist bureaucrat recalls the period 1966–79 as one during which the Canadian federal state was open to translating women's demands into public policy outputs and "demonstrated a commitment to consult with the women of Canada" (Findlay 1987: 31). In particular, second-wave feminism enjoyed regular engagement in public policymaking because of the provision of state funding to women's groups. Jenson and Phillips (1996: 118) claim that this legitimation of the advocacy sector through state funding programs "may comprise one of the distinctive characteristic of Canada's [postwar] citizenship regime." Created in 1973, the Secretary of State Women's Program channelled government monies to grassroots women's groups. This ready availability of funding in the early years of the program instilled a view in feminist circles, at least in English-speaking Canada, that the Canadian federal state was the logical focal point for their activist energies. Such circumstances, however, also reinforced the dependency of national women's organizations on the Canadian state (Burt 1997: 259), a fact that would surface as increasingly important when Canada's political landscape later became dominated by neoliberal principles and practices, and one that retains critical importance in the Internet era.

Brodie explains that "[k]ey front-line women's organizations recognized, from the early 1980s, that the neoliberal vision of a minimalist state and unfettered market-driven development threatened the very foundations of second-wave feminism's equity agenda" (1995: 21). Indeed, women's organizations first began to absorb the deleterious impact of state restructuring under the Mulroney regime (1984–93). Equality-seeking organizations within and outside the state were excluded gradually from the policy process and the women's movement, in particular, was slowly squeezed financially through successive budget reductions (Bashevkin 1998). Between 1986 and 1990, the Women's Program endured budget cuts of 40 percent (Bonnet 1996: 70). In tandem with the emerging neoliberal climate that narrowed the Canadian women's movement's access to the policy process, the funding withdrawal during the Mulroney years affected the grassroots movement acutely (Morris 1999: 31).

The optimism that accompanied the re-election of the Liberal Party in 1993 soon dissipated as a zealous concentration on fiscal responsibility and deficit elimination made it more difficult to place women's equality on the policy agenda. Paquet and Shepherd (1996) explain that the Chrétien government faced two crises upon election in 1993: a public finance crisis and a crisis of governance. The urgency of reacting to these twin crises led to a flurry of reforms designed to "get government right" through increasing the efficiency, effectiveness and accountability of government actions and by creating a more results-oriented public service working in "partnership" with citizens, business, subnational governments and local communities.

The government's Program Review downsized the federal public service by 45,000 employees and instituted cuts worth an accumulated $29 billion; the reforms were cast as a gender-neutral exercise; yet the impact of these changes was significantly gendered (Brodie 1998). Along with other social movements in Canada, women's groups faced additional attacks under this new regime both financially, through the gradual elimination of public funding, as well as on an ideological level. Intense rhetoric from the then Reform Party of Canada decried the public funding of "special interest groups" and castigated advocacy organizations as "threats to representational democracy in Canada" (Brodie 1995: 69). Devastating budget reductions to women's organizations continued, and their effects were compounded by the refusal of the government to index funding of women's groups to inflation after 1995–96 (Bush 2001).

The impact of this funding loss was profound, threatening the capacity of women's advocacy groups to mobilize amongst themselves, to maintain their internal operations, sponsor events and initiate public education campaigns. Within feminist circles, the dismantling of established funding practices was interpreted as a blatant effort to silence criticism of Liberal policies, constrain the capacity of grassroots women to hold the government accountable for its domestic and international commitments and inhibit effective interventions in public policy debates.

With its introduction of the 1995 *Federal Plan for Gender Equality*, the Liberal government withdrew from its longstanding commitment to advance women's equality through institutional means. Since the tabling of the *Report of the Royal Commission on the Status of Women in Canada* in 1970, the federal Liberals had promoted the advancement of women's equality within the federal government through a set of bureaucratic mechanisms (Findlay 1987). The institutionalization of a network of national machinery for the advancement of women, as well as positive measures such as the creation of programs, policies and legislation targeted to address women's systemic inequality, had functioned as defining characteristics of post-1960s Canadian feminism. In 1995, in a move argued to reduce duplication of services and provide a more comprehensive approach to women's equality, the federal government quietly dissolved one pillar of its status-of-women institutions, the Canadian Advisory Council on the Status of Women. It was created in 1973 to provide advice on women's issues to the federal government and to educate and communicate with Canadians. The remaining women's policy machinery was restructured in ways that significantly reduced their influence within government. In the process, this narrowed the institutional framework within which women's equality demands were funnelled, further exacerbating tensions between the federal government and the women's movements.

The messaging around these changes was set squarely within an economic rationalist discourse citing the enhanced efficiency and effectiveness of the new arrangements. As Canadian feminist scholars argue, however, the redefinition of citizenship that accompanied the federal state's embrace of neoliberalism by extension meant that while advocacy efforts were dismissed as undermining to democracy, groups with mandates incorporating service delivery were exalted as pivotal to the public good. The new "partnership regime" between the state and civil society, therefore, endorsed service organizations over advocacy groups, now denigrated as exerting undue pressure on an already-overburdened state (Jenson and Phillips 1996).

The dislodging of women's organizations as accepted actors on the Canadian political landscape, coupled with the severing of the historic links between the women's movement and the federal state, forced feminist activists to confront the pressing need for new channels through which to pursue equality agendas in this altered political environment. To sustain their viability as social movement actors in "hard times," the turn to Internet activism has been one noticeable shift in the strategic practice of women's movements. In the section below, we highlight one particular example of how feminists across Canada employ Internet technology for activist purposes and probe the capacity of online activism to translate into tangible social change and transcend dependency on the Canadian federal state.

THE EXPERIENCE OF PAR-L

Our purpose in this section is not to survey the burgeoning range of online opportunities available for feminist activism in Canada. Instead, we focus on one Canadian listserv and website and examine the opportunities and constraints associated with this single activist venue. We conclude that the role of the state that loomed so large throughout the history of feminist activism in Canada has not been diminished, even with the shift to online organizing. For a growing number of feminists in Canada and across a dozen other countries, daily messages from the bilingual electronic discussion list PAR-L, launched on International Women's Day in 1995, now forms an integral element of regular connection with the domestic and global women's community. Covering upcoming events, engaging debates about pressing national and international political issues and provoking discussions about feminist theory and activist strategies, PAR-L serves a crucial role of linking the feminist academic and activist communities.

PAR-L's origins lay not in the efforts of technologically savvy activists, but rather PAR-L was a project launched and funded by the research department of the Canadian Advisory Council on the Status of Women (CACSW), one of the federal government institutions that formed part of the "women's state." Ironically, the original impetus for organizing an email list for feminists was to create a new tool for combating what in 1995 were persistent rumours about further impending funding cuts to women's organizations (Ollivier and Robbins 1997). As the organizers admit, the list "utterly failed" as a means of saving the CACSW. Within months of the list's founding, the Chrétien Liberal government closed the Advisory Council (Ollivier, Robbins, Brayton and Sauvé 2002: 3). Feminists lost the council that had long facilitated interaction between feminists and the federal government, and the new electronic resource was vulnerable. In this context of shrinking access to public policymaking and vanishing resources, PAR-L was quick to gain popularity and soon boasted a growing network of subscribers across Canada and abroad. In 1997, when the listserv's future was at risk, financial support was secured through a Strategic Research Grant from the Social Sciences and Humanities Research Council of Canada. Although PAR-L organizers were delighted with the guarantee of another three years of funding (which eventually continued until 2005), the list, like so many other elements of women's movements, quickly institutionalized a reliance on state funding for its very existence.

Since its creation, PAR-L expanded to support a discussion list, comprehensive website and online publications. In 1997, eight feminist organizations joined to form the PAR-L Strategic Research Network. Today, the partner network includes twenty-one Canadian feminist research organizations and two international feminist organizations. PAR-L's website[13] includes detailed advice for women's groups on how best to mobilize online activism, an inventory of useful research links and an array of information on recent public policy initiatives. The list archives boast over 15,000 messages. The mainstay of PAR-L, however, remains the electronic discussion list that supplies daily news of activist work across the country and on the international stage and retains a focus on social, political and economic issues.

As PAR-L developed into a core tool of organizing, it attracted an almost even distribution of university and community users. List members have mobilized around events such as the 2000 World March of Women, the closing of the Toronto Women's College Hospital, the Multilateral Agreement on Investment (MAI), the Global March Against Child Labor and, most recently, the Harper government's cuts to Status of Women Canada (among others, see Regan Shade 2002; Ollivier et al. 2006). They have debated pressing policy issues such as welfare reform, child poverty and national childcare. Arguably, one of the most important functions that PAR-L serves is to offer a safe forum where competing views on difficult, complex issues are aired. One survey of PAR-L's effectiveness revealed that many *"Parleuses"* reported that the online discussions had been instrumental in modifying and clarifying their positions on topics as diverse as transgenderism and assisted suicide (Ollivier et al. 2002: 9). In short, the interactive exchanges and comprehensive online information clearinghouse facilitated by PAR-L have made it a vital tool for its 1500 subscribers, a necessity in a large, sparsely populated country in which face-to-face communication is often time-consuming and prohibitively expensive.

PAR-L now assumes a lead role in coordinating activist initiatives and re-establishing connections among Canadian women's groups weakened by the sustained attack levelled by the federal government against the advocacy sector. With its focus on the interconnections among public policy outputs, research and action, however, PAR-L illustrates very clearly the state-centric tradition of women's movements in Canada, which identifies the need to influence government action as its primary function. Towards this end, the network facilitates instantaneous and inexpensive coordination and collaboration on social, political and economic issues and allows groups to deploy their diminished resources much more effectively. Particularly useful is the cross-sectoral cooperation generated by the simultaneous focus on academic and activist communities. While a majority of postings are in English, PAR-L's bilingual mandate allows the list to serve as a tool to bridge historic divisions between anglophone and francophone feminists. Finally, one of PAR-L's most significant contributions is in its role as an umbrella list that includes posting on events and issues of concern to groups historically marginalized within mainstream feminism. At a moment in which the prior visibility of English-speaking Canada's principal feminist organization, the National Action Committee on the Status of Women (NAC), has waned dramatically, PAR-L allows for interaction and coordination among groups that previously relied heavily on NAC. In their reflections of PAR-L's early years, Ollivier and Robbins (1999: 49) conclude that

> among women who have time and access to equipment and train-
> ing, participating in a feminist electronic discussion list may cre-
> ate a new form of community which includes women previously
> isolated or separated from one another, often bridging the gap
> between community and university-based activists. It may also
> foster empowerment by giving voice to a larger segment of the
> feminist community than has usually been possible, and forge a
> valuable tool in organizing for change.

In a more recent assessment of PAR-L, Ollivier et al. (2006: 462) conclude that such forms of communication technology also offer women a "lifeline — between the political, professional and personal elements of their often isolated, fragmented, run-ragged lives." These substantial contributions notwithstanding, the capacity of electronic organizing to facilitate offline action remains subject to considerable debate. Given the severing of the federal state's historic support of women's advocacy, which defined Canadian politics from the 1970s through the 1990s, PAR-L's reliance on the state for sustaining funds is troubling and suggests that the *virtual* women's movements may be subject to the same fate as their offline counterparts.

More broadly, the ease of individual participation in online activism through vehicles such as PAR-L risks substituting cybersphere participation for public sphere, collective action. Electronic lists such as PAR-L that readily supply information on feminist initiatives may inadvertently contribute to the movement's further demobilization as the technology allows social movement supporters, especially those involved in movements experiencing serious crises, to maintain a comfortable stance as "passive activists" with engagement limited to sympathetic, but only virtual, support for women's equality campaigns. As one respondent to the PAR-L 2002 survey reported, "I use PAR-L primarily as a passive form of networking, i.e., to observe what are current issues for Canadian feminists, and to receive information" (Ollivier et al. 2002).

Despite the vibrancy of PAR-L, the growing panoply of active, online discussion groups and comprehensive websites related to feminist activism are not attached necessarily to viable organizations with the financial and human resources needed to mount substantive activist initiatives. Increasingly, the Web presence of organizations may bear little relationship to the group's capacity to pursue its mandate beyond cyberspace and may mask the extent to which women's movements continue to be demobilized due to the federal state's restructuring efforts.

The capacity of women's groups to use Internet activism effectively to influence government policy is affected also by the spread of e-government. Throughout the Chrétien/Martin years, the Liberals promoted online government and its commitment to "connect Canadians" with the goal of making Canada the most cyber-connected country. ICT analysts Pollock and Sutton argue that Canadian women were a forgotten population in this process. They noted "the enormous resources being spent to get a whole population online without any serious attempt to ensure women and girls are included" and called on the Canadian government to realize "that access to the Internet is an equality issue, and that there is a long fight under way just to ensure women have the resources to get online; [there is a] need for an inclusive approach, building networks and making the Internet a welcoming and relevant place for a diversity of women where we can work together" (Pollock and Sutton 1998: 42). Women's groups, for example, pointed to the unwillingness of the Canadian government to add a women's portal to the federal government's main website, despite making available comprehensive portals for Aboriginals, seniors, youth and persons with disabilities. Not only is this a telling example of the federal government's hesitancy to implement concrete measures for advancing women's equality; it also points to the inability of Canadian women's groups to convince the federal government of the significance of this portal in an era of e-government.

CONCLUSION

Already reeling from cutbacks in state funding, the negative impact of two decades of neoliberal policies and a growing backlash against feminism, the era of Internet activism, once seen as promising and full of hope, potentially raises further obstacles for feminist movements. The Canadian women's movements have not been able to benefit from the potential offered by the new ICTs. In continuing to decry the demise of state funding, women's groups reinforce observations that the advent of such technologies are not liberating in and of themselves, since they lack the resources to fully engage with the new technologies. Despite the federal government's rhetoric of citizen engagement, the historically dependent relationship between women and the state persists. We therefore must ask if the new era of Internet activism can provide new mobilization opportunities for movements facing serious demobilizing pressures.

The PAR-L case shows that we need to exercise caution when gauging the potential of the new ICTs for promoting social change. We must probe the impact of the new ICTs in various contexts and increase our body of case studies, particularly with groups that historically have faced severe mobilization and access challenges. Far from enhancing or improving their position, the new ICTs may serve to reinforce their marginalized status.

We agree with Kahn and Kellner (2004: 183) who argue in their analysis of online activism that given the ongoing role of the Internet as a potential tool for activists, online communities need to be "continually theorized from a standpoint that is both critical and reconstructive." Analysis of the specificities of particular social movements must accompany any pronouncements about the potential transformative impact of online activism. Assessing women's movements and their relationship to online activism illustrates that while depoliticized and demobilized movements may eagerly embrace the opportunities available from Internet organizing, the challenges endemic to such movements are not resolved simply through a shift to online activity. Although the gender and technology literature does indicate the enormous potential of online communication for individual women, whether or not this translates into measurable gains for women's movements requires systematic, empirical investigation.

Stewart-Miller (1998: 67) argues for a "feminist politics of anticipation," in which women would not simply respond to change but anticipate it. This is a useful approach to look at women's online activism in Canada. It is insufficient for activists in women's movements to simply "catch up" and replicate what other groups are doing with the Internet. Rather, they must continually look forward to developing strategies that promote women's equality agendas and, in particular, tailor those strategies to respond to the social, political and economic context within which that activism is undertaken.

This is consistent with our analysis of online activism more generally. The new ICTs have given groups different tools, but these tools have not radically altered the nature of organizing and acting for social change. As we argue, one must examine the impact and possibilities of the new ICTs within the broader sociopolitical setting. The case of women's movements in Canada shows that marginalization, linked to historic structural and economic questions, including a steady focus on state lobbying and a simultaneous reliance on state funding is likely to continue despite the appearance of the new ICTs.

Two key issues still need examination in order to understand the relationship between the new ICTs and activism and social change more fully. First, Ayres (1999: 141–42) questions if "wired activism" necessarily will replace the important cultural and personal linkages of activists, and suggests that Internet activism might also signal a return to old-style protest — mass and sporadic. This debate is central to understanding if online activity enhances a sense of community, as cyber-feminists argue, or if the question is one of organizing along traditional lines, using the new ICTs to supplement such efforts.

In fact, we might be witnessing an emerging complementary relationship between traditionally organized and contemporary wired women's organizations. In this scenario, established feminist institutions may continue to play an important role in Canadian feminism with their name recognition, long institutional memory and deeply rooted ties to the broad range of women's groups. As we have shown, however, such organizations are now preoccupied with their own survival in light of the tremendous pressures facing women's movements, and their continuing orientation towards changing public policy, particularly given the economic and social restructuring that marked Canadian society over the past decade. Thus, there is a potential space — contingent upon securing stable funding preferably beyond the governmental sphere — for alternative feminist networks like PAR-L that provide instant communication among activists and improve knowledge sharing considerably.

Second, we need to increase our repertoire of comparative case studies to understand these issues. For example, we know there are important structural, political and ideological differences between the Canadian and U.S. women's movements (Backhouse and Flaherty 1992). These differences would, we suspect, emerge in matters of online activism as well. For instance, can a social movement that is largely state-centric contribute to true social change? If activists in a wealthy country like Canada continue to face serious obstacles, what of the challenges faced by activists in the developing world? There is also the matter of online activism across spheres of social change and policy communities. We also must consider the impact of the new ICTs across movements — for example, the labour movement versus the environmental movement — to help us theorize at a more general level the overall impact of the ICTs on social change movements.

In conclusion, it is clear that the full impact of the new ICTs has not yet been felt or seen. If anything, the experiences of Canadian women's movements indicate a need for greater caution with respect to ICT's and social change: empirical analyses must be grounded squarely in the broader sociopolitical environment in which the ongoing struggle for social change takes place. This requires research that considers *simultaneously* the multiple, interconnected spheres — cyber and otherwise — in which social movements fight for survival and change.

NOTES

1. Michèle Ollivier and Wendy Robbins, "PAR-L enters 13th year of service — notre anniversaire," message to PAR-L listserv, March 8, 2007. See <www.unb.ca/PAR-L>.

2. In 2003, a group of female professors tabled a complaint with the Canadian Human Rights Commission concerning women's low level of representation in the ranks of holders of the Canada Research Chairs Program, a program that funds over 1600 research professorships in Canadian universities. Country-wide mobilization for that complaint began on PAR-L in 2002 when the co-moderators of the list, Wendy Robbins and Michèle Ollivier, solicited support for this issue, citing the fact that women received only 14 percent of the Chairs in the program's first year of operation. As a result of the complaint, a new agreement on equity in the nomination process for chairholders was ratified in November 2006.

3. Honourable Bev Oda, Minister of Canadian Heritage and Status of Women. Witness, Standing Committee on the Status of Women, Government of Canada, 39th Parliament, 1st session, October 5, 2006.

4. In a letter to the editor of the *Ottawa Citizen* on February 2, 2007, Minister Oda stated that "'the promotion of gender equality' has never been part of the original mandate of Status of Women Canada." Since that time, the phrase "the federal government agency which promotes gender equality" has been reinstated on the home page of the Status of Women Canada website <www.swc-cfc.gc.ca>.

5. The "women's state" refers to the creation of programs and institutional spaces throughout the federal and provincial/territorial governments beginning in the 1970s. Such mechanisms acted as conduits through which women and women's groups could communicate their perspectives to bureaucrats and politicians; in establishing the "women's state," Canadian governments replicated similar international efforts to construct women's bureaucratic machinery. In most Canadian jurisdictions, the "women's state" included women's policy offices and arm's-length advisory councils.

6. The Internet is used by numerous causes, not all progressive. For example, the anonymity of the new technologies has allowed racist groups and radical anti-abortionists to spread their messages and promote hate in a rather anonymous fashion.

7. Hacktivism comprises various tactics in the effort to hack into the electronic networks of powerful organizations. Disruptions may damage electronic records or may simply interfere with their proper operation. This wide range of tactics raises many political, ethical, territorial and legal issues, and not all groups agree with the propriety of these tactics. See Samuel (2004) for a detailed examination of hacktivism.

8. Other key events include the 2001 protests at the Free Trade of the Americas

meeting in Quebec City, growing recognition of the plight of the Zapatistas following their successful awareness raising campaign on the Internet and the Council of Canadians employment of email to defeat the Multilateral Agreement on Investment in 1997 (described in Smith and Smythe 2003: 189–92).

9. Most candidates for office have blogs that invite supporters to contribute to policy platforms. The most prominent include Howard Dean's 2004 campaign to become the presidential candidate of the Democratic Party and the Ségolène Royal presidential campaign in France in 2006–07.

10. See for example, the Canadian Security Intelligence Service, *Anti-Globalization — A Spreading Phenomenon* (August 22, 2000) <www.csis-scrs.gc.ca/en/publications/perspectives/200008.asp> (accessed April 28, 2007).

11. For example, only 68% percent of Canadians reported using the Internet for personal, non-business reasons (Statistics Canada 2006). The survey notes that a "digital divide," affected by income, education, age and family factors exists for certain groups, and rural Canadians use the Internet less than urban Canadians do. Moreover, as Barney (2005: 155) notes, connectivity is a superficial measure of the relationship between the new technologies and the political system.

12. In some cases, elites simply refuse to publicize events in order to avoid media and activist attention. This was the case in the controversial meetings discussing North American integration (the North American Summit), held in Banff September 12–14, 2006, which featured leading business, political and military leaders from Canada, the United States and Mexico.

13. <www.unb.ca/PAR-L>.

CHAPTER FOUR

COLONIALISM, RESISTANCE AND INDIGENOUS POST-SECONDARY EDUCATION IN CANADA

Amie McLean

As objects of colonial oppression and subjects of resistance in Canadian society, Aboriginal peoples[1] have a long and continuing history of people trying to "make them up." These constructions of selfhood are currently finding new modes of expression through post-secondary education policies for Aboriginal students. Education can play a critical role in opening up possibilities for engagement with power; it can enrich the "tools" through which resistance might be exercised by familiarizing individuals with the discursive tactics of the dominant power mechanisms in society. Education can thus be understood as a means to alter the very power-knowledge relations that structure and determine realms of possibility for Aboriginal peoples in Canada. As a result, education has been a key sight of struggle for Aboriginal resistance movements.

Increasing the numbers of well-educated Aboriginal individuals is seen as key in facilitating the decolonization of Canadian society and current education systems. Proposed methods for accomplishing these goals include the creation and expansion of education systems grounded in Aboriginal languages and cultural values. Furthermore, Aboriginal individuals and communities are increasingly called upon to communicate Aboriginal perspectives to the Canadian public, governments and the media; to participate in policy development and implementation; and to carry out various self-government initiatives (Assembly of First Nations (AFN) 2005). Education is therefore seen as one mechanism for empowering Canadian Indigenous movements by providing the tools necessary for actualizing Aboriginal peoples' self-determination.

Historically, education has been a key mechanism for the instillation and expansion of colonial control over and within Indigenous nations, communities and individuals within the borders of what has come to be Canada. At the same time, education has been and is an important component of Indigenous resistance to oppressive colonial governance, a site where deeply unequal power relations may be revealed and contested. On one hand, Indigenous leaders fought to ensure education rights in the numbered treaties and many now see education as an important tool for cultural and communal revitalization (Stonechild 2006). On the other, colonial applications of European education systems have had devastating results for Aboriginal peoples, most notoriously through the imposition of the residential school system.[2]

While Indigenous peoples in what came to be Canada have defended their rights to self-determination and autonomy since the onset of imperialism and colonialism,[3] government consolidation of public services in the 1970s coincided with the rise of strong First Nations' organizations to create a political environment conducive to greater First Nations' input over programs and services that impact their communities (Satzewich and Wotherspoon, 2000: 131). Through wide-ranging political practices and discursive strategies, Indigenous resistance movements have highlighted Canada's authoritarian and oppressive relationship with Indigenous peoples. The incongruity of these governing practices with liberal ideals of individual freedom has led to a gradual shift away from overtly paternalistic and authoritarian modes of governance within and upon Aboriginal communities, perhaps most notably through self-government initiatives allowing for local control over education and education program administration.

For Aboriginal peoples in Canada, self-government can represent freedom from a long history of oppressive colonial governance: "ever since they were forcibly deprived of self-government by colonial powers, Indians have hoped to reclaim it. An offer of self-government is one they can hardly resist" (Boldt and Long 1988: 47). The counterfoil, or disciplinary tactic, underlying this particular mode of governance-through-freedom is the threat of the loss or further limitation of what hard-won autonomy First Nations have been "awarded." Therefore, government control of the finances upon which First Nations communities rely is a central mechanism for disciplinary practices. To avoid the disciplinary "whip," First Nations are compelled to structure their governments in a manner that re-creates liberal ideals of limited and accountable government.

Devolutionary processes at the heart of current self-government initiatives can be understood to mould First Nations governments into "municipal-type structures that can be readily slotted into existing federal and provincial systems" (Boldt and Long 1988: 28). First Nations bands and organizations, having finally won a degree of autonomy from the (post) colonial government, have a vested interest in maintaining and enhancing the current relationship — despite the difficulties of inadequate support structures and funding. Radical solutions or new experiments in social and political practices are curtailed as emergent structures of First Nations governance increasingly come under the disciplinary and supervisory gaze of the Canadian government.

The Post-Secondary Student Support Program (PSSSP), which can provide financial aid to First Nations and Inuit students attending post-secondary institutions, is among those programs devolved from the Department of Indian and Northern Development (INAC) to the band level. Referring to the PSSSP in a textbook on Aboriginal peoples in Canada, Frideres (1998) recites a popularly held misconception as "truth": "all Indians and Inuit who have been accepted in a post-secondary school qualify for financial support that covers tuition, tutorial assistance, books, supplies, and transportation" (161–63). However, not all Aboriginal peoples are eligible; many eligible students are denied funding; and students who do secure funding receive, on average, only enough to cover 48 percent of the estimated average cost of higher education per year (British Columbia Ministry of Advanced Education 2006: 13). In the three years from 1999–2000 to 2001–02, the PSSSP funded between 25,300 and 26,500 students (INAC 2005: 19). INAC's (2005) *Evaluation of the Post-Secondary Education Program* estimates that about 20–22 percent of applicants are deferred each year (40). Of the students interviewed for the study, 77.4 percent (or 304 out of 394 students) asserted they would not have attended post-secondary if it were not for PSSSP funding (33).

This chapter examines the current post-secondary education funding policies for Aboriginal students within the context of liberalism and colonialism, which shape Canadian understandings of and approaches to citizenship, rights, education, the welfare state and Aboriginal peoples. Neoliberal political practices increasingly emphasize individual over societal responsibility for "success" in arenas such as social welfare and education. This has led to funding restrictions and means- and performance-based eligibility requirements being introduced to the PSSSP. Such changes effectively sidestep the issue of "education as a treaty right" through a neoliberal emphasis on fiscal accountability and competition. In this context, the PSSSP can be understood as a political tactic for the exercise of power. The general aim of this exercise is the constitution of First Nations and Inuit students into self-disciplining liberal rational actors and the constitution of First Nations governments according to the liberalist ideal of limited, accountable government.[4]

LIBERALISM

Liberalism is a classic political philosophical doctrine that came to prominence in Europe in the 1700s and that remains the dominant regime of governance in Canadian society (Brym 2001: 249). Liberalism views society as a collection of individuals with individual rights and freedoms, with the role of government being to protect those rights and freedoms. In recent decades, a variant of liberalism, neoliberalism, has become a guiding force in many Western industrial nations and trans- and multi-national corporations (Hiller 2006: 127; Brym 2001: 249–50). Neoliberalism retains a liberalist focus on individual liberty but further disdains state interference.

Neoliberalism is associated with the rise of the New Right, neoconservatism, fiscal restraint, government restructuring, and emphasis on the free-markets and monetarism.

Liberal ideals and governmentality rely heavily on a particular conceptualization of what an individual citizen is and should be. The ideal liberal individual is independent, responsible, self-disciplining and capable of rational thought (Ruhl 1999: 110). Scholars have pointed out that this model of the citizen is based on the attributes of elite white males (Orloff 1993: 308; Ruhl 1999: 110–11). Breitkreuz (2005) contends that neoliberalism has led to a shift away from social citizenship models, "where all citizens are entitled to a base level of benefits, to a model of market citizenship, where citizenship entitlement is contingent upon a person's attachment to the labour market" (148).

Liberal technologies of power facilitate governance through the constitution of individuals — they attempt to "create" citizens in the image of the liberal rational actor. Autonomous liberal actors are free in the sense that they possess the capacity of choice; at the same time, they are subjectified inasmuch as their, "subjugation works through the promotion and calculated regulation of spaces in which choice is exercised" (Dean 1995: 562). Foucault utilizes the concept of governmentality to explain these processes. Governmentality is the '"conduct of conduct," or more specifically, "the relation between government and conduct" (1978: 560). Governmentality refers to the complex array of mechanisms through which the government of populations is linked to self-government, or the means by which individuals work on the constitution of their own subjectivity (Garland 1997: 174). Bio-politics and bio-power are linked to governmentality and address themselves to the regulation of populations and the maximization of those populations' productive capacities.

Bio-power relies on disciplinary regimes, since a power focused on the control of life must have a complementary series of corrective and regulatory mechanisms that facilitate its ability to normalize society (Foucault 1978: 144). Discipline seeks to inculcate specific behaviour patterns in the individual. Surveillance is linked to discipline and constitutes a technique of power, as it confers power onto the observer while disempowering the observed through their visibility. Surveillance in the form of detailed observation "feeds" bio-power — it helps create knowledge that in turn facilitates governance. While the existence and expansion of regulatory mechanisms may seem antithetical to a liberal insistence on individual liberty, liberal governance in fact necessitates them:

> The liberal arts of government specify the content of individual freedom, give it a particular form and turn it to various goals. They employ techniques ranging from earlier disciplines found in institutional settings to contemporary practices of individual and

mutual empowerment, participation, self-help and community development and care. (Dean 2002:38)

Neoliberalism understands the welfare state to be "costly, inefficient, and culpable in the creation of economic dependences"; therefore, a central focus of neoliberal politics has been welfare-state reform (Hiller 2006: 127). This genre of reform moves away from social guarantees against poverty for citizens towards an "empowerment to work" model that stresses equality of opportunity rather than outcome. In a political environment constituted by an increasing movement towards neoliberal economics and right-wing policy endeavours, calls for governments to enforce obligations on those receiving social services (such as welfare and education benefits) are growing: "in practice, this means governing substantial minorities... in a way that emphasizes increased surveillance, detailed administration and sanction" (Dean 2002: 55). Such developments are evident in programs and services (often administered at the band level) available in Indigenous communities. Transforming Aboriginal individuals into educated and competitive labour-force participants is constructed as being good for them, their communities and the federal bottom line.

Accountability relations and actuarial practices are central aspects of this shift, as actuarial practices entail assessments of risk, assessments that are often utilized to make and justify administrative decisions. At the same time, actuarial practices place responsibility (for behaviour, achievement or failure) squarely on individuals, as they are understood as having chosen to behave in a certain manner. Ruhl (1999) argues:

> the actuarial model of government... has a clear political lineage. In its use of an ahistorical, de-contextualized 'rational actor' as a model of behavior, it draws on a model of the citizen that is emblematic of liberal regimes. In its emphasis on risk, which is after all based on the rational assessment of costs verses benefits, it echoes the utilitarianism that is again a hallmark of liberalism. Finally... it puts forth a world view in which individuals, not society, take responsibility for not just their actions, but for their environments as well. (110)

Responsibility is equated with rationality and the capacity to engage in a cost-benefit analysis of ones' actions: "[i]n this sense, responsibility talk within liberal regimes is also morality talk; behaving responsibly is a moral act" (96).

Relating these formulations specifically to education, neoliberal understandings of education are linked with human capital theory, which argues for a highly educated workforce in an increasingly globalized society and associates education with economic autonomy in the marketplace. The human capital approach to education emerges from liberalism and is inherently optimistic and economic; it stresses correlations between "success at school and success at work" and, therefore, emphasizes the economic rewards of individual and societal investment in education (Brym 2001: 325). Education systems provide human resources, which drive economic productivity, and, "those with the most human capital will be the most attractive to employers, and will be paid the highest wages, indicating the greater contribution they make to the economy" (325). Therefore, human capital theory views the economic and social successes or failures of social groups as indicative of group members' abilities to "adapt to prevailing social norms and to compete on an equal basis with other individuals" (Satzewich and Wotherspoon 2000: 114).

Mudge (2003) suggests that in a meritocratic system, educational spending may reinforce constructions of the "worthy" and "unworthy" poor, since the impoverished are perceived to have had "every opportunity" to improve their situation. She further notes:

> The emerging welfare state agenda in many countries now emphasizes active participation in labour markets rather than passive receipt of benefits, individual citizen responsibilities rather than group rights, more targeted benefits to segmented groups, and empowerment to work (via education, training, and employment services) rather than entitlement to a certain living standard. (4)

Accordingly, individual autonomy is understood to reduce (real or potential) government (fiscal) responsibility for citizens. In current liberal and neoliberal Canadian contexts, education is understood as a mechanism for creating ideal liberal citizens (i.e., productive workers and consumers) (British Columbia Ministry of Advanced Education 2006; Satzewich and Wotherspoon 2000: 112). This formulation effectively equates education with freedom while leaving the nature and processes of education unproblematized. Freedom is defined as the attainment of economic autonomy — economic autonomy which may be achieved through (the right kind and amount of) education.

COLONIALISM

Colonialism "is the implanting of settlements on distant territory" and is almost always the consequence of imperialism, or "the practice, the theory, and the attitudes of a dominating metropolitan centre ruling a distant territory" (Ashcroft, Grifiths and Tiffin 2000: 45). Colonial practices carried out by liberal societies reveal that, despite an emphasis on limited government, authoritarian exercises of power are not antithetical to liberal governance. As Dean (2002) points out, colonial liberal governance has a long history of authoritarianism: in "*Considerations on Representative Government,* Mill argues for the necessity of a 'good despot,' provided under the benign dominion of a 'more civilized people,' for those nations incapable of 'spontaneous improvement' [of] themselves" (47).

Smith (1999) argues that European notions of modernity and accompanying assumptions of human progress emerging from the Enlightenment are credited with stimulating the Industrial Revolution, liberal philosophy, the development of the disciplines and public education; however, this view of history ignores that imperialism and imperialistic practices were central to such developments (58). As imperialist and empire-building projects were carried out, conceptions of modernity were utilized in colonial discourses to define Indigenous peoples as (somewhat paradoxically) uncivilized, childlike,[5] irrational, incapable of autonomy and ominously threatening to the social order (Ruhl 1999: 111; Dean 2002: 48–49). The de-valuing and/or demonizing of Aboriginal individuals, societies and cultures functionally served colonialism by casting them as an impediment to the "natural" processes of economy and civilization.

In Canada, colonization "occurred in simultaneous, overlapping, spatially distinct waves of different European imperial regimes" and had both heterogenous and shared implications for the territory's diverse Indigenous populations (Stevenson 1999: 50). The necessity of "civilizing" Aboriginal peoples in Canada was explicitly addressed in 1914 by Duncan Campbell Scott, one of Canada's Confederation Poets and then Deputy Minister of the Indian Department:

> The happiest future for the Indian Race is absorption into the general population, and this is the object of the policy of our government. The great forces of intermarriage and education will finally overcome the lingering traces of native custom and tradition. (quoted in Neu and Therrien 2003: 102)

From the early stages of the Canadian colonial project, colonial authorities saw education as a functional mechanism for the creation of liberal citizens out of the "weird and waning race"[6] of First Nations peoples in Canada (Scott 1898: 93). Such discourses justified the implementation of residential schools and the imposition of colonial education systems.

Colonial liberal conceptualizations of Aboriginal peoples as childlike, irrational and dependent are antithetical to the liberal rational actor, making them particular targets in neoliberal campaigns for dependency reduction. Smith (1999) argues:

> Once Indigenous peoples had been rounded up and put on reserves the "Indigenous problem" became embedded as a policy discourse which reached out across all aspects of government's attempt to control the natives.... The natives were, according to this view, to

blame for not accepting the terms of their colonisation. In time social policies — for example, in health and education — were also viewed as remedies for the "Indigenous problem." By the 1960's this approach had been theorized repeatedly around notions of cultural deprivation or cultural deficit which laid the blame for Indigenous poverty and marginalisation even more securely on the people themselves. (91)

The discursive construction of Aboriginal peoples as culturally incapable of "spontaneous improvement" is alive and well in current neoliberal political practices, which view First Nations' historically enforced dependency on the state as worrisome at best and, at worst, as a marker of inherently flawed peoples and societies. Aboriginal peoples' lower levels of participation in the economy, high use of social assistance, limited tax exemption and receipt of funding from programs such as the PSSSP are taken as markers of a "culture of dependency" that must be replaced by independence and industry.

At the same time, as First Nations status has come to be attached with rights and entitlements different than those of other Canadian citizens, liberal and neoliberal frameworks increasingly view Indian status as repre-senting an unfair advantage "enjoyed" by First Nations peoples. Such trends are implied in Lawrence's (2004) reference to "the amount of work it takes to actually claim treaty rights because of the tremendous racism that is gener-ated when individuals pull out their Indian card for tax exemption" (222).

FIRST NATIONS CITIZENSHIP

Citizenship control is often viewed as a fundamental aspect of self-deter-mination; therefore, emergent structures of First Nations governance assert their right to determine and impose citizenship criteria (Green 2001: 727). The category of status Indian, meanwhile, was deliberately created as a means and mechanism for the governance of Aboriginal peoples in Canada. In 1869 the federal government passed the *Gradual Enfranchisement Act*, later called the *Indian Act* (Gehl 2004: 59). Through the *Indian Act*, the Canadian state employed its own criteria to define who was — and who was not — Indian through the ascription of the binary legal identities of "status" and "non-status" (Napoleon 2001: 2). Status Indians are afforded certain entitlements under the *Indian Act*, including tax exemption on reserve land, the right to live and be buried on-reserve, and certain health and education benefits (3).

Through a process called "enfranchisement," and in accordance with the original *Gradual Enfranchisement Act*, a status Indian woman marrying a non-status man lost Indian status, as did her children. At the same time, a non-status woman marrying a status Indian man received Indian status, as did her children (Lawrence 2003: 11–12). In addition to "enfranchisement," many individuals were convinced to give up Indian status for certain rights (such as the right to vote or drink alcohol) and others were not present at the time of registration for their band and area and therefore never received status in the first place (Smith 2000). The 1876 *Indian Act* included a provision whereby First Nations individuals who received a post-secondary education could be forced to give up Indian status (Napoleon 2001: 4; Dyck 1991: 53; Gehl 2004: 61). As the colonial governments' authority to define Indigenous identity was reinforced through legal, social and political channels, First Nations' understandings and criteria for citizenship were overwritten. Lawrence (2004) argues that this tactic of individualization sidestepped the issue of sovereignty "by replacing 'the nation' with 'the Indian'" (229).

Over time, the rights and entitlements status entails have come to produce real differences between those individuals (and communities) with status and those without (Fiske 1993: 22; Lawrence 2004). In 1985, after a Maliseet woman named Sandra Lovelace fought and won her case regarding loss of Indian status in a United Nations Human Rights Committee, Canada took measures to amend the *Indian Act* and enacted the controversial Bill C-31 (Lawrence 2003: 16). The Bill allowed people who had previously lost their status to regain it. However, the move was not universally welcomed by the Aboriginal community. Many First Nations protested Bill C-31 for a variety of reasons, including that it violated their constitutional rights to self-determination (Green 2001: 723–24; Napoleon 2001: 4). Since the practical administration of rights and entitlements has been devolved to the band level, First Nations citizenship is often conflated with band membership. Band membership, meanwhile, was uncoupled from Indian status through Bill C-31, which allowed First Nations to determine their own membership codes — codes that may or may not be different from the government's status criteria. As a result, in certain instances some status Indian women have been denied band membership and the concomitant rights and entitlements that go along with it (Green 2001: 723 n20).

Bill C-31 has consistently been framed as a women's issue, primarily since it was mainly Aboriginal women who lost status prior to the Bill's implementation. Bill C-31 shifted concerns over loss of status from women onto their children and grandchildren by introducing stacking provisions whereby a child who has two status Indian parents has status under Section C (1) of the *Indian Act* and a child who has one status Indian parent has status under Section C (2) of the *Indian Act*. If a C (1) person has a child with a non-status person, their child has C (2) Indian status. If a C (2) person has a child with a non-status person, their child does not receive Indian status. Individual status categorisations have been applied in varied ways historically and subject to individual and local contexts (Schissel and Wotherspoon 2003: 8; Gehl 2004; Green 2001; Napoleon 2001). Thus, Indian status as determined by the federal government purports to be based on a blood-quantum system that in reality amounts to defining and construct-ing individuals on the basis of the government's own pre-set bureaucratic categorizations and legal interpretations. Blood-quantum measures are applied over historically inconsistently applied status categorizations, meaning current categorizations cannot be assumed to reflect the "reality" of an individual's Indigenous biological heritage. Napoleon (2001) argues that these categorizations amount to "extinction by number" and points out that regulating Indian status legalized the taking of First Nations' land and resources and limits federal obligations to First Nations peoples "by limit-ing the number of people who qualify as Indians" (4, 9). While bands can set their own membership codes, by far the majority rely on some form of blood-quantum citizenship determination (6).[7]

Napoleon (2001) argues that restrictive federal funding of programs may discourage First Nations from engaging in inclusive membership models and create support for restrictive criteria for band membership (23–24). The situation of non-status Indians is emblematic of this tension. In her (unsuccessful) application for band membership in an Algonquin Nation, Indigenous scholar Lynn Gehl (2004) recounts, "I expected to be denied, as I am aware that funds provided to bands are based on the number of registered Indians" (68). Gehl's connection to the community itself, her own self-identity and the perspectives of the community as to her suitability for membership are all overwritten or ignored on the basis of the federal government's fiscal allocation process.

The citizenship categorization you fall into (or out of) determines your eligibility for PSSSP funding: Inuit and status Indians are eligible; Métis and non-status Indians are not. The exclusionary tactics used in the dissemina-tion of post-secondary funding may be part of an important resistance that seeks to re-create and rebuild Aboriginal communities, but it can also be understood to be reinforcing, or at least leaving unchallenged, the federal government's authority to define who is and is not "Indian." Indian status is a key mechanism in the claims making of Aboriginal governments and individuals (Cairns 2000: 97). Regarding post-secondary education, First Nations organizations have argued that free access to education is a treaty right, basing their arguments on provisions included in the numbered trea-ties and oral traditions that maintain treaty negotiations promised First Nations who signed the treaties far more than was contained in written versions (Stonechild 2006: 7–29). Legal arguments based on provisions in the *Indian Act* and moral arguments related to the impacts of colonialism extend the argument for free provision of post-secondary education to all status Indian peoples (National Indian Brotherhood 1972: 5; Stonechild 2006). According to the Assembly of First Nations (2000), "education at all levels is an inherent Aboriginal and treaty right that is recognized in the Canadian Constitution [and] the federal government has a fiduciary responsibility to uphold the rights of all First Nations" (quoted in INAC 2005: 34).

The federal government, meanwhile, maintains that, "education is a privilege and not a right" (Lanceley 1999: 4). In its (2005) evaluation of the PSSSP, INAC re-positions this argument in terms of neoliberal understandings of citizenship and education:

> Generally speaking, western governments have moved to the concept of a cost-shared approach in which the recipients of advanced education, who tend to reap lifelong benefits by way of an enhanced economic status, are expected to bear a significant portion of the costs of their own post-secondary education.... PSSSP has in the past decade evolved from a program intended to provide complete support for eligible students into a cost-shared program, although this policy has never been explicitly declared. (iv–v)

Lanceley (1999) explains that tensions between Aboriginal rights and First Nations policies result from "the contradiction in how devolution of post-secondary education resulted in First Nations administering a program that does not recognize treaty right to education" (4). As a result, "First Nations struggle to honor the perceived right to education while being forced to create a policy that limits the number of students who may enter universities" (24). Devolutionary processes can thus be seen to directly undermine First Nations' claims to free post-secondary education as a right.

DEVOLUTION OF SERVICES, DEVOLUTION OF BLAME

In 1972, the National Indian Brotherhood (precursor to the Assembly of First Nations) presented its policy paper, *Indian Control of Indian Education,* to the federal government (Hiller 2006: 211). It re-asserted the federal government's legal responsibility for First Nations' education and demanded immediate reforms in the areas of responsibility, programs, teachers, facilities and local control. The paper also outlined the need for administrative training to ensure the success of self-governing endeavours:

> Training must be made available to those reserves desiring local control of education. This training must include every aspect of educational administration. It is important that Bands moving towards local control have the opportunity to prepare themselves for the move... continuing guidance during the operational phase is equally important and necessary. (National Indian Brotherhood 1972: 7)

Although INAC adopted the National Indian Brotherhood's proposals in 1973 and subsequently introduced a mega-policy that focused on participation with First Nations and devolution of program administration to the band level, training for band administrative staff never materialized (Matthew 2001: 73; Frideres 1998: 224–25; Comeau and Santin 1990; British Columbia Ministry of Advanced Education 2006). This has led Comeau and Santin (1990) to argue: "[d]evolution thus created a cadre of untrained band officials who found themselves unable to do any more than carry out government orders on reserve. Budget deficits and service delays became routine" (55). The role that the federal government has played in these processes is overlooked and ignored as neoliberal discourses call for open and accountable governance in reserve communities (Flanagan 2000; Sandberg 2005; Canadian Taxpayer's Federation 2003).

Frideres (1998) notes that devolution served the marked function of transferring critical attention from INAC and the federal government onto band governments and administrators. At the same time, the benefits that many non-First Nations groups and organizations (such as educational institutions) receive from such programs are generally overlooked or ignored (223–26). With the transfer of fiscal responsibility and program administration, the federal government is no longer understood as being "at fault" for program shortcomings at the band level — whether those shortcomings are a result of fiscal mismanagement, a lack of resources, improperly trained staff, the desperately inadequate housing and infrastructural situation found on many reserves and/or past or present government policies. Fleras and Elliott (1992) point out that, "from the federal perspective, there is much to be gained by displacing public displeasure and transferring Aboriginal dissatisfaction from Ottawa to the provinces and local communities" (49). First Nations may be subjected to a range of criticisms from their communities for PSSSP administration and the application of exclusionary measures. Examining the effects of a failed self-government educational initiative, Dyck (1991) recalls,

> The overall expenditures undertaken on the reserve during these years were quite unremarkable. The more serious blows were to the pride, confidence, and unity of the band. Every project mounted on a reserve or on behalf of Indians is subjected to intense scrutiny by local non-Indians. Just as too great a degree of success in such projects could be expected to encounter criticism from those who contend that Indians are being given too much by government, so too is any indication of failure seized upon by some non-Indians as evidence of the supposed inherent deficiencies of Indians as a people. (135)

Such issues may be further complicated since some First Nation peoples may see Chief and council structures of governance as impositions of colonial rule rather than representative bodies accountable to their membership (Napoleon 2001: 11).

Block-funding arrangements that have accompanied devolutionary processes can add to public perceptions of First Nations governments receiving vast amounts of federal dollars. However, in order to qualify for block funding such as Fiscal Transfer Arrangements and Alternative Funding mechanisms, "a band or tribal council must have participatory and governing procedures that are satisfactory to [INAC], and the band and tribal council must also agree to submit a yearly audit of its financial affairs" (Satzewich and Wotherspoon 2000: 235). Thus, federal control of First Nations' finances means that they are compelled to structure their governments to match liberal ideals of limited and accountable government. Lanceley reflects that, "[i]n 1988, PSSSP began with an announcement to increase dollars spent on First Nations education" (Lanceley 1999: 14). The rhetorical impact of large numbers hides the fact that, once divided among all First Nation communities and all programs, fiscal transfers may not be enough to adequately administer individual initiatives such as the PSSSP.

This is especially true since PSSSP funds are "core" funds in block funding allotments, allowing the money to be reallocated according to local priorities. Currently, heavy reporting burdens require a significant amount of time and energy at the band level: in 2002, the Auditor General found that four federal departments required at least 168 reports from First Nations communities (many of which had fewer than 500 residents). Many of the reports were unnecessary and not used by the government (Office of the Auditor General 2006: 163). However, INAC's extensive monitoring of First Nations' financial affairs does not necessarily translate into program-specific requirements. Satzewich and Wotherspoon (2000) observe that,

> Funds directed to specific purposes such as education are often diverted to more pressing community requirements for local administration and infrastructural services, often with the tacit consent of the Indian Affairs Department, which seeks little or no financial information or monitoring of programs delivered at the band level. (143–44)

Many First Nations communities are coping with pressing issues such as a lack of clean water, housing shortages, extremely poor housing conditions and a multitude of other communal and infrastructural challenges. When issues of funding prioritization are negotiated at the band level, the re-allocation of post-secondary funds may seem a necessary evil. INAC is protected from scrutiny while First Nations are locally, politically and publicly held to blame for program's administrative inadequacies.

Meanwhile, in an environment of neoliberal cutbacks and fiscal restraint, public resentment may be fostered over First Nation peoples' perceived "financial advantage" regarding post-secondary funding and other social programs, as it occurs at a time when non-Aboriginals are being required to "tighten the belt." Thomas Flanagan (2000), a political scientist, senior fellow at the Fraser Institute and advisor to Prime Minister Steven Harper, echoes such sentiments in his argument that Aboriginal peoples have,

> little sense of the real-world trade-offs because everything their governments do for them is paid for by other people. They never have to give up anything in order to get additional government programs. If they had to make the same choices that other Canadians routinely make, they would, I predict, take the axe to many of the government programs proliferating luxuriantly in their communities. (197–98)

Ironically, First Nations are increasingly subject to such criticisms although they may have little or no control over program administration. Despite devolutionary processes, many First Nations do not have control over federal transfer payments to their band. Close to 10 percent of First Nations in Canada are in co-management or third-party management as a result of serious or chronic fiscal imbalances. Co-management involves a First Nation and INAC agreeing on a third party who mutually approves band expenditures; under third-party management, INAC appoints a third party who must approve all band expenditures (Graham 2000: 1). Under third-party management, a First Nation may not even have access to the contractual agreement between INAC and the administering group or organization, although the fees paid for their services come out of the overall band budget (Office of the Auditor General 2003: 9). Third-party managers often live off-reserve; therefore, tracking them down to approve expenditures can be a problem. Chief Irvin McIvor recounts:

> When a school bus broke down, we had to find him. We had to get him to send a fax over to another city for them to release the parts. The school was closed sometimes two or three times a week. (Barnsely 2004)

Problems such as these have led to third-party managers being called the "new Indian agents," referring to INAC-appointed individuals who were responsible for band-level administration of all aspects of the *Indian Act* from its inception until the position was gradually phased out during the 1960s (Barnsely 2004; OCAP 2004; Report of the Royal Commission on Aboriginal Peoples 1996: 39). As third party managers are not agents of the federal government, the government is not seen as being "responsible" for their actions and First Nations remain in the spotlight for receipt of critical attention.

Devolutionary processes and block-funding strategies (promoted as allowing First Nations the 'flexibility' to respond to local priorities) taking place under the rubric of self-government mirror other financial allocation processes through which the federal government is attempting to carry out its overall objective of promoting fiscal restraint. Brodie (2002) contends that decentralization in Canada has resulted in "a scurry of fiscal off-loading onto newly-designated 'shock absorbers'" (103). In devolutionary processes tied to self-government initiatives such as the PSSSP, it is frequently noted that the cost of, in addition to control over, service delivery is downloaded to the regional level (Slowey 2001: 3). Lanceley (1991) contends that through PSSSP devolution, INAC's intent has always been to reduce its fiscal expenditures on Aboriginal education (245). Block-funding arrangements have reduced government costs through funding regulation mechanisms whereby fiscal transfers are no longer tied to specific programs or the population eligible for program funding. The federal government saves on administration and staffing costs for programs such as the PSSSP while funding restrictions result in the increasing regulation of program accessibility — further resulting in longer student waiting lists (Lanceley 1999: 21). In this and other areas, First Nations struggle to maintain the current levels of service provision and often cannot match that which was previously provided directly through the government (Slowey 2001: 3). Comeau and Santin (1990) argue that in these processes, the federal government gives

> Indian people bits and pieces of control, some of it in response
> to native demands, but most of it as a way of satisfying its own
> agenda of reducing its financial and constitutional responsibilities
> while ensuring that the division of power remains intact. (quoted
> in Pompana 1997: 56)

THE POST-SECONDARY STUDENT SUPPORT SYSTEM

Contrary to popular Canadian beliefs about "free education for Indians," First Nation-students trying to access funding negotiate a complex web of structured power relations. Currently, federal funding for the PSSSP is transferred to INAC's regional offices, which re-allocate funds to First Nations. Funding allocation methods from INAC to First Nations vary regionally. British Columbia, which is home to 198 of 615 federally recognized First Nations, constitutes one region according to current funding strategies. The situation in British Columbia provides insight into current forms of PSSSP administration. In 1994–95, INAC introduced per-capita funding allocation methods in the region. These amendments untied PSSSP funding from the actual number of eligible students, as the regional budget distributes funds on the basis of band membership as a proportion of the total band population of British Columbia (Matthew 2001: 58). The new funding mechanisms save on INAC expenditures while putting some bands in a much better position to fund their students than others.

In releasing administrative control of the PSSSP to First Nations bands and tribal councils, the federal government has also restricted funding and imposed national guidelines on program administration. INAC's (2003) *Post-Secondary Education: National Program Guidelines* presents a framework for policy implementation for the PSSSP. The guidelines allow First Nations to develop local operating policies for PSSSP administration. However, such policies are subject to INAC approval, are required to incorporate specific criteria and must be able to pass a compliance review process (First Nations Education Steering Committee 2005). They may increase eligibility requirements and/or decrease the maximum per-student funding allowances set by the *National Program Guidelines*, but are not permitted to lower the eligibility requirements or to increase the maximum funding permitted per student. Funding caps have been imposed at the same time as tuition fees have skyrocketed and the number of eligible students is increasing rapidly.[8] As a result, decisions as to resource allocation — that is, how to fund an increasing number of students with a decreasing[9] amount of money — must be negotiated at the band level (Rounce 2004: 4; Schuetze and Day 2001: 8; Satzewich and Wotherspoon 2000: 143).

Faced with funding restrictions, rising numbers of eligible students and increasing tuition and education expenses, many First Nations have developed local operating policies (LOPs) to guide student sponsorship decisions since, increasingly, not all students can be funded. Many First Nations are "forced to choose between funding many students at a low level of assistance, or a few students at a higher level of assistance" (INAC 2005: 31). Accounting and insurential techniques are used to make administrative judgments of individuals' relative suitability for funding. Where LOPs are in place, students must meet a series of qualifications before receiving funding and may be placed in competition with each other for funding. "Rituals of truth" relying on knowledges about students help to "make and justify administrative decisions about individuals that are inescapably determinist in their consequences" (Rose 1998: 181).

Ironically, techniques of governance employed by the LOPs may significantly impede students' abilities to replicate the behaviour patterns they are designed to promote. Heavy course load requirements, overall funding restrictions and low living allowances add to the "normal" stresses Indigenous students encounter when attending post-secondary education within a colonial society (see Guno 1996; R.A. Malatest and Associates 2004; Association of Canadian Community Colleges 2005; Verjee 2003). On top of this LOPs generally require students to dedicate a significant degree of time and energy to the production of knowledge about themselves (such as providing transcripts, progress reports, budget sheets, receipts, etc.). Failure to carry out such knowledge-production activities often carries the potential for loss of funding. These and other techniques of governance in the LOPs enlist students as the primary agents responsible for their "successful" educational experiences.

In current contexts, "responsible budgeting" may require students to attempt to live off funding amounts too small to meet their basic needs. *National Program Guidelines* (INAC 2003) specify the *maximum* living allowance permitted as that established by the (annually updated) Canada Student Loan Program (20). However, due to funding restrictions, many First Nations use the guidelines in INAC's (1989) PSSSP *Terms and Conditions.* In its (2005) evaluation of the PSSSP, INAC notes that these "'rates for resourcing monthly allowances' were introduced in 1989 and have never been changed" (31). It further found,

> PSSSP students are, on average, receiving between $500 and $4000 less per academic year than they are paying in living expenses; and... current per student allowances are below the national average established under the Canada Student Loan Program five years ago. (iv)

The trends are exacerbated for more remote bands, as students' high travel costs leave little in the post-secondary budget (31).

National Program Guidelines (INAC 2003) stipulate that, to be eligible for PSSSP funding, students must "maintain continued satisfactory academic standing within that institution" (8). They also require funding be stopped for students placed on academic probation or otherwise restricted from continuing in their program of study (5). Bands may require students to meet additional grade-based performance measures in order to receive funding. Failure to meet such standards is often linked to disciplinary action, namely probation or termination of funding. If current trends continue, raising GPA (grade point average) requirements may seem inevitable — especially in a neoliberal policy environment requiring standardized, quantifiable measures of educational success. Such performance measures are meant to ensure that individuals are not "riding the system" and thereby failing to fulfil their social obligations. Through such measures, academic standing becomes the primary indicator of individual success and the primary determinant of whether one is worthy of aid. "Doing well" is equated with meeting certain standards, standards that serve the wider society. Alternative measures or understandings of success are lost even as conceptualizations of the worthy and unworthy poor are reinforced.

These processes are all the more disconcerting since they are being applied to Indigenous students within a colonial education system. Verjee (2003) contends:

> Standardized tests... have been used to classify large proportions of Aboriginal students as "learning disabled" or unteachable, and to

stream these students into non-academic and vocationally limited programs. The small amount of psychological and educational literature reveals Aboriginal learners as right-brained, having aberrant learning styles, suffering from fetal alcohol effects, learning disabled, and in general less intelligent than almost everyone else. Most of these conclusions have been reached through the misuse of tests. (13)

Verjee also argues that measurement practices can facilitate racism through the perpetuation of stereotypes (15). Accountability regimes that force First Nations to justify methods of program administration, combined with restrictive PSSSP budgets, mean that Aboriginal students must meet colonial standards of "success" to justify their access to post-secondary funds.

Band funding prioritizations are influenced by the *National Program Guidelines,* which offer "Strategic Studies Scholarships." These incentives discipline First Nation students into rationalizing the choices they make while encouraging them to adopt a framework for analysis that emphasizes economics above all else. The eligible programs are reflective of current market prioritizations, particularly as they apply to the needs of First Nations to engage in economic development programs. They include commerce, public or business administration, physical science, mathematics, computer sciences, forestry and engineering. Since colonialism and neoliberalism structure current capitalist markets and the enterprises they deem of value, these aspects of current policies may significantly limit potential ways of being for Indigenous students. The Union of British Columbia Indian Chiefs has argued that funding preferences and incentives for students enrolled in courses favoured by the federal government are intended to "create Indians in the image of federal bureaucrats who can take over many of the functions and values of the Department of Indian Affairs" (*Saskatchewan Indian* 1989).

Restrictions on amount and length of funding are accompanied by course load requirements. In order to receive a living allowance, students must maintain a full course load, and LOPs may increase or impose their own definitions of full-time studies. Attendance provisions further discipline students' use of time by connecting absences and even lateness with the potential suspension or loss of funding. As women are more likely to be the primary caregiver of young children, heavy course loads, timed completion and disciplinary measures tied to absence and lateness may have a stronger impact on their access to funding, particularly as women are the majority of part-time students at the graduate and undergraduate levels (Statistics Canada 2006b: 93). These trends may be exacerbated for Aboriginal women, who are noted to have more children and larger families than non-Aboriginal women (189).

While guidelines and protocols vary among provinces, territories, tribal councils, and First Nations bands, in order to receive or maintain funding, students may be required to submit budgets; to grant detailed financial disclosure regarding themselves, their spouses and their dependants (including wages, employment insurance, rental costs, etc.); and/or to have previously applied for student loans (McLean 2007). A First Nation may impose restrictions on course or program changes, may retract funding if students do not apply for a set number of scholarships per year, may place time limits on program completion, and may require students to take study or life skills courses on top of regular classes. Students may be prioritized based on whether they live on- or off-reserve, whether they re-gained status through Bill C-31 or on the perceived benefit of their area of study to First Nation's social and economic development. Students may be required to work for the band for a set number of years after graduation; some policies outline that students' funding will be docked or terminated for "accumulated tardiness," and others require monthly progress and attendance reports. These provisions are inherently disciplinary inasmuch as the threat of losing funding — and therefore the threat losing access to higher education — is always present.

The devolution of programs also has widespread implications for student resistance to current methods of program administration and federal support. In 1988–89, Aboriginal students across Canada engaged in widespread resistance to government attempts to alter post-secondary funding arrangements in a way that would see funding capped, access limited and benefits slashed: "[d]uring the 1988-89 academic year, the voice of Indian students struck the Canadian public with intense force. Collectively, many students across the country fasted, demonstrated, and participated in peaceful sit-ins at [INAC] offices and were subsequently arrested" (Lanceley 1991: 235). Although the students did win some important concessions (including increasing the amount and length of assistance provided), major areas of contention — such as the funding cap — remained in place (Lanceley 1999; Satzewich and Wotherspoon 2000: 140). Devolution of funding and administrative functions to individual First Nations means that student resistance to the imposition of disciplinary, actuarial and surveillance techniques of power through the program has been fragmented.

By specifying that "students may not appeal to INAC" regarding their funding application, the federal government avoids blatantly paternalistic practices and simultaneously transfers students' potential criticisms of the program onto their First Nation (INAC 2003: 23). Students are faced with lobbying their individual First Nation or tribal council, which in turn has little or no control over their PSSSP budget. Such processes can be divisive at the band level and are more complex within the context of self-government. Aboriginal students unhappy with the status quo may now be seen as criticizing their own governments and thereby undermining the degrees of hard-won autonomy that First Nations have re-gained. When students encounter difficulty negotiating funding dilemmas at the band level, their belief in First Nations' capacities for exercising autonomy may be directly undermined (McLean 2007: 100).

CONCLUSION

In utilizing the limited tools selectively made available to them by the federal government, First Nations are attempting to rebuild their communities and societies on the foundations of an educated citizenry. The creation of well-educated Indigenous populations is seen as key in facilitating not only First Nations' autonomy and self-determination, but the decolonization of the education system as well. In order to do so as effectively as possible and in consideration of the limited funds available, disciplining students in their use of those resources becomes a priority. Indigenous students are being asked to assume all the attributes of the liberal rational actor, a conceptualization based on the characteristics of elite white males. Criteria for probation, suspension and termination of funding clearly demarcate between accept-able and unacceptable behaviour for funded Aboriginal students. Through responsibilization, Aboriginal students are cast as the fundamental agents in creating positive educational outcomes for themselves. Recognizing the capabilities and agency of Aboriginal individuals has been a core component of the Indigenous (or Fourth World) movement in Canada and internation-ally. However, this shift must also be contextualized within a neoliberal move towards market citizenship where social problems are individualized; that is to say, the responsibility for overcoming social barriers is laid on the individual rather than society as a whole.

Limited funding has produced limited choices for First Nations — and limiting possibilities for Aboriginal students. The irony is that in the "suc-cess" of such endeavours, Aboriginal peoples are told their very freedom is at stake; engaging in "rational" governance practices and capacity-building exercises is considered a pre-requisite to enhancing First Nations' institu-tional capacities for self-determination. Rather than recognizing Aboriginal peoples' inherent rights to self-determination, self-government in the cur-rent neoliberal environment looks suspiciously like contracting-out federal obligations and downloading responsibility for colonialism onto individual First Nation students.

Disciplinary measures in current post-secondary education funding policies for Aboriginal students are designed to facilitate the creation of responsible, self-regulating, economically autonomous individuals. Foucault explains:

> [i]n discipline, punishment is only one element of a double system: gratification-punishment.... Through this micro-economy of a

> perpetual penalty operates a differentiation that is not one of acts, but of individuals themselves, of their nature, their potentialities, their level or their value. (180–81)

The policies use a market-based approach to regulating and disciplining human behaviour to force individuals to calculate their actions on a cost/benefit analysis. The program enmeshes students within a web of authority relations; a system of individualization, standardized measurement, supervision and personal accountability for fulfilment of obligation completes the process. Performance-measurement and evaluation are key; Ormiston (2002) explains:

> In the case of reward, there is promoted a pride of self, a pleasure in one's performance recognized as meritorious. Similarly punishments are directed at provoking feelings of shame and dissatisfaction with self. One strives to be "deserving" of the privileges one sees granted to one's peers... one reacts against one's own self. One strives to become that which is recognized and rewarded in a positive way. (8, emphasis in original)

The use of such rationalities in the constitution of Aboriginal students through the PSSSP is clear. What is perhaps most disturbing about the applicability of this analysis, however, is that Ormiston is in fact referencing teaching strategies applied by the Oblate Fathers of Canada in residential schools during the 1950s. Although the terminology may have changed — from Indian to Aboriginal, from assimilation to autonomy — the "making up" of Aboriginal peoples in Canada is far from over.

NOTES

1. Policymakers have utilized various legal and non-legal terms to define and administer over and to Indigenous peoples in Canada. As a result, terminologies are controversial and subject to ongoing debate (Guno 1996: 1 n1). I use the term "First Nation" to refer to a federally recognized Indian Band as this term is utilized by the AFN in self-description and indicates respect and recognition of pre-existing and autonomous Indigenous nations within the borders of what is now Canada. "First Nations individual" refers to status Indian peoples. I have attempted to limit the use of the terms "Indian" and "native" to those instances when I am referring to the legal categorization of status Indian peoples or when quoting another source. This research makes limited reference to Inuit or Métis and I use the term "Aboriginal" to refer to Inuit, Métis, status and non-status Indian peoples inclusively. I also use the term "Indigenous peoples" inclusively and virtually interchangeably with "Aboriginal peoples" (see Smith 1999: 7).

2. As a result of these and other political, social and historical factors, Aboriginal peoples' relationship with the European school system in Canada remains ambiguous. In 2001, 40 percent of Aboriginal women and 44 percent of Aboriginal men over the age of twenty-five had not graduated from high school (Statistics Canada

2006b: 196). Although the numbers of Aboriginal post-secondary students have continued to rise, a relative gap with non-Aboriginal population remains and is increasing (Hull 2005: 12–13). A report estimated that the education gap between First Nations peoples living on reserve and the rest of the Canadian population would take twenty-eight years to close (Office of the Auditor General 2004).

3. See, for example, Dyck 1991; Maaka and Fleras 2005; Manuel and Posluns 1974; McFarlane 1993; Miller 2000; Stonechild 2006.

4. This chapter does not address aspects of PSSSP policy administration in contexts specific to Inuit, Métis and non-status peoples. It also is unable to account for the specifics of land claims settlements. This focus may be seen to homogenize diverse First Nations while simultaneously neglecting large portions of Canada's Indigenous peoples. My intention is not to overlook local, cultural and social contexts of policy implementation, but to examine the effects of uniform federal policies applied to these diverse populations.

5. First Nations peoples' childlike status is also a legal categorization, as they are "wards of the state" under the *Indian Act.*

6. This phrase is derived from Scott's (1898) "Onandaga Madonna," a poem relying heavily on colonial conceptions of Indigenous women (93).

7. Bill C-31 also directly regulates the sexuality of First Nation women when it comes to paternity. If, for any reason, a mother does not wish to list the father of her child on the birth certificate, Bill C-31 requires that Indian Affairs assume the father is non-status, meaning the child either receives no status or the "lesser" status afforded by Section 6(2) (Gabriel et al. 2005: 16). Either way, a woman's choice of partner (or choice to keep that partner's identity to herself) is regulated and constrained by provisions that have the potential to limit the ability of her children to access the rights and entitlements associated with Indian status, including PSSSP funding.

8. Between 1990 and 2000, tuition fees at universities have increased by as much as 125 percent (Rounce 2004: 4). As a result, student debt has risen by an estimated 277 percent (Schuetze and Day 2001: 8). From 1960–61 to the early 1990s, the number of Aboriginal students completing high school rose from 3.4 to 47 percent (Satzewich and Wotherspoon 2000: 131). Aboriginal youth are also the fastest growing segment of Canada's population — half of all Aboriginal people are under the age of twenty-five (Frances, 2004: 17). The Aboriginal population had a growth rate of 22 percent between 1996 and 2001, around 70 percent higher than that of non-Aboriginal Canadians (Frances, 2004: 6; R.A. Malatest and Associates 2004: 12).

9. Relative to inflation, accounting for the increasing Aboriginal population and somewhat dependent on individual First Nations' decisions regarding program funding mechanisms.

SECTION II – CASE STUDIES OF SOCIAL MOVEMENTS

CHAPTER FIVE

"BLAIRMORE EXPECTS THIS DAY EVERY WAGE EARNER TO DO HIS DUTY"

DEPRESSION RELIEF AND THE RADICAL ADMINISTRATION OF BLAIRMORE ALBERTA, 1933–1936

Kyle R. Franz

Until 1933, Mrs. Rossi was not a well-known person outside of Blairmore, Alberta. An eighty-year-old Italian immigrant, Rossi typified the silent majority of this bituminous coal mining centre: non-British, impoverished and trying to survive the Depression as best she could. Yet it was not for her struggle against poverty or her hard work as a wife and mother that she would be remembered, but her simple actions on municipal election day, Monday February 13, 1933. Unable to speak a word of English, Rossi entered the polling station with a lump of coal firmly in her grasp to signify her vote for the miners' slate of Red candidates (*The Worker* June 3, 1933).[1] The election was contentious, but by 2 a.m. a slim victory was announced for the Red slate. Sweeping the previous pro-business council from power, Communists were elected to every available seat on town council as well as the mayor's chair. "Never in the history of any town in western Canada," the *Blairmore Enterprise* reported, has "such a degree of interest manifested itself in a municipal election" (*Blairmore Enterprise* February 16, 1933; hereafter *BE*). Mayor Bill Knight won re-election in 1935, with Red government continuing at Blairmore until February 14, 1936.[2] This chapter examines the social policies and ideological practices of Canada's first Red town council, arguing that it was able to work within the established legislative boundaries of municipal authority to fundamentally alter the social experience for the working class at Blairmore while simultaneously challenging the dominant political ideologies of the Canadian nation state in the 1930s.

Bill Knight and councillors Joseph Aschacher, Joseph Krkosky, Albert Olson and returning councillor Romano Peressini took power at the peak of anti-Communist activity by the Canadian state. In 1931 the federal government arrested eight senior members of the Communist Party of Canada (CCP), including their leader Tim Buck, and charged them under Section 98 of the Criminal Code of Canada. Section 98 made it illegal to advocate "'governmental, industrial, or economic change within Canada by use of force, violence, or physical injury...' even if the accused did nothing to bring about such changes" (Thompson and Seager 1985: 227). Until its repeal by Prime Minister William Lyon Mackenzie King, Section 98 effectively made it illegal to be a Communist in Canada. Under these circumstances, the CCP leadership went underground, continuing to advocate change through the formation of front organizations such as the Canadian Labour Defence League (CLDL) and the Workers' Unity League (WUL) (Angus 1981: 269, 281). The party demanded non-contributory unemployment insurance, the abandonment of the relief camp scheme, the institution of a seven-hour work day with no reduction in income and the payment of union wages to the unemployed working on government relief projects (Avakumovic 1975: 75). The increased expense could be offset, according to the CCP, by the introduction of a "sharply graduated income tax," a "graduated capital levy" and the reduction of "official salaries" and defence expenditures (*The Worker* October 3, 1931). While some of these proposals overlapped with other left-leaning political parties, the CCP never shied away from its ultimate goal of a Canadian revolution.

It was under the auspices of Section 98 and the perceived threat of revolution that "local bosses, clergy and reactionaries" called for the provincial government to declare Blairmore's election invalid and appoint a provincial administrator for the town. The Anglican Reverend Parkington was reported to have been "traveling around making scarifying speeches about 'life and property' being in danger," while United Farmers of Alberta Premier John Brownlee was so displeased with the election results that his government ordered an audit of the town's finances (*The Worker* March 3, 1933; *The Worker* March 11, 1933). Under provincial legislation, a municipal government in or near bankruptcy automatically qualified to be put under provincial management (*Medicine Hat News* February 28, 1933). It was against this backdrop of uncertainty that the council made their first dramatic decisions.

After their inaugural council meeting, the new Red administration issued what the press dubbed the "Knight Manifesto," outlining its new relief and taxation policies. With the bold headline "Blairmore Expects This Day Every Wage Earner To Do His Duty," the document stated: "It is quite evident that the [federal and provincial] government cannot or will not make adequate provisions for the unemployed, and until such time as their relief scheme functions at a better manner than present, it is up to us" (*BE* March 2, 1933). Mayor Knight also indicated how the town would pay for the increased support: a "voluntary" 5 percent contribution by every wage earner in Blairmore. It was announced that the local miners, under the auspices of the Red-affiliated Mine Workers' Union of Canada (MWUC), had already agreed to contribute 5 percent of their pay, as had teachers in the Blairmore School District and the employees of F.M. Thompson's store (*BE* March 2, 1933). Should 5 percent "donations" not be forthcoming from the remaining segments of the population, the council warned that it would take whatever action was required to finance the necessary relief (*BE* March 2, 1933).

Knight also carefully and deliberately addressed the "Redness" of the new council: "After a great deal of deliberation, [it has been decided by council] that redness is a state of the stomach. It is time that people's opinion regarding this colour business were changed, and we get together as before" (*BE* March 2, 1933). While this may have been an effort to unite the town after a politically charged election, it is more likely that this denial was intended to avoid any legal complications under Section 98. It was this awareness of the possible legal implications from statements like these, coupled with the town's relatively good financial position, that prevented the authorities from immediately acting against the Communist councillors.

The Knight Manifesto marked the beginning of substantive change to the systems of taxation and relief at Blairmore. When the local merchants and independent business owners refused to voluntarily contribute 5 percent of their income towards a more comprehensive relief program, Knight and his council introduced Business Tax Bylaw Number Nine, to legislate a 5 percent increase in business taxes while providing for a decrease in municipal taxes for homeowners.[3] Quickly passing first, second and third reading, this bylaw represents a fundamental change in the reason taxes were collected at Blairmore. Whereas until 1933 public funds were used to pay for civic projects demanded by boosters, the upper classes and the West Canadian Collieries (the largest employer in town), this bylaw reversed the imperative, with taxes being collected from the local business interests to finance programs that benefitted the working class.

The assumption that the rich should pay for relief was reinforced some weeks later with the adoption of a bylaw that levied taxes on purebred dogs.[4] While superficially about animal control, this bylaw effectively implied that if you could afford a purebred dog during the Depression, you could afford to pay more towards the costs of providing relief programs to the unemployed and underemployed of Blairmore. Ben Swanky, a Communist Party of Canada organizer who was sent to Blairmore, recalled years later:

> They couldn't figure out how to get at the mine owners, so the question came up "what kind of dogs are there in town?" They found that it was the mine owners that had the pedigree dogs and the miners that owned the mongrels, so they put a tax on the pedigree dogs. (Bouzek 2005)

This attack on the upper classes was not limited to the owners of expensive canines. Knight removed any question regarding his stance on capital and landlords by proposing that "any work given to tenants for the purpose of paying for rent be regarded as granted for the purpose of paying arrears of taxes owing by the landlord [to the Town of Blairmore]."[5] This was not simply an effort to collect unpaid taxes owing the town treasury but a pointed attempt to extract money from a particular group of people. There was not, nor would there be, an accompanying motion that forced miners or those on assistance to hand over their relief payments to finance outstanding arrears on personal property taxes. During their first weeks in office the council served notice that the tax burden was to be borne by the upper classes and those who made a living by providing services to the working-class community.

This fundamental alteration in Blairmore's taxation policy was accompanied by a complete overhaul of the municipal relief apparatus. Once in office, the new administration repeatedly telegrammed the provincial Relief Commissioner, asking him to visit Blairmore to personally discuss how a more comprehensive yet humane system of relief could be implemented. Having received no response to their many letters, council finally decided that the suffering of Blairmoreites could not wait for action by the provincial and federal governments, and unilaterally increased the wages of the unemployed working for the town "from thirty cents per hour to fifty cents per hour."[6] Though not indicating how this increase would be paid for in the long term, the town assumed the immediate costs and sent a telegram to the federal and provincial governments advising them that the council had increased their financial liabilities to the people of Blairmore. This telegram did get a response from A.A. McKenzie, provincial minister of charity and relief, who demanded that "all efforts must be made to reduce expenses as far as the married unemployed were concerned."[7] This answer was unacceptable to Knight and his associates, who found the minister's demands to be "impossible" to meet and enclosed with their reply a list of "all single and married unemployed so that they might receive financial help."[8] Despite no increase in funding from the provincial or federal governments, the Red council continued to finance relief at the rate of fifty cents per hour. This marked the beginning of an aggressive campaign to force favourable action from government for the residents of Blairmore.

This new approach was not reflected in the form of lofty petitions or demands for new and unrealistic programs; most of the correspondence between the administration and the authorities involved detailed cases and sought specific retribution. Given the dangerous nature of bituminous coal mining, the Workmen's Compensation Board (wcb) was often the recipient of such communications. Mr. Camile Canet was the first to appeal to the "council for help getting justice from the wcb" and was certainly not the last.[9] In what had previously been a process between the injured miner and the wcb, the town took an active role by writing to the board on Canet's behalf. When the adjudication of the file took longer than the council deemed necessary, they took the matter further by petitioning the government, the minister and the MLA for "justice."[10] The municipal authority's resources extended beyond those seeking compensation from the WCB; they also included collecting money for those who were awarded settlement but had not been paid.[11] Such actions were simple but important for many residents, particularly if English was not their first language. The council had the staff, resources, time and understanding of the issues to successfully pursue cases for many who would have otherwise never received the "justice" they deserved from the WCB and other government bodies.

The administration also facilitated dialogue between the citizens themselves. Mr. O. Kurri came before council on August 7, 1933, seeking legal advice, not retribution or advocacy. Kurri had been renting a house from Mr. Kubic but was unable to pay his rent because he was unemployed. He had been threatened with eviction and did not know what to do. Council "advised him that the only way he could be evicted was on a judge's order" and Kurri left the chamber.[12] When Kubic came to council the next month, he said that he had decided to sell the house which Kurri was renting, and the new owners did not want a tenant.[13] Kubic did not want to evict Kurri, but did not know that there was any other choice. The administration intervened and agreed to find a new home for Kurri.[14] Council's mediation would later extend to fences, porches and other squabbles between neighbours.

Council chambers also functioned as a *de facto* court of appeal for provincial and federal relief. For many who were challenging relief settlements awarded to them by the provincial or federal government, the appeals process proved lengthy and they could not provide for themselves in the interim. The Red administration made a point of listening to their problems and providing what they could in short term relief to keep the men out of relief camps, or "slave camps," as the labour press and local Single Unemployed Association called them (*The Worker* Nov. 11, 1932).[15] Mr. Stella, for example, approached council on June 19, 1933, seeking assistance in dealing with the provincial government's relief program. After hearing about his situation, the council agreed that he was indeed justified in seeking further aid from the provincial authorities and granted him the sack of flour he requested to sustain him and his family in the short term.[16] Similar actions were taken on July 3 1933, for example, when immediate help was granted to Mrs. Mishalski and Mr. F.O. Peters, who were not receiving "sufficient relief" from the province.[17]

For Knight and his associates relief was not only about the allocation of money but also the right to support oneself with dignity. Oral histories clearly indicate the need to hunt, fish and garden to supplement dietary intake. Beatrice Peressini remembers that as a child her father (Councillor Romano Peressini) not only worked in the mine, but that "we had half a block... and we grew vegetables, and that gave us any vegetable you wanted, and even some of the vegetables went on in the winter time."[18] Being able to grow your own food was important in an economy where many were starving or barely subsisting, and it was from this personal experience that Councillor Peressini proposed the town make available all unused public property "for the purpose of growing gardens."[19] The rent per annum per lot was to be "free to the first applicant for the year 1933, understanding that they are to be properly cultivated."[20] It was through these provisions that many of the town's empty lots were converted to vegetable gardens to feed the unemployed and underemployed. Residents were later permitted to also have chicken runs on these vacant properties. Moreover, although council had made provisions to "cancel the lease in the event of a sale," the town did not sell any of the properties being used as gardens despite receiving offers on at least one of them.[21]

The sale of property owned by the municipality was carefully considered when an offer was made before agreeing or declining the tender. Whereas previous councils sold property based on the price offered in comparison to its market value, the Knight administration put the social value of the property first and foremost. An offer from C. Sartoris of $100 for a house owned by the town and in relatively poor repair was received by council, and though the offer was considered to be fair market value, council did not permit Sartoris to buy the house.[22] Instead the council chose to find out how much it would cost to repair the house so that the unemployed or under-employed might be able to live there; the renovations were later done and the house was used for this purpose.[23] They believed that the use or sale of town-owned property should be for the good of the residents, not based on an economic formula that only considered the value of the property based on market conditions.

Council did not limit its agenda to strictly local concerns, but rather demanded action on issues that extended well beyond Blairmore's munici-pal boundaries. While the mayor and councillors carefully avoided saying anything that could be construed as anti-Canadian, anti-British or "revolu-tionary," the council endorsed the aims of several petitions and resolutions brought forward by the Red-affiliated Mine Workers Union of Canada and other radical bodies demanding change. Perhaps the most important and controversial change demanded by council was a call for the dissolution of the Royal Canadian Mounted Police.[24] While it would have been illegal to demand the disillusion of the force as a part of a revolutionary or anti-capitalist program, the council instead based its demands squarely on the RCMP's heavy-handed and violent actions during the Crowsnest Pass miners' strike of 1932.[25] It was the careful grammatical and contextual framing of the petition that allowed the council to endorse a resolution that was in its implications revolutionary, but in its literal and legal constitution a protest against the excessive violence exhibited by police during a contentious and prolonged strike. Similarly, when the administration demanded the repeal of Section 98 of the Criminal Code of Canada, it did so under the banner of free speech, not in support of a legal basis for the Communist Party of Canada. Council also gave moral support to radical striking miners at Stratford, Ontario (citing fair wages), called for the return of tobacco to provincial jails (citing humanitarian concerns) and protested the arrest of picketing labourers in Calgary (again citing freedom of speech).[26] Though such petitions had little practical chance of success, they were effective vehicles for council to express its political beliefs to a larger audience. The petitions could be carefully worded to avoid problems with the authorities and had no cost attached to them, making them a relatively safe way of expressing council's opinions. In addition, they were usually controversial enough to gain free press both in the home market and sometimes in provincial and national papers as well.

The administration was not afraid, however, to put public funds towards projects that were overtly political. When Harvey Murphy, who was neither a resident of the town nor a councillor but a political activist for the Communist Party of Canada, suggested that the council should send a delegate to the Red-associated National Unemployed Congress in Ottawa, Councillor Albert Olson was selected and unapologetically sent to the conference with a budget of $200 (Betcherman 1982: 42–43).[27]

These actions — in terms of taxation, relief and criticism of the capitalist order — were actively challenged by the business community in Blairmore. The *Blairmore Enterprise* and several other companies refused to pay the increased taxes, hoping to appeal the validity of Tax Bylaw Number Nine in court, declaring "when the Blairmore town council undertakes to collect a tax from the business concerns of Blairmore, which must be considered a tax spread over the year for the benefit of the unemployed, they are practically guaranteeing that the unemployed will remain unemployed for at least the year" (*BE* April 13, 1933). The imposition of a new tax regime also prompted the formation of the Blairmore Business and Professional Man's Association (BBPMA) in April of 1933 to promote the interests of the "commercial and professional classes" (*BE* April 27, 1933). The BBPMA used the *Enterprise* as a platform from which to challenge the Knight administration, declaring they would take "steps to test the legality of the Blairmore Council's actions" (*BE* April 27, 1933). When business owners challenged their tax assessments, they found themselves appealing their rate of taxation to the very council that had imposed the increase in the first place, sitting as a court of revision. When they complained that the appeal process was unfair, the mayor advised the town secretary to record that the complainants were "asking for relief," and if corporate relief were to be granted another increase in business taxes would have to be investigated (*BE* May 4, 1933). Businesses that did not pay their taxes were issued writs of enforcement that were upheld in court. Though the change in taxation was revolutionary in its concept and implications, it did not violate the letter of the law.

There was one notable absence from the BBPMA, the West Canadian Collieries (WCC). Though the town's largest employer had been critical of the Red movement in the past, it was basic economic considerations and not reconciliation between the radicals and the company that caused its absence. In a company document addressing potential cost-saving measures, author and WCC board member Raoul Green concluded: "Common sense dictates that cutting down any quantity of men at [Blairmore's] Greenhill [mine] is not worth trying at present. Idle men go on relief and I for one would assume that the company would have to pay for them indirectly by taxation."[28] The WCC may not have been pleased with the priorities of the new administration, but it had decided that given the recent tax increase, antagonizing the council was not worthwhile. The company turned elsewhere in an effort to reduce costs. Green had reported that parts of the timbering at the Blairmore mine required "immediate repairs" and suggested an innovative and cost-effective solution: "steel rails are every bit as suitable as I beams, since they cost nothing for purchase... there must still be quite a few rails at Lille."[29] Green was later sent to the abandoned town site to assess the availability of rails there, and found that "2000 ft. are well worth a try at re-claiming... they are angular #60 steel, and are well suited for mine timbers."[30] Instead of cutting staff, an expedition was sent up the abandoned railway line to Lille to extract the remaining 2000 ft. of rail as a cost-saving measure.

Thus equilibrium had been achieved by the Red council by the end of its first term in office. The radical action advocated by Communists at the provincial or national level was balanced by a hands-on, paternalistic system of relief administered at the grassroots level. Knight and his associates, in a populist sense, successfully established an outside power bloc against which to define themselves (Laycock 1990: 17; Harrison 2000: 108). By linking the economic hardships being experienced by residents with the relief programs of the capitalist governments at Edmonton and Ottawa (and by extension the economic systems they represented), the council successfully established these outside elements as a bloc that threatened "the people" and was therefore to be opposed (Harrison 2000: 108).[31]

By the end of its first term in office, the council had succeeded in reversing the governmental norm at Blairmore: taxes were collected from the rich and spent on programs for the poor. These relief programs were administered in a paternalistic way by a council who personally attended to the needs of residents at its weekly meetings. Knight and his colleagues actively cultivated a new civic culture where Blairmoreites could, and did, come to council seeking help with their personal and social problems. It was on this record of advocacy for residents and the implementation of a pragmatic system of relief that the councillors sought and received a second mandate.

Although the majority of fundamental social and governmental changes were initiated during the council's first mandate, its current notoriety stems from what started as improvements to the town's main thoroughfare, Victoria Avenue. Part of Highway Three, Victoria Avenue was in rough shape by spring of 1934, and council wrote to the Hon. O.L. McPherson (minister responsible for infrastructure) to demand that improvements be forthcoming. Despite receiving a letter indicating that "a provincial engineer would be in shortly to look at it," no repairs were done and council took matters into their own hands, making improvements to the existing sidewalks and then to the road itself.[32] Breaking with its criticism of municipal spending and the Red council in general, the *Blairmore Enterprise* called the work "entirely necessary," reporting "a determined effort to improve the streets of the town can be seen in various directions... sidewalks of shale and plank are also being installed, and the work is considerably relieving the unemployment situation" (*BE* May 23, 1934). While this support for improvements represents a departure from the larger anti-Knight position of the paper, it is in line with editor William Bartlett's demands that the council stop spending money on direct relief and spend it on town improvements that might attract further monetary investment. For the conservative Bartlett, the upgrades represented progress, unlike the money spent on direct relief.

The support from the business and commercial interests of Blairmore ended in the fall of 1934 when the council announced it would do more than simply upgrade roadways or improve the sidewalks: council wanted to unofficially rename Victoria Avenue in honour of Tim Buck, the imprisoned leader of the Communist Party of Canada. The street could not be officially renamed as it was a provincial highway, and as such was not within council's jurisdiction, but that did not stop them (*BE* November 29, 1934). During the public rededication ceremony A.E. Smith of Toronto, Secretary of the Red Workers' Unity League, cut the tape, broke a bottle of ginger ale and pronounced Tim Buck Boulevard open to traffic (*Maclean's* April 15, 1935). The town tried to make it a boulevard by widening it, adding streetlights and installing a new sprinkler system at the cost of $80 per block.[33] Flowers were planted along the route, and the council finished the job by ordering two large, neon "Tim Buck Boulevard" signs to be installed at the beginning and the end of the boulevard. *Maclean's* reported:

> Whereas Victoria Avenue boasted only five ordinary streetlights, the boulevard is a blaze of glory at night, being illuminated by a row of about eighty arc-lights of high candle power. A new project is underway at present to erect at either end of the boulevard a large neon sign bearing the name "Tim Buck," and announcing to all and sundry that here is no mean city but one which proudly boasts the communist leader as patron saint. (April 15, 1935)

Having established this monument to Tim Buck, the mayor instructed the secretary to draw up a bylaw that "impos[ed] parallel parking and [another] bylaw concerning driving to danger the public, fine for first offence under the parking bylaw $1.00, and for driving to danger the public $10.00."[34] Driving on the sidewalks with either a bicycle or automobile was also banned.[35] The council showed it was serious about the enforcement of these bylaws by reading them a first, second and third time and passing them within four days.

The boulevard was not meant for everyone to enjoy. When the sprinkler system and streetlight improvements to Tim Buck Boulevard were announced, the West Canadian Collieries asked that the amenities be extended the length of the highway to include the Westside residences occupied by the mine managers and other mine officials; the prosperous Westside residences were separated from the working-class Eastside residences by a Canadian Pacific Railway spurline. In the discussion that followed, town council decided that "improvements be made only to the east side of the CPR spurline… West Canadian Collieries' request for improvements to the Westside not granted."[36]

The council went even further in November of 1934 when it declared, in conjunction with the school board, a school and civic holiday on the anniversary of the Russian Revolution. The *Regina Leader Post* declared the decision to be "unprecedented in the educational life of [the] whole continent" while the *Fernie Free Press* questioned "if it isn't time for [Blairmore] to be transported lock, stock and barrel to Russia where most of its citizens seem to belong" (cited in *BE* November 22, 1934). The situation was further enflamed by the board's refusal to grant a holiday on Armistice Day or for the royal wedding of the Duke of Kent to Princess Marina. "To put it mildly," *Maclean's* editorialized, these actions were "an affront to the sensibilities of all thinking Canadians" (April 15, 1935). The Hon. Perrin Baker, Minister of Education, acknowledged that while the actions taken at Blairmore were offensive to many, they were not in fact illegal. Baker admitted "a school board has the authority to declare any day a holiday, subject to the limitations prescribed in the School Act, [and] it was never contemplated that this prerogative would be used by a public body to commemorate officially a foreign revolution" (*Maclean's* April 15, 1935).

Council also continued to pass resolutions protesting conditions encountered by other radical groups across the country. Overnight lettergrams were sent to the miners at Flin Flon and Noranda, supporting them in their strike against mine owners and condemning the violent actions of the Royal Canadian Mounted Police.[37] Council continued to take up the case of known Communists who were facing persecution, calling for the release of Tim Buck and expressing outrage over the tarring and feathering experienced by George Palmer of Innisfree, Alberta, for his political beliefs (*BE* November

22, 1934). Delegates were again sent to a national conference with Red ties, this time to the National Congress against War and Fascism, held in Toronto (*BE* September 20, 1934).

While Tim Buck Boulevard and the newly realized holiday on the anniversary of the Russian Revolution dominated the headlines, the day-to-day administration of relief programs and other local considerations occupied most of the council's regular business in 1934. Residents continued to come to the council seeking specific items to help them through everyday life. Mr. D. Mills had no stove and had not been able to locate a used one for his home, so he came to council seeking help. Knight and his colleagues agreed to find him a used stove at reasonable cost, and when they could not locate one either they granted Mills the sum of $20 to purchase a new one.[38] A similar grant was made to Mr. A. Pondelicek Sr., who had appeared before council to request repairs for his artificial limb.[39] Free memberships to the Blairmore Public Library were provided to anyone on relief (*BE* May 23, 1934).

Though such requests and their solutions are similar to those granted by council in 1933, the administration's second year in office saw the introduction of more complex expectations of those applying for relief. Council had previously acted on a moral obligation to help all who were in need, regardless of their situation or personal actions. This changed in 1934, with applicants increasingly being required to demonstrate not only need but also that an attempt had been made to address the problem before asking for help. Mills, for example, tried to find a stove before going to council, and Pondelicek could not have anticipated needing repairs to his prosthetic. When cases arose where residents had made no effort to help themselves or demonstrated that they felt entitled to relief, Knight and his colleagues began to adopt a firmer approach. When Mr. Wislet of the Unemployed Association enquired why Mr. F. Amatto had not been issued his regular relief payment, "it was stated F. Amatto had refused to work when called upon to do so. Mayor Knight stated that in that case Mr. Amatto would be off relief until he was willing to work."[40]

The year 1934 represented not only the introduction of a moral standard for the delivery of relief, but also the beginning of a more aggressive legislative agenda. Previously, the council had simply responded to concerns brought forward to them by members of the public, and when the council did initiate change it was in regard to taxes or other initiatives aimed directly at the upper classes. This new agenda affected everyone. Concerned about the possible health problems caused by living in close proximity to cattle, the administration decided to inspect all cows within its jurisdiction. Having found eight families living within the town limits with more than one cow, Mayor Knight "suggested that all cows be Tuberculosis tested and registered."[41] Council insisted that vaccination and registration of all cattle be completed within a one-month period, including "outside dairies selling milk in town."[42]

Residents' health was also invoked when council sought to regulate the town's sex trade. Hill Sixty, as it was called, was located between the townsites of Blairmore and Frank and was well-known to contain two brothels. Though Knight did not seek to end prostitution, nor was Hill Sixty within the legal municipal boundaries of Blairmore, council demanded "that the Chief of Police notify the two landladies that they and all the girls on the premises must have a photo of themselves, to which is attached a certificate certifying they have been medically examined at least once every week."[43] Though professing the action was in the interest of public health, the *Enterprise* asked "why such interest on the part of the town council in Hill Sixty? The town grading apparatus is trying to make the approaches easier" (*BE* August 23, 1934).

Concern for the health and social welfare of Blairmoreites did not erupt overnight, nor did council's worry that some individuals were abusing the reformed relief process. Faced with the massive task of completely restructuring the systems of taxation and relief — and to do so against formidable resistance from local business and the provincial and the federal governments — Knight and his colleagues did not have the time or political resources at their disposal to enact such additional changes in 1933. Once the new taxation and relief apparatuses were successfully implemented and operating smoothly, the council then became able to proceed in other areas. Actions such as questing the legitimacy of a relief applicant or insisting that prostitutes and bovine obtain a clean bill of health were, in the case of the former, a response to perceived demands from the working class that action be taken on a particular issue, and in the latter, a realization that under the new relief scheme the town hall was likely to end up paying for medical treatment miners could not afford on their own. Therefore, although the council's introduction of a moral standard for the delivery of relief and increasingly active legislative agenda may at first consideration be seemingly divergent from their initial manifesto, the actions were in reality both a populist response to local demands and the paternalistic enactment of reforms designed to keep the population in good health.

The council also acted politically against the only non-Red member of the Blairmore School Board, local solicitor and well-known member of the Masonic Lodge S.G. Bannan. Accusing Bannan of stealing electricity from the town utilities by connecting his line before the meter, charges of theft were laid against the individual. While these charges were originally upheld by the magistrate at Blairmore, Bannan won on appeal to the District Court in Fort MacLeod. Furious, the mayor and council declared that they were denied justice by the courts because the administration was Red and issued the following notice to the citizens of Blairmore:

You are hereby warned that from midnight Friday April 13th, 1934, the Town of Blairmore will discontinue to supply electricity. The action has been brought about by the inability of the town to obtain justice in cases where customers are taking juice from ahead of the meter. Any complaints should be registered with the Attorney-General. Signed, Mayor and Council of Blairmore (*BE* April 12, 1934).

Though the Knight town hall did not follow through on the threats to discontinue electricity to the residents of Blairmore, they were swiftly condemned for having made them at all. The *Enterprise* asked "why worry about the drastic action threatened by the mayor and council? It's just their natural way of expressing love for the people," and even Communist organizer Harvey Murphy called the threat "crazy" (*BE* April 12, 1934; *BE* April 19, 1934).

Refusing to acknowledge their loss, the town appealed the decision to the Supreme Court at Lethbridge. In his ruling, Mr. Justice Simmons found against the Town of Blairmore, awarding the defendant $100 and expenses (*BE* October 25, 1934). The judge also took the time to chastise the municipal government for threatening to cut off power to the residents of Blairmore when the decision at MacLeod had not gone in their favour, stating that "actions which might endanger the life and property of citizens would not be tolerated, whatever one might obtain in Moscow" (*BE* November 1, 1934). Despite this setback and public rebuke, Knight made himself available to the media. In an interview with the *Lethbridge Herald* he pointed out "the splendid financial position of the town of Blairmore. Practically all debt and all debentures have been paid. Blairmore is a model town," he declared, indicating that "ninety percent of citizens are behind the municipal government" (cited in *BE* October 25 1934; also see *Lethbridge Herald* October 23, 1934). In spite of the legal setback, the council did not stop prosecuting individuals for stealing electricity. The council soon thereafter brought similar charges against Mr. M. Giacommuzzi.[44]

If there was any real opposition to the council's increasingly active social and political agenda it was not evident in February of 1935, when the Red slate proposed for both council and school board was returned by acclamation.[45] The Knight administration's policies may have been controversial, but there was no denying that the town was in excellent financial shape after two years of Red administration. In January 1935 the Town of Blairmore announced that it had an audited bank statement of over $18,000 at fiscal year end (*BE* February 7, 1935). This compared to a surplus of just $2109.41 at Coleman and an administration in provincial receivership at Fernie (*BE* January 31, 1935; Norton 2002: 131–46). The *Coleman Journal* offered its opinion, stating that "people get the type of government they deserve, therefore it is presumed Blairmore is content" (cited in *BE* February 7, 1935). In comparison to the acclamations at Blairmore, fourteen candidates were vying for six vacancies in Coleman (*BE* February 7, 1935).

Perhaps equating their electoral acclamation with support for their increasingly high profile Red agenda, the council and school board jointly issued a new manifesto that reflected on the accomplishments and short-comings of their two years in power, and laid out their agenda for 1935 (*BE* February 14, 1935). Among the achievements noted were the attendance of A.E. Cross, Secretary of the WUL at the rededication of Tim Buck Boulevard, protesting against the conditions in relief camps and providing cash for delegates to the National Conference Against War and Fascism. When analyzing their shortcomings, the manifesto noted that Reds "did not take full advantage of their elected positions to organize and mobilize the workers," pledging to address this problem by pursuing a higher degree of integration between the Mine Workers' Union of Canada, the workers, the school board and the town council (*BE* February 14, 1935). Relief programs were not mentioned once in the document. This redefinition of priorities fundamentally shifted the council's primary focus from changing the local experience to effecting change on a national and international level.

The administration lost no time in implementing its new agenda by declaring a civic holiday to honour Tim Buck. Recently released from jail, Buck travelled to Blairmore on March 21, 1935, and spoke to a large audience. Council gave all employees and school children the day off so that they could attend the day's events (*BE* March 21, 1935). The Communist leader was feted during the day and handed the keys to the city during an evening celebration.

Knight and his councillors also continued to pass resolutions pertaining to the plight of workers elsewhere in the country, but unlike previous proclamations, the council moved to accompany these statements of solidarity with public education on the matter in question. It was in this vein that the administration endorsed a resolution "protesting the government's actions in connection with the Regina Riot."[46] In order that a broader understanding and sympathy for the issue be present at Blairmore, Knight scheduled a "public meeting of the town council" to discuss matters pertaining to the Regina Riot and the On-to-Ottawa trekkers.[47] Though there had been general mention of the trek in the *Blairmore Enterprise*, this public meeting explained from a working-class perspective that the march to Ottawa had been caused by the appalling conditions faced by the single unemployed in federal relief camps, the same camps that were eliminated at Blairmore by council's changes to the relief system in 1933. The crowd learned that although the protesters had been proceeding in an orderly fashion, they were stopped by the RCMP in Regina and forced to disband because the federal government feared that by the time they reached Ottawa there could be serious revolutionary implications for the government; the Regina Riot resulted. While the mainstream press had portrayed the Regina Riot as the result of the trekkers, Knight insisted that they were forced to violence in self defence, and by so doing he followed the lead of the Citizens Defence Committee and the Communist Party of Canada in trying to regain public support for the trekkers.

The Soviet-inspired struggle against war and Fascism was also embraced by council. When it was learned in November that Mussolini had invaded Ethiopia, the administration lost no time endorsing the following cable to be sent to the Ethiopian emperor:

> Mayor and Council convey best wishes for success over Mussolini, the oppressor of the Italian people and war-monger. We pray for your victory which will help to free the Italian people and the world. Blairmore salutes you. [signed] Mayor William Knight[48]

Despite being advised by the town secretary that "he considered this an illegal expense, [as] money spent for political purposes [was] out of order," the council passed the motion anyhow and directed that copies be sent to the *New York Times, the Toronto Star* and *Pravda* by costly overnight telegram.[49]

There was also growing concern among Reds that there might be an attempt from within the town's bureaucracy to stall the council's agenda: "Councillor Packer recommended a change in auditor, and stated his reason for wishing same [was] that in his opinion E.D. Bantrum, Auditor, was collaborating with the provincial government."[50] Having disposed of the suspected government spy, the council occupied itself with requests from the union local and other workers' groups, granting subsidies to the Young Workers Gymnasium and the Workers' Sports Association.[51] These grants were made by council despite the town secretary advising that such grants were being "made illegally."[52] Financial support was also extended to help pay for a second visit from Tim Buck, with the Secretary of the Communist Party of Canada being led from the train station to the location where he was to speak in a dramatic torchlight procession.[53]

Time that had previously been used to address the day-to-day concerns of the residents was now dominated by council's national and international ambitions. When Mrs. Diamond, for example, came to council on April 15, 1935, to request a new pair of glasses, she was informed that her appeal could not be dealt with in council, and the matter was referred to the relief committee.[54] Mr. Rossi — perhaps a relative of Mrs. Rossi, who famously brought a lump of coal with her to the polling booth in 1933 — came to council to seek assistance in finding a stove to heat his home, but unlike Mills the preceding year, the council again left Rossi's request to the relief committee.[55] When Mr. Zubersky sought mediation between himself and his neighbour Mrs. Doubek regarding a fence that ran between their properties, the council again declined to act where it had previously, stating that "a fence was not a matter that could be settled by council."[56]

While there is no evidence to suggest that the key provisions of council's relief policy were altered by its increasing focus on national and international issues — people on relief continued to receive the same types and amounts of relief as before — relief was now being dominantly administered by the relief committee and not the council itself. When council first come to power in 1933 they clearly defined improvements to the relief system as their top priority, and though they based systemic reforms around radical principles, it was this personal attention to the local situation that the residents identified with. Even with the declaration of Tim Buck Boulevard and a holiday for the Russian Revolution, the citizens were content to re-elect the council because it was concurrently addressing the relief problem in a practical, hands-on way.

Though the residents of Blairmore could easily identify with the priorities laid out by Knight in 1933 — the need to fix a flawed system of relief imposed on Blairmore by the federal and provincial governments — the provisions of the second manifesto were more abstract and difficult to conceptualize. Because a struggle against war and fascism was not something that manifested itself in everyday life at Blairmore, it became exceedingly difficult to link local unemployment, underemployment and suffering to the external elements with which the council was doing battle. Though this revolutionary (and pro-CCP) agenda had existed within the administration from the beginning, the combination of legal restraint via Section 98 of the Criminal Code and the implementation of major local reforms restricted the council's ability to act (beyond symbolic petitions and demands) on a national and international level. With McKenzie King taking office in 1935, Knight and his colleagues had a major barrier to their radical agenda removed. Concurrently, the relief and taxation measures implemented by council were, by late 1934, effective without direct supervision, therefore permitting council more time to pursue their radical program on the national and international stage. As the administration increasingly left the relief apparatus on autopilot, the delivery of aid became less associated with the ideological preoccupations of the administration, and the immediacy of the threat from outside decreased accordingly.

Throughout 1935 the council also experienced a number of scandals that tarnished its reputation as a grounded, responsible administration. Early in the year the council initiated a plebiscite that if passed would have seen the mayor and councillors paid for every meeting they attended; until this point they served for free. The vote came back decisively against the proposal, with an approval rating of only one third (*BE* March 28, 1935). Shortly thereafter, the Red-appointed chief of police was arrested and charged with extortion, the RCMP claiming that he had been working with a local prostitute to blackmail her clientele (*BE* June 20, 1935). The police chief was found guilty and sentenced to two years hard labour, while the prostitute committed suicide days before the trail began (*BE* December 5, 1935).[57] The ethics of Knight himself were directly challenged when the mayor appealed — and won his appeal — for a lower tax assessment.[58] Knight also was offered an option to purchase a piece of town-owned property at a price that was considered to be well below its actual value.[59]

Thus, when the Red council faced re-election in 1936 they were in a much different position than they had been a year earlier. While the relief apparatus had not fundamentally changed, the councillors were no longer associated with the ambitious social justice agenda for which they were once known and faced a backlash over the expenses and scandals of the previous year. Their spectacular downfall in February 1936 suggests that they misjudged their mandate of 1935, and while there was clearly some support within the community for radical action on multiple levels, the administration's increasing distance from "bread and butter" issues — local relief and local-ized social change — caused Knight and his councillors to lose the support of much of their electoral base. The gap between the expectations of the grassroots community and the program of Knight's town hall was reinforced by scandals that brought the council province-wide notoriety and portrayed Blairmore's civic leaders not as "average" people but individuals using their elected offices to their own benefit.

It is possible that Knight and his associates were unaware of their coming peril given the timing of the 1936 civic election. There had been no large-scale public meeting held in the last three months of 1935, and the first chance for the public to interact with their mayor and councillors *en masse* was two weeks before the election at the town's annual general meet-ing in January. It was at this meeting that voters learned of the town's large budget deficit and heard for the first time the auditor's allegations of illegal expenditures made for political reasons. The turnout for the AGM was so large that the meeting had to be adjourned until a bigger venue was found (*BE* February 7, 1936). Media reports suggest the crowd arrived displeased with the council, but upon hearing of the town's poor financial situation, became enraged and "pulled [Mayor Knight] from the platform" (*MacLeod Gazette* cited in *BE*, February 7, 1936). By the time Knight and the other Red candidates realized the strength of the opposition to their candidacy, their political futures were sealed. Facing tremendous social pressure from the citizens of this small mining town, the Red councillors withdrew their nominations and were replaced by a compromise slate of both miners and business owners (*BE* February 7, 1936). The Red administration at Blairmore ended as quickly as it had begun, in a bloodless coup.

The experience at Blairmore from 1933–36 has important implications for the historiography of the Crowsnest Pass and the history of the Canadian left. The Crowsnest experience is frequently compared to mining or working-class communities elsewhere. A. Ross McCormack, for example, argues that the Crowsnest Pass was a part of a larger Canadian regional labour history, which included the hard rock miners in the interior of British Columbia and coal miners on Vancouver Island (1977: 43). Allen Seager similarly places the Crowsnest Pass within a larger regional framework, comparing "common experiences" at Vancouver, Nanaimo and the Kootenays with the Crowsnest Pass (1985: 56). John Manley also cites the creation of Communist play groups at Blairmore as evidence that the third period objectives of the CCP were becoming successful with party members (2002: 220–46). This tendency to use the Crowsnest Pass experience in support of a larger radical or political argument is problematic for two reasons. Such arguments fail to address the realities of geographic location or the ethnic differences in the populations involved. It is insufficient to point out that labour unrest occurred at certain points within a region without clearly establishing that the agitation in question was derived from the same circumstances or motivations. Second, such comparisons take for granted that the working class in different places were affected in the same way by larger events, thus robbing them of individual agency and obscuring an opportunity to explore other reasons for local radicalism. By making such comparisons between the experiences at Blairmore or the Crowsnest Pass with other locations, the existing literature succeeds in highlighting common labour anxieties but does not address the root causes of such sentiments.

This study is not strictly intended to be a history of Communism at Blairmore; nor is it an investigation of the links between radical action in the Crowsnest Pass and elsewhere. Rather, this chapter supports the perspective of Gregory Kealey, who argues that is it necessary to conceptualize the experiences of the Canadian working-class in a framework "that avoids the teleologies of old left analyses, be they social democratic or Stalinist... [while also dismissing] the cynicism of most contemporary bourgeois scholars and the burgeoning pessimism of many left-wing scholars" (Kealey 1995: 151). The events at Blairmore demonstrate that each leftist movement, or perceived leftist movement, is "defined by time, place, demography, [and the] types of institutions" from which they create their own experiment in "living otherwise" (McKay 2005: 35). For the majority of Blairmoreites, their experience from 1933–36 was not defined by a strict socialist or Communist dogma, but as McKay terms it, a desire to "live otherwise."

This case study also highlights several important realizations about the abilities of radical social movements during the Depression. It is evident that at Blairmore, despite the rigidly defined role of town councils in provincial legislation and the strict limits to the amount of relief provided by the senior levels of government, it was in fact possible to use the existing municipal apparatus to significantly and fundamentally force social change. The redefinition of both taxation and relief was a direct challenge to the social norms dictated by the state and, despite business leaders' loud calls for provincial government intervention, the council's close attention to legal loopholes and technicalities prevented such intervention. Taxation reforms, while revolutionary in concept, were within the letter of the law, as were the headline-grabbing proclamations of Tim Buck Boulevard, a holiday to celebrate the Russian Revolution and the many council-backed petitions for controversial change. Though the Red majority on council did not continue after 1936 — nor did Tim Buck Boulevard or the Revolutionary holiday — the basic provisions of the relief and taxation program as defined and implemented by this radical administration were left largely intact until the beginning of the Second World War. Ultimately, the Red administration at Blairmore, Alberta, was able to work within the legal parameters imposed on it to enact revolutionary taxation and relief measures for its citizens, leaving opponents — business leaders, the provincial government and the federal government — largely impotent to oppose its actions. This case study of Blairmore demonstrates that a social movement can use the levers of existing political power to accomplish its goals while working within the political system it seeks to fundamentally change.

PRIMARY SOURCES AND NEWSPAPER ARTICLES CITED

Blairmore Enterprise. 1933. "Blairmore Expects This Day Every Wage Earner To Do His Duty." March 2.

_____. 1933. "Business Men Organize." April 27.

_____. 1934. "Local and General Items." August 23.

_____. 1933. "Correspondence." April 13.

_____. 1933. "Council Declines to Entertain Appeals Against Assessments." May 4.

_____. 1933. "William Knight Chief Magistrate." February 16.

_____. 1934. "A 'Red' School Board." November 22.

_____. 1934. "Actions of Blairmore School Board Arouse Protest." November 29.

_____. 1934. "Blairmore Mayor Proud of His Town." October 25.

_____. 1934. "Correspondence." December 6.

_____. 1934. "Here's the Latest Rave!" April 12.

_____. 1934. "Local and General Items." May 23.

_____. 1934. "Local and General Items." November 22.

_____. 1935. "Blairmore Council Suspends Police Chief." June 20.

_____. 1935. "Blairmore Issues Absolutely Red Manifesto." February 14.

_____. 1935. "Civic Holiday for Buck." March 21.

_____. 1935. "Correspondence.." February 7.

_____. 1935. "Local and General Items." February 7.

_____. 1935. "Local and General Items." January 31.

_____. 1935. Two years, less a day, for Fitzpatrick." December 5.

_____. 1936. "Correspondence." February 7.

J.W. 1933. "Blairmore, A Union Camp." *The Worker*, June 3.

Knight, W., and C. Shaw. 1934. "Local Appeal for Fight Against War and Fascism." *Blairmore Enterprise*, September 20.

Lethbridge Herald. 1934. "Suit Against Town of Blairmore Opens in Supreme Court

Here." October 23.

Medicine Hat News. 1933. "That Blairmore Trouble." February 28.

Miles, Florence Elder. 1935. "Is This a Soviet?" *Maclean's,* April 15.

NOTES

1. The slate was officially known as "workers' candidates," but were commonly referred to as the "Red miners' slate" or the "miners' slate of Red candidates."
2. Both mayor and councillors were elected for two-year terms. The terms were staggered, so that one year three councillors and the mayor would be elected, and the next only three councillors would be elected.
3. Blairmore Town Council Meeting Minutes, March 6, 1933. The meeting minutes are in the possession of the Municipality of the Crowsnest Pass, and are stored in their document vault; there is no accession number. Hereafter "Town Council Meeting Minutes."
4. Town Council Meeting Minutes, March 20, 1933.
5. Town Council Meeting Minutes, February 20, 1933.
6. Town Council Meeting Minutes, April 13, 1933.
7. Town Council Meeting Minutes, April 24, 1933.
8. Ibid.
9. Town Council Meeting Minutes, June 19, 1933.
10. Blairmore Town Council Meeting Minutes, November 6, 1933.
11. Blairmore Town Council Meeting Minutes, November 20, 1933.
12. Town Council Meeting Minutes, August 7, 1933.
13. Town Council Meeting Minutes, September 18, 1933.
14. Ibid.
15. Town Council Meeting Minutes, March 5, 1934.
16. Town Council Meeting Minutes, June 19, 1933.
17. Town Council Meeting Minutes, July 7, 1933.
18. Interview with author, May 26, 2006.
19. Town Council Meeting Minutes, March 20, 1933.
20. Town Council Meeting Minutes, April 3, 1933.
21. Ibid.
22. Blairmore Town Council Meeting Minutes, June 19, 1933.
23. Ibid.
24. Town Council Meeting Minutes, May 15, 1933; October 30, 1933.
25. The strike of 1932 was organized by the Mine Worker's Union of Canada and at its height involved all major coal operations on the Alberta side of the Crowsnest Pass. The strike did not last very long at the International Coal and Coke Company or the McGillivary Creek Coal and Coke Company — both located in Coleman — but was bitter and protracted at the West Canadian Collieries operations at both Blairmore and Bellevue.
26. Town Council Meeting Minutes, May 15, 1933.
27. Town Council Meeting Minutes, August 7, 1933.
28. Raoul Green, "Greenhill Mine Report," March 14, 1933. Crowsnest Pass Historical Society, accession number 88.13.33 Kerr J+H.
29. Raoul Green to G.A. Vissac, March 14, 1933. Crowsnest Pass Historical Association, accession number 88.18.33 Kerr J+H.
30. Raoul Green to J.A. Brusset, September 6, 1933, Crowsnest Pass Historical Association, accession number 88-18-33 Kerr J+H.

31. According to Harrison, the basic tenets of a populist movement "involve a personal appeal by a leader to a mass audience... central to the leader's appeal is the notion of 'the people.' A group defined by its historic, geographic, and/or cultural roots. This appeal is made urgent by the precipitation of a crisis threatening 'the people.' Finally, the source of this threat is another group — sometimes termed 'power bloc' — viewed as physically or culturally external to 'the people.'" All of these circumstances were existent in Blairmore.

32. Town Council Meeting Minutes, May 31, 1934.

33. Town Council Meeting Minutes, July 17, 1934; August 6, 1934.

34. Town Council Meeting Minutes, August 20, 1934.

35. Town Council Meeting Minutes, June 21, 1934.

36. Town Council Meeting Minutes, August 29, 1934.

37. Town Council Meeting Minutes, April 23, 1934.

38. Town Council Meeting Minutes, April 3, 1934.

39. Town Council Meeting Minutes, November 19, 1934.

40. Town Council Meeting Minutes, January 26, 1935.

41. Town Council Meeting Minutes, August 20, 1934.

42. Ibid.

43. Town Council Meeting Minutes, May 31, 1934.

44. Town Council Meeting Minutes, June 4, 1934.

45. Town Council Meeting Minutes, February 5, 1935.

46. Town Council Meeting Minutes, August 26, 1935.

47. Town Council Meeting Minutes, October 17, 1935.

48. Town Council Meeting Minutes, November 4, 1935.

49. Ibid.

50. Town Council Meeting Minutes, March 4, 1935.

51. Town Council Meeting Minutes, June 3, 1935.

52. Ibid.

53. Town Council Meeting Minutes, August 22, 1935; August 19, 1935.

54. Town Council Meeting Minutes, April 15, 1935.

55. Town Council Meeting Minutes, April 3, 1935.

56. Town Council Meeting Minutes, July 2, 1935.

57. Cudmore's suicide is confirmed on her Certificate of Death, issued by Alberta Government Services — Vital Statistics.

58. Town Council Meeting Minutes, September 16, 1935.

59. Town Council Meeting Minutes, November 6, 1935.

CHAPTER SIX

THE COMMUNITY OF SCHOLARS
THE ENGLISH-CANADIAN STUDENT
MOVEMENT AND UNIVERSITY GOVERNANCE

Roberta Lexier

On November 16, 1972, approximately three hundred students at the University of Saskatchewan, Regina Campus, occupied the office of the Dean of Arts and Science, Sir Edgar Vaughan. While a number of issues, including budgetary cutbacks, autonomy for the Regina Campus and concerns over the university's research program, were raised during the occupation, the primary motivation for this political action stemmed from student demands for parity, or equal student-faculty representation on decision-making bodies. Believing that they "were one half of the equation of the university,"[1] these students demanded that they have an equal say with faculty in how it was run. Parity was necessary, they argued, because an effective voice in decision-making would make the educational process more meaningful to students and to the provincial community (*The Carillon*, January 26, 1973: 1). Although the university administration initially rejected student demands for parity, on November 22, 1972, Regina Campus Principal John Archer stated that he favoured greater participation by faculty members, students and the public in the governance of the university, and was prepared to urge a review of the nature and level of student participation to ensure that students have opportunity to make a full contribution.[2] The occupation finally came to an end when Archer agreed to establish a committee composed of students, faculty members and members of the public to implement necessary changes to the governing structure of the university.[3]

This occupation at the University of Saskatchewan, Regina Campus was an important moment in the history of the student movement at that institution; it was the culmination of an almost decade-long struggle for increased student participation in university governing structures. In fact, at all three universities included in this chapter — University of Toronto, University of Saskatchewan, Regina Campus (now University of Regina), and Simon Fraser University[4] — demands for greater student involvement in university decision-making processes dominated the student movements throughout the sixties.[5] Before this time, students had little political involvement in their universities and, in actuality, were treated as children by university administrators. However, by the mid-1960s student movements had emerged on university campuses throughout English Canada to challenge the traditional place of students within the university community and demand the democratization of university governing bodies. Although student activists, the small and amorphous group of politically active students who sought to guide the debates on campus, often attempted to raise wider societal issues, including the war in Vietnam and the subjugation of the First Nations population, their demands for increased student involvement in university governing structures provided the means to create alliances among a varied and complex student population and enabled the development of influential student movements. As a result, the democratization of university campuses remained the primary issue for the student movements in English Canada throughout the sixties.

Despite the centrality of governance issues to the student movements of the sixties, scholars have yet to provide a comprehensive examination of this aspect of these movements. In fact, sixties scholars have tended to focus on the international and social justice aspects of the student movements of the period, including the anti-Vietnam War protests and the Civil Rights Movement (Gitlin 1987; Gosse 2005; Marwick 1998; Suri 2003). As well, while very little scholarly attention has been paid to the student movements in English Canada during the sixties, those works that do exist tend to underplay the importance of governance issues. Books such as Doug Owram's *Born at the Right Time: A History of the Baby Boom Generation*, which focuses on the development of a generational identity, and Cyril Levitt's *Children of Privilege: Student Revolt in the Sixties*, which compares Canadian, West German and American student movements, both overlook the importance of demands for greater student participation in university governance (Owram 1996; Levitt 1984). As well, a number of recent institutional histories of Canadian universities make reference to the student movements of this era, including governance issues, but rarely discuss the events and actions related to these movements in great detail, generally placing university administrators and faculty members, rather than students, at the centre of their studies (Friedland 2002; Johnston 2005; Pitsula 2006). Thus, while drawing from these various works, this study seeks to highlight the importance of governance issues to the sixties student movements in English Canada, contributing to the history of this period.

EMERGENCE OF ENGLISH-CANADIAN STUDENT MOVEMENTS

The student movements at English-Canadian universities developed in the sixties for a variety of reasons. One of the most important factors was the enormous economic boom of the postwar period, which saw almost continuous economic growth and expansion until the early 1970s. This prosperity enabled people, no longer concerned with basic economic survival, to consider broader issues of social change (Marwick 1998; Norrie, Owram and Emery 2002; Owram 1996). Also central to the emergence of student movements during the sixties was the enormous population expansion that took place following the Second World War, often referred to as the Baby Boom Generation (Owram 1996: ix, 4). This generation, according to a number of scholars, shared common experiences and developed a generational identity, exerting power and influence over all institutions with which they came into contact (Owram 1996; Ricard 1994). One such institution was the university; universities in the sixties, as a result of the expanding youth population and changing expectations regarding higher education, experienced tremendous growth and change. They became increasingly important institutions in the modern and technological world and emerging as focal points for the activism of the period (Massolin 2001). However, the student movements in Canada also developed in response to the widespread social movements that emerged all across the globe, including decolonization movements in Africa, Asia and Latin America and the massive uprisings in Paris, Prague, Mexico City and Chicago. Especially influential were the movements in the United States, including the Civil Rights Movement and the student movement, led by the Students for a Democratic Society (SDS). Students in Canada drew much of their inspiration, issues and organizational strategies from these movements and were greatly influenced by the large numbers of Americans who to came to Canada during the period, either as draft dodgers and military deserters or as staff members and students in the expanding universities (Marwick 1998; Owram 1996; Gosse 2005; Suri 2007; Kurlansky 2004). Overall, the student movements at English-Canadian universities developed in response to these enormous changes occurring around the world.

UNIVERSITY STRUCTURES PRIOR TO THE SIXTIES

Universities, as many scholars have pointed out, were very traditional and conservative institutions prior to the sixties (Owram 1996; Gidney 2004; Allyn 2001; Bailey 1998; Lansley 2004). Of particular importance was the relationship between the university administration and its students based on the concept of *in loco parentis*, where the university regulated students' behaviour in the place of their parents. As David Allyn explained in his book on the sexual revolution: "for decades — indeed for centuries — school administrators had served as foster parents, entrusted with the responsibility of guiding and governing their charges as they made the transition from adolescence into adulthood" (Allyn 2001: 94). Rules were thus put in place covering areas such as sexual relations, alcohol, swearing, smoking and, especially in the case of female students, residence life (Owram 1996: 178; Bailey 1998: 194; Lansely 2004: 12). As well, in the early sixties, students had little or no involvement in the bodies responsible for governing the university.

They had no voice in determining which classes would be offered, in setting the curriculum or in evaluating teachers. In fact, students were not involved in the university in any political way (Owram 1996: 178).

However, by the mid-1960s this relationship between the university and its students came increasingly under attack. Students, attending universities in growing numbers and challenging traditional conceptions of adolescence, viewed themselves not as children but as adults who could regulate their own behaviour. "Students," recalled Doug Ward, the 1963–64 University of Toronto Students' Administrative Council (SAC) President, "felt that they were old enough to have some responsibility but there was very little responsibility for them to have.... [S]tudents wanted to be treated as adults."[6] Although students also continued to participate in a number of non-political extra-curricular activities, including dances and frosh activities, they increasingly demanded recognition as adult members of the university community and insisted that administrators stop regulating their personal behaviour. At the three universities included in this study, hundreds of students, not merely student activists, participated in the actions aimed at achieving such demands. Universities were forced to alter their relationships with their students.

Facing pressure from rising university enrolments, as well as changing conceptions of adolescence and widespread demands by to students to be treated as adults, university administrators were ultimately forced to abandon the principle of *in loco parentis*. By the mid-1960s it became increasingly difficult for administrators to justify the regulation of personal behaviour and by 1966 the dean of students at University of Toronto admitted that "[m]ost of the girls [living in residences] are adults and we have to treat them as such. They have to learn how to control their own lives" (*The Varsity*, January 26, 1966: 1). As well, at Simon Fraser University, a statement was added to the university calendar in 1966–67 acknowledging that the university no longer assumed parental responsibilities for its students, trusting them to regulate their own social behaviour.[7] Large numbers of students all across campus had demanded that the university recognize them as adults with the right and responsibility to make decisions regarding their own behaviour and had succeeded in destroying *in loco parentis*.

EARLY DEMANDS: OPENNESS AND REPRESENTATION

Once accepted as adult members of the university community, student activists, with the widespread support of most students on campus, then began to demand the right to participate in university governing structures. As students insisted upon recognition as adults, and the rights and responsibilities associated with adulthood, their demands naturally evolved to include the basic political rights supposedly held by all adult members of a democratic society. Drawing upon international demands for democratization, including the Civil Rights Movement in the American South and decolonization movements around the world, students argued that, like all people in a democratic society, they should participate in the governing bodies of their community and should contribute to the decisions that affect their lives. As the Regina Campus Students' Union argued, "students are integral members of the university and as such have a legitimate claim and a positive contribution to make to university government."[8]

In forwarding these demands, students were encouraged not only by the broader political context but also by many of the faculty members on their campuses. In fact, within Canadian universities, faculty members largely spearheaded demands for structural changes and greater democratization. In a report commissioned in 1962 and published in 1966 by the Canadian Association of University Teachers (CAUT) and the National Conference of Canadian Universities and Colleges, later renamed the Association of Universities and Colleges of Canada (AUCC), co-chairs Sir James Duff and Robert Berdahl supported calls for greater faculty representation in university government (Johnston 2005: 37). Their recommendations included minority faculty representation on the Board of Governors, faculty control of the Senate and faculty involvement in the selection of deans and department chairs. Although the Duff-Berdahl commission addressed the growing concerns of faculty members about their positions within the university governing structure, by the time of its release in 1966 it was already considered out-dated and viewed by both faculty members and students as "an ultra-conservative document" (Ross 1984: 35). The students complained that although the commission claimed to have been sponsored by the entire university community in Canada (*University Government in Canada* 1966: v), it had in fact been sponsored only by the representatives of university administrations and faculty associations; students had played no part in initiating, financing or setting up the commission.

The commission had, however, commented on the role of students within the university governing structure because Duff-Berdahl

> saw enough symptoms of student dissatisfaction with the self-perceived status as "customers" of the universities to know that there will be increasing demands made in Canada for their elevation to partners (albeit unequal ones) in the "community of scholars and students".... The issue, then, is not whether to welcome or stifle this new wave of student sentiment, but rather how to develop channels into which it can flow constructively. (*University Government in Canada* 1966: 65)

The commissioners thus recommended the establishment of joint faculty/student committees at the departmental and faculty level of the university to discuss issues of direct relevance to students, such as course offerings, teaching methods and library facilities. As a result of concerns over the rapid turnover in student leadership, issues of confidentiality in Board of Governors deliberations, and the time commitment which would be a hardship for busy student leaders, Duff-Berdahl recommended that Canadian universities follow the example of Scottish universities and have students elect a non-student rector who could represent them on the Board of Governors. As for student representation on the Senate, Duff-Berdahl recommended that students sit on Senate committees that dealt with issues of interest to students, but not sit as representatives directly on the Senate itself (*University Government in Canada* 1966: 66–67).

To the older generation Duff-Berdahl was a significant step toward reforming the academy. However, student activists largely rejected the Duff-Berdahl recommendations, arguing that the report failed to acknowledge the role students played within the university community or the contributions they could make to that community.[9] Critiques of Duff-Berdahl also used the rhetoric of democracy, particularly the right of political participation. As University of Toronto student activist Howard Adelman argued at the time of the report's publication, "The Duff-Berdahl report is based on a fundamental lack of faith in democracy and the ability of people, no matter how well educated, to govern themselves."[10] Although the report claimed that faculty and students comprise the university community, Adelman thought that the commissioners showed "no belief that the members of a community, and of the university community in particular, should have the right to create and control the destiny and aspirations of their own environment."[11] Instead, students were not considered responsible and mature enough to make the decisions that affected their lives at the university. "Universities," Adelman argued, "must and should be governed by the members of their own community — the faculty and students which make it up."[12] This demand was based on the emerging belief that students were members of the so-called "community of scholars" and should, therefore, have the right and responsibility to participate in the governance of their community.

One of the first demands made by students regarding university government was that all decision-making bodies be opened to the public. As a 1966 University of Toronto Students' Administrative Council (SAC) brief on student participation in university government argued, open meetings are a prerequisite for democratic governance.[13] Demands were initially restricted to the publication of minutes of meetings and the ability of faculty and student representatives to attend all meetings on campus, but, as this interpretation of openness went into operation, students discovered that it did not provide the information they desired and did not, in their opinion, create an atmosphere for democratic participation.[14] Thus, their definition of openness further evolved and they demanded in a second brief that meetings of decision-making bodies of the university be open to any member of the university community.[15] At Simon Fraser University, student Senator Sharon Yandle argued that "[e]nding Senate secrecy is a preliminary move, long denied us, in the direction of meaningful democratic process and towards the realization of the demand now heard from students all across Canada: decisions must be made by those affected by them" (Yandle 1968: 6). As well, the Students' Union at the University of Saskatchewan, Regina Campus argued that since secrecy "only leads to suspicion and misunderstanding... it would be in the interests of all members of the university community for decisions to be made openly and for the scrutiny of all."[16] Thus, early demands for greater student involvement in university governance, supported by many students on campus, centred on the necessity of openness and accountability in university governing structures.

Along with these appeals for openness, student activists also demanded representation on university governing bodies. At the University of Toronto, SAC demanded direct student representation on the Board of Governors, on the Senate, on Presidential Advisory Committees, on college, residence and departmental bodies, and on any bodies struck to discuss the reform of the governing structure in its entirety.[17] They refused to sit on any body in which deliberations were closed to the public and, although this was never clearly defined, demanded significant, rather than token, representation.[18] At Simon Fraser University, student activists demanded representation on the University Senate, arguing that the university, "as Canada's newest university, [it] is the logical place to pioneer a student representative" (The Peak, March 2, 1966: 4). These activists also demanded positions on various committees that dealt directly with student issues, such as food services, housing and library facilities. In Regina, activists demanded direct representation on decision-making bodies, especially within the departments and faculties and on committees of express interest to students.[19] Student activists at all three universities, with significant support from the general student body, continued to argue that students should be involved in making all decisions that affected them and thus demanded the right to participate in university governing structures.

University administrators on the whole proved responsive to these early demands. Although administrators, along with many faculty members, did not always support student claims that the university was a political or democratic institution (Corry 1969: 569–70),[20] they did agree that students should participate in the university's decision-making processes. In fact, as Beth Bailey argued, the role of administrators in fostering personal growth and responsibility led them to encourage students to take greater roles in the governance of the university (Bailey 1998: 192). "No one," a brief by the University of Toronto Association of the Teaching Staff stated, "doubts that students deserve some voice in the government of the university."[21] Another possibility was that the university administration granted student representation in order to quell what might have become a more radical student movement; administrators realized that there was significant support among students for increased involvement in university governance and acknowledged that they therefore must accept this participation or risk further escalations in demands.[22]

At the University of Toronto, for example, President Claude Bissell offered students seats on the President's Council and on the Senate, although SAC rejected the offers because meetings of both bodies were closed to the public and membership was seen as token rather than significant representation.[23] Students were, however, granted representation on a number of committees as well as on faculty, department, and college boards.[24] As well, in Regina, the Faculty Council proved relatively amenable to student demands and created committees to study possible ways of improving student participation.[25] Regina Campus Principal William Riddell also sent a letter in 1968 encouraging the faculties and departments to find ways of involving students in the decision-making process.[26] However, this approach was "exploratory and on an ad hoc experimental basis,"[27] leading to different procedures being adopted in the various units on campus. In the years that followed, the provincial government also recognized demands for student representation on the top decision-making bodies of the university and amended the *University Act* in 1970 to include students on the Senate and again in 1971 to add student representatives to the Board of Governors.

At Simon Fraser University, following student demands for seats on the university Senate, university administrators ultimately decided in February 1967 to seat three students on that body (*The Peak*, February 8, 1967: 1). With this, Simon Fraser became the first university in Canada with student representatives on the Senate (Johnston 2005: 120). As well, administrators granted students representation on committees dealing directly with student issues. However, SFU activists continued to press for greater representation through both the Student Implementation Committee and the Student Affairs Committee; both of these committees recommended direct student representation on decision-making bodies throughout the university.[28] As at Toronto and Regina, university administrators were relatively responsive to certain student demands for representation on university governing bodies.

However, Simon Fraser was also the site of a significant confrontation in the summer of 1968. Using the controversy created by the Canadian Association of University Teachers' (CAUT) censure of the university, students presented demands for representation on university decision-making boards and a general democratization of university structures. The censure emerged from an investigation, requested by the Simon Fraser Faculty Association, into "the breakdown in communications between the Faculty Association and the President" (Milner et al. 1968: 4). After recommendations that faculty members be given greater control over university deci-sion-making procedures were largely ignored, the CAUT voted to censure the Board of Governors and the President of SFU (Milner et al. 1968: 26-–27).[29] This was the first censure ever issued by the CAUT.

While faculty members responded by endorsing the censure and de-manding the immediate resignation of SFU president, Patrick McTaggart-Cowan (Smith 1968: 25), the Student Society, dominated by members of the radical Students for a Democratic University (SDU), presented a motion to the general student body that called for sweeping structural changes of the university. They presented eight demands, endorsed by a number of stu-dent organizations (Pill 1968: 1), including a restructuring of the Board of Governors and Senate with faculty and student majority control, abolition of the offices of President and Chancellor, democratization of departmental structures and establishment of a joint student-faculty committee to super-vise the implementation of these demands.[30] "What we want," explained student Senator Sharon Yandle, "is control over the decisions which affect us" (Pill 1968: 1).

Although students had initially sought to work with faculty members to achieve structural changes within the university, it soon became clear that the faculty "take-over" of the university did not include the students. Although students had felt that cooperation between students and faculty members was essential,[31] the faculty voted to exclude the students from the entire process (Rossi 2003: 133), defeating six attempts to give the students a voice (Doupe 1968: 1). When it became clear that efforts to use "proper channels" had failed and that faculty members would not support the inclusion of students in the decision-making processes of the university, student activists organized a "non-obstructive sit-in" at the entrance to the Administration Building (*The Peak*, June 12, 1968: 1). As well, forty students, mostly members of SDU, occupied the Board of Governors meeting room on June 6, 1968. The purpose of the occupation, explained SDU member Jim Harding, was to present the argument that "[p]ower relations must change for real democracy to come to this campus. Board power and student power are not reconcilable... If we lose sight of our overall goals — BOG [Board of Governors'] resignation and total democratic restructuring — then student power demands will be smothered."[32] After receiving promises that their demands would be addressed, students vacated the room, effectively ending the occupation (*The Peak*, June 12, 1968: 2).

For student activists, the CAUT censure provided an opportunity to demand dramatic structural changes that would recognize their right to par-ticipate in university decision-making processes. The student government, elected on a platform of democratization, gained widespread support from a number of groups on campus, including such non-obvious allies as the Progressive Conservative and Social Credit clubs. As well, over 1600 students voted in a referendum that overwhelmingly demanded the resignation of the Board of Governors (Pill 1968: 1).[33] This indicates the degree to which students throughout the university supported demands for greater student participation. Despite this widespread support amongst students on campus, many faculty members ultimately proved interested only in increasing their own power within the university and reneged on what students viewed as promises to grant student representation; activists ultimately felt betrayed by faculty members. As one student argued, "faculty representatives sold out to the [Board of Governors] in return for a slice of the privileged pie."[34] According to historian Michiel Horn, faculty members, who had only recently obtained some power within the university, were unwilling to share this power with their students (Horn 1999: 26). This crisis, however, was an early indication of the centrality of governance issues to the student movements of the period.

ESCALATION OF DEMANDS: PARITY

While student activists had, with the support of the general student population, pressed for dramatic changes in the governing structures of English-Canadian universities, many soon came to realize the minimal influence they could have as minority members of committees and boards. By the latter part of the 1960s, student activists began demanding greater representation, often in the form of parity, or equal representation with faculty members and administrators. These activists believed students were central to the operations of the university and should therefore have a significant voice in how it was run.[35] As student government leaders in Toronto argued, "there must be parity between faculty and students...in recognition of the fact that faculty and students have essentially equal, albeit different, contributions to make in the teaching-learning process."[36] Overall, the students demanded that they "be accepted as full and necessary members of the university community, with the power to participate on an equal basis with faculty in making decisions" (*The Varsity*, January 22, 1971: 4).

At the University of Toronto, for example, these debates emerged when a commission was established with the task of examining and recommending radical changes to the university's governing structures. The Commission on University Government (CUG) was created in 1968 by University of Toronto President Claude Bissell to address what he considered to be an unworkable governing structure (Ross 1984: 39). As originally proposed by Bissell, this committee would be composed of two faculty members, two students, two administrators, two alumni and two members of the Board of Governors.[37] However, SAC rejected this composition and demanded a parity structure; they proposed that the committee consist of four students and four faculty members, with non-voting memberships for the president and two administrative appointees. "The students and faculty must have the right to decide on the future of the university," argued SAC member (and future Ontario premier) Bob Rae in justifying this demand, "or else our hopes for democracy are nothing at all" (Varsity SAC Bureau 1968: 1).

The SAC, hoping to form an alliance with faculty members that could exercise greater power in the negotiations with the administration, took this proposal to the Association of the Teaching Staff (ATS) on October 3, 1968. The ATS, already frustrated with the administration's failure to address their own demands for greater involvement in university governing structures, supported these demands for a parity structure (Bissell 1974: 135). Thus the Commission on University Government, which was to decide the future of the governing structure of the University of Toronto, was organized along a parity structure with equal representation between faculty and students. As Claude Bissell claimed in his memoirs, "[t]he final form of the Commission on University Government represented a victory for the radical students" (Bissell 1974: 160).

After nearly 400 hours of meetings, the CUG released its report, titled *Toward Community in University Government*, in October 1969. The commissioners agreed that the university was a community of scholars, which included administrators, faculty members and students. The goal that faced the university, then, was to determine operating principles that would make it possible for these groups to work together within the community (Commission on the Government of the University of Toronto 1970: 32). "Power, authority and responsibility," the commissioners argued, "must be shared between the central structure and departments; between faculty and students; between deans, chairmen and their councils; between academics and general support staff" (40). The commissioners also argued that some form of democracy should guide the operations of the university. "What the Report argues for," explained Bissell, "is the open society where all the estates participate in decisions at various levels, where discussions in official bodies are open, where all decisions are made known as quickly as possible."[38] As well, the commissioners recommended the creation of a single governing body composed of equal numbers of students, academic staff and lay members (Commission on the Government of the University of Toronto 1970: 214). Thus, the Commission on University Government had conceded that students were equal members of the university community and should, therefore, have equal representation on decision-making bodies.

However, when it came time to make final decisions regarding the university's governing structure in 1970, it became apparent that there existed a "deep split" between students and faculty members of the issue of parity (Ross 1984: 51). Although many members of the ATS had initially accepted that students were equal members of the university community and had used an alliance with students to press their own demands for representative government, by the time the CUG reported faculty members were increasingly divided over the issue and many bitterly opposed the principle of parity (Bissell 1974: 155). For their part, student activists, led by SAC, continued to push for parity, pressuring the provincial government to accept the principle when drafting the new *University Act*. Provincial politicians facing an upcoming election in which eighteen-year-olds were eligible to vote for the first time were aware of the potential political benefits of conceding to the students' demands. However, in response to continued pressure from faculty members on campus, including threats to disrupt the university if students were given parity, the government conceded the point and students were denied parity on the newly created Governing Council.[39] On July 23, 1971, the new *University Act* was passed by the Ontario Legislative Assembly to come into effect July 1, 1972. The final composition of the Governing Council included sixteen lay members appointed by the provincial government, eight alumni, twelve teaching staff, eight students, two presidential appointees, two administrative staff members and the President and Chancellor as ex-officio members (Ross 1984: 55). Student activists had failed to achieve parity in the university's ultimate governing structure.

Similar demands for parity also emerged at Simon Fraser University in the fall of 1969. At SFU, the issue of parity was most actively debated in the context of the Political Science, Sociology and Anthropology (PSA) Department, which had developed a radical perspective and a reputation for radical politics.[40] This radical orientation often brought the department into conflict with the university administration and created an environment of distrust within the university (Johnston 2005: 300–301). This situation reached a crisis point during the fall semester 1969, when a number of PSA students and faculty members went on strike, largely in an attempt to defend the parity system that had been established within the department.

Committed to a radical vision of education that stressed democratic control, including the principle of student-faculty parity, members of the PSA Department sought to put these theories into practice by revising the department's governing structures to allow for greater democratization and joint student-faculty control. Following the CAUT censure in 1968, seen by many students and faculty members in the university as only the first step on the road to democratization,[41] the decision was taken by faculty members in the PSA Department to open all departmental meetings and move aggressively towards a parity structure. The PSA course union, a student organization dominated by members of the SDU, developed suggestions for a new departmental structure based on the goal of creating "an academic *community* of equals, without role or status distinctions" by "maximiz[ing] the *real* power of students."[42] Based on the course union's recommendations, the PSA Department put into operation a parity structure, which gave students and faculty members equal say in all decisions made within the department.

The university administration grew increasingly uncomfortable with these changes, as did a number of faculty members in other departments (Harding 2005: 109). Of greatest concern for the more moderate faculty members and the university administration was the issue of student parity in the area of personnel decisions, that is, decisions regarding tenure, promotion and contract renewal. In July 1968 the University Tenure Committee (UTC) refused to accept recommendations made by the parity committee within the PSA Department, arguing that while students could contribute their opinions to personnel decisions, parity was not acceptable.[43] When the majority of PSA faculty members remained committed to student parity,[44] the university administration placed the department under an administrative trusteeship. "The decision by the administration," reflected SDU activist John Conway, "was... to smash the experiment. They were saying, 'You can't have parity. You can't have democracy. You have to go back to the acceptable model.'"[45]

When the newly formed PSA Tenure Committee, under the control of the administrative trustees, decided in August to reverse some of the original recommendations made by the department's parity committee, fuelling suspicions that the administration was conducting a political purge of the department (*The Peak*, September 3, 1969: 1),[46] PSA faculty members presented four "inseparable" demands to President Kenneth Strand. These included an immediate end to the administrative trusteeship and the reinstatement of the department's elected chair; the immediate rescinding of the recommendations made on tenure, promotion and renewals by the Department Tenure Committee and the University Tenure Committee; acceptance of the recommendations on tenure, promotions and renewals put forward by the PSA Department's elected tenure committee in May 1969; and a fundamental recognition at SFU of decentralized experimentation among faculty and students in organization and educational procedures, with such experimentation encouraged and not repressed.[47] Strand rejected all four demands.[48] In response, over 400 student and faculty members of the PSA department met and decided to abolish the separate student and faculty organizations, creating a General Assembly, which would emphasize the "common unity of faculty and students in their struggle with the administration" (*The Peak*, September 17, 1969). Faculty members and student activists within the department found common cause and formed an alliance that could press for democratic change. This General Assembly set a deadline of September 22 for the administration to respond to its demands and, when such a response was not forthcoming, voted to strike on September 24, 1969. Having failed to accomplish their goals through the use of so-called "proper channels," students and faculty members within the PSA Department attempted to use a more radical and confrontational approach to advance their agenda.

Throughout the strike, which included the withdrawal of services by a number of professors and teaching assistants, the creation of "counter-courses," the obstruction of classes by picketers and a hunger strike (Harding 2005: 110; Rossi 2003: 191–92, *The Peak*, October 1, 1969: 1, and October 29, 1969: 1), student participation in university governance remained the central issue, at least for students. "We cannot surrender the parity issue," stated Simon Fraser Student Society (SFSS) President Norm Wickstrom in explaining student council's decision to support the department's demands.[49] "[T]he central issue in this crisis," a motion by students in the Economics and Commerce Department confirmed, "is the defense of the right of student participation." These students supported the PSA Department "in its struggle to preserve this right for all students" (*The Peak*, October 6, 1969:). Arguing that students were equal members of the university community and therefore, based on the principles of representative government and self-determination, had a right to participate in equal numbers in the university's governing structures, many students on campus supported the strike in the PSA Department.

Despite this support, administrative pressure proved too strong for the PSA Department. On October 3, 1969, eight days into the strike, the administration suspended nine PSA faculty members. Three days later the Senate met and called for the non-suspended faculty members in the department to select a new chairman as a necessary step towards removing the trusteeship.[50] Given that faculty members held the majority of seats in the SFU Senate, it is clear that most faculty members in the university did not accept students as equal members of the university community. As well, acting upon a request made by SFU President Strand, the British Columbia Supreme Court granted an injunction on October 24 against fourteen strikers, including eleven students and three faculty members,[51] to prevent picketing outside and disruptions inside classrooms (*The Peak*, October 22, 1969: 1). Striking professors and students decided three days later to respect the injunction and to halt all pickets (*The Peak*, October 29, 1969: 1). The strike was officially ended by a vote of the Joint Strike Assembly, a body comprised of student activists and faculty members in the PSA Department that provided leadership during the strike, on November 4, 1969 (*The Peak*, November 5, 1969: 1). Student activists and faculty members within the PSA Department had failed to convince other members of the university community to accept students as equal members of the community of scholars with a right to participate equally in governing structures.

Similarly, student activists at the University of Saskatchewan, Regina Campus failed to persuade faculty members and administrators to accept parity on decision-making bodies in the university. Despite the use of an occupation to forward these demands, along with support from many students on campus, students were ultimately denied equal representation on university governing boards. Following the end of the occupation on November 22, 1972, based on an agreement to use "proper channels" to resolve the crisis, it was not until January 1974 that any final decisions were made regarding student demands for parity. A "tripartite" committee, composed of student, faculty and public representatives, began meeting in February 1973 and agreed in March of that year that "in principle students have the right to participate in a department up to the level of, and including, parity."[52] However, the faculty members of the committee submitted a minority report in which they stated their disagreement with the principle of parity (*The Carillon*, June 1, 1973: 1). Another committee, a subcommittee of the Senior Academic Committee of Council, which had been established prior to the occupation, released its report in November 1973. Its primary conclusion was that students need to be involved in some forms of university decision-making, but that this involvement should be primarily in the areas related to course content, curriculum and teaching. They argued that each department should find its own means to allow for student participation, but recommended that student participation be limited to 20 percent of the number of faculty.[53] Faculty members in Arts and Science ultimately accepted the recommendations of this latter report. It was decided on January 30, 1974, that student representatives would number no more than 20 percent of the faculty, except in departments where parity had already been accepted.[54] Thus, as at Toronto and Simon Fraser, while faculty members and administrators in Regina were generally willing to support the idea that students should, as members of the community, participate in the university's decision-making processes, they were unwilling to accept students as their equals within the university community. Failure to gain the support of not only students but also faculty members and administrators meant that such radical changes to the university's governing structures could not be achieved.

CONCLUSION

Throughout the sixties, governance issues remained central to the student movements at English-Canadian universities. At all three universities included in this study, students continually questioned their place within the university and demanded the right to participate in the governing structures of their community. Although the actions surrounding these demands differed slightly at each university, with students at Toronto working largely through so-called "proper channels" and students at Regina and Simon Fraser adopting more confrontational methods to press their demands, the issues played out in a relatively similar manner at all three schools. In all three cases, students initially demanded that university decision-making bodies operate in an open manner and include direct student representation. As faculty members and administrators could accept students as members of the university community, as well as their right to participate in the governing structures of that community, such demands were generally granted. However, as students continued to press for greater representation, including *equal* representation with faculty members, the support of faculty members and administrators could no longer be maintained. In particular, faculty members, seeking greater power for themselves within the university community, were often unwilling to support student demands for parity. Without such support, students failed to achieve equality within the community of scholars. This history of the student movements at the University of Toronto, University of Saskatchewan, Regina Campus and Simon Fraser University illustrates, then, the power relations in operation within the university community as well as the necessity of obtaining the support of the various estates, including students, faculty members and administrators, to achieve radical structural change. However, students did successfully challenge their place within the community of scholars, achieving recognition of their membership within this community and did contribute to the dramatic transformation of English-Canadian universities.

PRIMARY SOURCES AND NEWSPAPER ARTICLES CITED

Doupe, David. 1968. "Faculty Decide No Student Voice." *The Peak.* June 6.

Pill, Jaan. 1968. "Drastic change demanded: Board, senate reform must come." *The Peak.* May 31.

Pill, John Jaan. 1968. "No boycott: Record vote fails to pass." *The Peak.* June 4.

Smith, J. Percy. 1968. "Developments at Simon Fraser University." *C.A.U.T. Bulletin* 17, 1 (October).

The Carillon. 1973. "Students Ask For Support." January 26.

The Peak. 1966. "Senate voice Mynott." March 2.

_____. 1967. "Senate accepts students." February 8.

_____. 1968. "Council sits on BoG room sit-in stand." June 12.

_____. 1968. "On the way." June 12.

_____. 1969. "Economics & Commerce Supports PSA." October 6.

_____. 1969. "Fasters fast." October 29.

_____. 1969. "PSA Begins Picketing Classes." October 1.

_____. 1969. "PSA Calls Off Strike." November 5.

_____. 1969. "PSA Considers Strike: Monday Deadline Set." September 17.

_____. 1969. "Strikers Face Civil Suits." October 22.

_____. 1969. "Strikers Face Contempt of Court." October 29.

_____. 1969. "Tenure — Criteria." September 3.

The Varsity. 1966. "Whitney Hall curfews abolished." January 26.

_____. 1971. "Why student opinion is not enough." January 22.

Varsity SAC Bureau. 1968. "SAC Counter Proposal: No vote for administration on presidents council," *The Varsity*, September 20.

Yandle, Sharon. 1968. "Senate Inside and out." *The Peak.* July 31.

NOTES

1. Barry Lipton, interview with the author, February 20, 2002.
2. University of Regina Archives (hereafter URA), Regina Council Minutes and Agendas 1970–May 1974. John Archer, Untitled, November 22, 1972.
3. John Archer, untitled.
4. The decision to study these universities was taken for a number of reasons: all three universities had active student movements in the sixties; each university came into existence at a different time and in various contexts; each had distinctive student populations and different relationships with their external environment; and, finally, these three universities were located in diverse regions throughout English Canada. The decision to study universities in English Canada addressed the reality that the student movements in Quebec followed a very different trajectory from those in English Canada, as they interacted with the important currents within the province, and provided an opportunity to examine the issues of importance to the students on these campuses and gain some sense of how students interacted with the dramatic transformations taking place within French Canada. For information on the French Canadian student movements of the sixties, see for example Marcel Martel, "'S'ils veulent faire la révolution, qu'ils aillent la faire chez eux à leurs risques et périls. Nos anarchistes masions sont suffisants': occupation et répression à Sir George-William," *Bulletin d'Histoire Politique* Vol. 15, No. 1 (automne 2006); Nicole Neatby, *Carabins ou Activistes? L'idéalisme et la radicalisation de la pensée étudiante à l'Université de Montréal au temps du duplessisme* (Kingston & Montreal: McGill-Queen's University Press, 1997); Karine Hébert, "From Tomorrow's Elite to Young Intellectual Workers: The Search for Identity among Montreal Students, 1900–1958," in Bettina Bradbury and Tamara Myers (eds.), *Between Public and Private: Identity, Nation and Governance in Quebec* (Vancouver: University of British Columbia Press, 2005); Karine Hébert, "Carabines, poutchinettes, co-eds ou freshettes sont-elles des étudiantes? Les filles à l'Université McGill et à l'Université de Montréal (1900–1960)," *Revue d'histoire de l'Amérique française* Vol. 57, No. 3 (hiver 2004); and Karine Hébert, "Between the Future and the Present: Montreal University Student Youth and the Postwar Years, 1945-1960," in Michael Gauvreau and Nancy Christie (eds.), *Cultures of Citizenship in Post-War Canada. 1940–1955* (Kingston & Montreal: McGill-Queen's University Press, 2003).
5. The period generally referred to as "the sixties" has been delineated in different ways by a variety of scholars. While the sixties is sometimes used to refer to the actual decade of the 1960s, from 1960 to 1969, historical eras do not generally conform to simple divisions. Instead, many scholars refer to the "long sixties." For example, Arthur Marwick argues that the sixties began around 1958–59 and ended in about 1973–74. In Canada, especially for a study of the student movements in the sixties, it is probably most accurate to conceive of the sixties as a period extending from approximately 1964 to 1974. During this ten-year period, the student movements at English-Canadian universities were established, evolved and changed, and ultimately fractured and disintegrated. See for example, Todd Gitlin, *The Sixties: Years of Hope, Days of Rage* (New York: Bantam Books, 1987); Joan Morrison and Robert K. Morrison, *From Camelot to Kent State: The Sixties in the Words of Those Who Lived It* (New York: Times Books, 1987); and Arthur Marwick, *The Sixties: Cultural Revolution in Britain, France, Italy, and the United States, c.1958–c.1974* (Oxford: Oxford University Press, 1998).

6. Doug Ward, interview with the author, January 31, 2006.
7. Simon Fraser University Archives (hereafter SFUA), *Simon Fraser University Calendar*, 1966–67, 159.
8. URA, 78-3 USRC Office of the Principal, Box 28, File 2000.1-2 "Student's Representative Council (S.R.C.) 1967–69." Brief , n.d.
9. University of Toronto Archives (hereafter UTA), A1972-0023 Students' Administrative Council, Box 31, File 7 "University Government." Howard Adelman, "A Report on the Duff-Berdahl Commission Report on 'University Government in Canada,'" 3.
10. Adelman, "A Report on the Duff-Berdahl Commission Report on 'University Government in Canada," 7.
11. Adelman, 4.
12. Adelman, 8.
13. UTA, A1972-0023 Students' Administrative Council, Box 029, File 02. University of Toronto Students' Administrative Council, "Student Participation in the Government of the University of Toronto," September 22, 1966, 5–6.
14. UTA, A1977-0020 Office of the Executive Vice-President and Provost, Box 023, File "SAC." Tom Faulkner, "Address to the University of Toronto Senate," February 9, 1968, 2.
15. UTA, A1985-0031 Office of the Registrar, Box 019, File "Student Participation, Part II." "Openness at the University of Toronto," May 15, 1969, 1.
16. URA, 78-3 USRC Office of the Principal, Box 28, File 2000.1-2 Students' Representative Council (S.R.C.) 1967–69. Students' Union, "Brief on 'Open Decision-Making in the University,'" January 1967.
17. "Student Participation in the Government of the University of Toronto," 7–8.
18. See UTA, B1989-0031 Claude Bissell collection, Box 012, File "1966–67 President's Council." Various letters between Tom Faulkner and Claude Bissell, 1966–1967 and "Address to the University of Toronto Senate," 2.
19. Student's Representative Council (S.R.C.) 1967-69, Brief , n.d.
20. See also UTA, A1978-0028 Office of the President, Box 010, File "Student Participation." Committee of Presidents of Universities of Ontario, "Student Participation in University Government," November 1967, 7–8.
21. UTA, A1971-0011 Office of the President, Box 096, File "Joint Staff-Student Committees." Memorandum to Deans, Principals, Directors, and Chairmen of Departments from Claude Bissell, President, September 22, 1966, 2.
22. UTA, B1989-0031 Claude Bissell collection, Box 005, File "CUG Personal Communications." Letter to M.W. McCutcheon from Claude Bissell, September 30,1968.
23. UTA, B1989-0031 Claude Bissell collection, Box 012, File "1966–67 President's Council." Various letters between Tom Faulkner and Claude Bissell, 1966–1967.
24. See UTA, A1977-0019 Office of the President, Box 016, File "CAPUT." "Notes by R. Ross on steps that might be taken against possible trouble in the university in the Fall," [1968], 3.
25. URA, 78-3 USRC Office of the Principal, File 400.9. Joint Committee on Student Participation in University Government, 1966–70.
26. URA, Regina Council Minutes and Agendas 1970–May 1974. Memorandum to all members of faculty from Principal W.A. Riddell, September 12, 1968.
27. URA, 80–38 Principal's Papers, File 404.10-1. W.A. Riddell, "Student Participation

in University Government, University of Saskatchewan," September 28, 1970.

28. SFUA, F-159 The British Columbia Student Federation Fonds, File F-159-1-2-3 "Meeting briefs and reports, [1968], 1969–70." "Student Implementation Committee Report," [1968] and SFUA, F-193 Office of the President Fonds, File F-193-18-1-0-1 "Dean of Student Affairs, 1964–68." "Student Affairs Committee Final Report," December 1968.

29. See also, SFUA, F-74 Simon Fraser Student Society Fonds, F-74-3-2-20 "Martin Loney — Correspondence, May–Aug. 1968." "Resolution of Censure Against the Board of Governors and the President of Simon Fraser University," May 26, 1968.

30. SFUA, F-74 Simon Fraser Student Society Fonds, File F-74-2-0-13 "Minutes May–Aug. 1968." Minutes of Special General Meeting, May 30, 1968.

31. SFUA, F-20 The Department of Political Science, Sociology and Anthropology Fonds, File F-20-3-4-22 "Faculty dispute — handouts, 1968–74." SDU Information Bulletin Vol. 1, No. 1, [1968].

32. SFUA, F-74 Simon Fraser Student Society Fonds, File F-74-9-0-11 "Ephemera, 1965–68." Jim Harding, "Where is the BOG???????" n.d.

33. See also SFUA, F-74 Simon Fraser Student Society Fonds, File F-74-3-3-6 "2nd Vice President — Correspondence, 1968." Jim Harding, "From Confrontation to Committees: Student Power at Simon Fraser University," June 1968, 2.

34. SFUA, F-20 The Department of Political Science, Sociology and Anthropology Fonds, File F-20-3-4-22 "Faculty dispute — handouts, 1968–74." John Conway, "Build Student Power," September 1968.

35. See, Barry Lipton, interview with the author, February 20, 2002 and Corry, 568.

36. UTA, P79-0169-01. Students' Administrative Council, *The Last Whole Student Catalogue* (1974–75), 105.

37. UTA, B1989-0031 Claude Bissell collection, Box 005, File "CUG Personal Comm." Claude Bissell, "The Natural History of the Commission on University Government: University of Toronto Alumni Association, September 9, 1969," 2.

38. UTA, A1978-0028 Office of the President, Box 001, File 04. Claude Bissell, "Letter on the Commission on University Government to the University of Toronto Bulletin," [1969], 8.

39. UTA, P78-0693-05. Students' Administrative Council, *Handbook '72, Volume 1: The Year of the Change*, 6.

40. The original faculty members in the department, along with many of their students, sought to develop an alternative vision of education based on three key principles: critical social science, which demanded that scholars engage with society as critics; democratic control, which affirmed the principle of faculty-student parity in decision-making and viewed education as a cooperative process between faculty and students; and community integration, which challenged social scientists to serve the needs of the community rather than the needs of the wealthy and powerful. See, "PSA Statement of Principles," *The Peak*, July 16, 1969, 8.

41. John Conway, interview with the author, January 24, 2006.

42. "Report of the Student Power Research Sub-Committee," PSA Department, Simon Fraser University, June 1968, 2–3.

43. SFUA, F-85 Office of the Registrar Fonds, File F-85-1-0-0-1 "PSA materials, 1969–70, vol. 1." Concerned Faculty and Students, "The Crunch," July 9, 1969, 1.

44. Concerned Faculty and Students, "The Crunch," July 9. 1969, 1.
45. John Conway, interview with the author, January 24, 2006.
46. See also Library and Archives of Canada (hereafter LAC), RG-146 Canadian Security Intelligence Service Records, File 96-A-00045, pt. 50. "Simon Fraser University," September 1, 1970, 5.
47. See SFUA, F-131 The Norman Swartz PSA Collection, File F-131-0-2 "PSA Binder 1 2/3, 1969." "An Open Letter to President Kenneth L. Strand," September 8, 1969.
48. SFUA, F-193 Office of the President Fonds, File F-193-10-8-0-9 "Political Science, Sociology and Anthropology, 1969." Letter to all faculty from Kenneth Strand, September 15, 1969.
49. SFUA, F-74 Simon Fraser Student Society Fonds, File F-74-3-2-27 "Norm Wickstrom — Correspondence (Out), Sept.–Dec. 1969." Letter to Miss Lynda Lyman from Norm Wickstrom, September 15, 1969, 3.
50. SFUA, F-150 Political Science, Sociology and Anthropology Collection, File F-150-0-1 "Press Releases, 1969–70." Press Release, October 7, 1969.
51. SFUA, F-150 Political Science, Sociology and Anthropology Collection, File F150-0-3 "Publications About PSA, 1970–1990." Don Payzant, "Dismembering a department: The history of PSA at SFU," "PSA Student Handbook," Spring 1990, 13.
52. URA, 85-54 USRC Faculty of Arts and Science, File 103-5.1. D. de Vlieger, "Tri-Partite Committee Tentative Recommendations," March 26, 1972, 4.
53. URA, University of Saskatchewan, Regina Campus Executive of Council Minutes and Agendas 1973–June 1974. "A Report on Student Participation in University Government, Regina Campus, University of Saskatchewan, by Senior Academic Committee of Council," November 1973, 23–26.
54. URA, University of Saskatchewan, Regina Campus Executive of Council Minutes and Agendas 1973–June 1974. January 30, 1974.

CHAPTER SEVEN

MAD AT HATFIELD'S TEA PARTY
FEDERALISM AND THE FIGHT FOR FRENCH
IMMERSION IN SACKVILLE, NEW BRUNSWICK, 1973–1982

Matthew Hayday

In 1980, the lobbying activities of a group of parents in the community of Sackville, New Brunswick, (pop. 5,000) prompted the mass resignation of their local school board and a major policy change by the provincial government of Premier Richard Hatfield. At issue was access to French immersion, which the parents considered to be key to their children's future French-language capacities in a province (and country) that had become officially bilingual a decade earlier. Their lobbying activities over the spring and summer resulted in a new provincial policy mandating that immersion classes had to be created by school boards where sufficient demand existed. How should we account for the success of this group? Why were these parents, organized as a local chapter of a nation-wide social movement, able to accomplish their goals? What can this case study tell us about the capacity of a local movement to effect social change?

Over the course of the 1960s and 1970s, Canadian politics was greatly influenced by the identity projects of the Liberal governments of Lester Pearson and Pierre Elliott Trudeau. Rejecting the exclusionary British-centric model that had dominated Canadian political discourse until the 1950s, these prime ministers sought to craft new identity models that responded not only to the rise of Quebec nationalism but also to a host of other groups demanding recognition of their status and rights, ranging from multicultural communities to women to Aboriginal peoples (Igartua 2006). Two of the key legislative planks of this identity project were the *Official Languages Act,* 1969 and the multiculturalism policy, announced in 1971.

The Office of the Commissioner of Official Languages and the Department of the Secretary of State were among the key institutional actors involved in promoting these identity policies. As Leslie Pal has noted, many civil society groups received funding from the Secretary of State to carry out their objectives. These groups ranged from the National Action Committee on the Status of Women to the Fédération des francophones hors-Québec (Pal 1993). These funding programs created the peculiar situation of government-funded social movements. Applying the neo-institutionalist theories developed by Theda Skocpol and others (Skocpol 1985), Pal observes that while government funding to these organizations led these groups to couch their demands in terms of rights and government services, centred around the federal government, it did not completely compromise their freedom of action. These groups remained ardent critics of several aspects of government policies. This funding also permitted the federal government to put indirect pressure on provincial governments to change their policies (Behiels 2004; Hayday 2005).

While the federal government's top priority in the realm of official languages was the promotion of minority language rights, particularly for the francophone minority communities outside of Quebec, it also created funding programs to promote opportunities for individual Canadians to become bilingual, under the auspices of the Official Languages in Education Program (OLEP). This program provided the provinces with funding for a number of education programs, including the recently piloted French immersion programs. To help foster the growth of French-as-a-second-language (FSL) programs, the Commissioner of Official Languages helped to sponsor the birth of a new organization: Canadian Parents for French (CPF). In the late 1970s and onward, Canadian Parents for French actively lobbied local school boards and provincial governments for the creation of new and enhanced opportunities for children to learn French as their second language.

While numerous pedagogical studies indicated that FSL programs such as French immersion can be followed equally well by children of a wide array of learning abilities, French immersion was often perceived as a program for the children of elite parents. The fact that CPF's provincial and federal executives were composed largely of upper-middle-class parents did little to dispel this impression. Does this mean that we should dismiss Canadian Parents for French, with its middle-class image and federal government funding, as not being a legitimate social movement? To do so would have the unfortunate effect of dismissing the manner in which social movement goals can be obtained through state channels. Rather, I propose to follow Miriam Smith's broader interpretation of collective action, which includes all movements that seek to transform the values and institutions of society, even in moderate ways (Smith 2005: 12–13). Indeed, it is difficult to classify Canadian Parents for French, an association that was not fighting for their own narrow self-interest, but the interests of their children, and in a broader sense, the national unity and social cohesion of the country. While it employed a rights-based discourse, CPF was a key actor in a movement that was seeking to reshape how Canadians conceived of their political community and the role of language within that polity.

In order to fully understand the manner in which Canadian Parents for French—Sackville and its supporters managed to accomplish its objectives, it is important to bear in mind a number of key factors and theoretical models. Of primary importance is the fact that these lobbying efforts were taking place within a federal system. Responsibility for language education was shared between three levels of government: the federal government, which provided funding to official languages education; the provincial government, which set policy and curriculum; and municipal governments, which implemented policy at the community level. To understand the roles these different levels of government played in this case study, historical institutionalist and neopluralist theories are useful (Smith 2005: 29–33). It will become clear that these governments were not simply acting as passive arbiters between interest groups, but rather each branch of the state had interests of its own.

This case study also examines the operation of Canadian federalism in response to social movements in terms of the multiple crack theory. This theory was first advanced by Morton Grodzin to describe the actions of interest groups in the U.S. federal system. Applied in the Canadian context by political scientists, including Alan Cairns, Richard Simeon and Hugh Thorburn (Thorburn 1985), it postulates that a federal system of government provides multiple opportunities for action by social movements, which will congregate around the level of government they believe is most likely to be responsive to their demands and attempt to shift responsibility for decision-making to this level. Writing in 1972, Simeon argued that this theory did not apply well in the Canadian context, since the rise of executive federalism in the late 1960s meant that most intergovernmental negotiations were taking place in private and at high levels of the executive, leaving little room for interest groups to influence the decision-making process (Simeon 1972: 144). This case study attempts to determine if this was in fact the case, given that CPF did employ a multi-pronged strategy to shift government policy.

Two other considerations come into play in terms of how Canadian Parents for French planned its strategy and how it was received by its target governments. Although the parents it represented came from a wide variety of class backgrounds, Canadian Parents for French was considered to be a middle-class, if not upper-class, organization. In the Sackville context, this had particular resonance in light of the "town and gown" dynamic of a university town in rural New Brunswick. While the parents involved in the organization were both mothers and fathers, many of the key leaders of Canadian Parents for French were women, particularly the well-educated wives of faculty members at Mount Allison University, which added a gendered dimension to this movement. The fact that this movement was concerned with education, historically considered to be the domain of mothers, also affected the social networks and strategies employed by this organization.

FRENCH IMMERSION AND THE ORIGINS
OF CANADIAN PARENTS FOR FRENCH

Although Canadian Parents for French was involved in the promotion of many different FSL programs, in the 1970s and 1980s it was most prominently associated with the campaign to expand French immersion programs. French immersion is a Canadian pedagogical innovation, which draws its name from the method it employs for language teaching — immersing young children in a second-language classroom environment. The most common form is what is often referred to as "early immersion." Non-French speaking children begin in either kindergarten or grade one in an educational environment where French is the primary language of communication and the language of instruction for all subjects (possibly excluding an English language arts class, depending on the program). This immersive experience continues for the first several years of a child's education.

This methodology is based on research that indicates that children are most receptive to new language acquisition at a young age (for example, see Swain 1978). Early research on French immersion also showed that while immersion children initially lagged slightly behind non-immersion children in English-language acquisition, they caught up to their peers by third or fourth grade, and their French-language skills, while not as strong as native speakers, were much stronger than control groups in the regular FSL programs. As a method of language teaching, French immersion is not without its pedagogical critics (Hammerly 1989), as even its supporters have noted that this type of learning environment may reinforce certain language errors (Fraser 2006). It is not my intention to engage this debate. What is important in the context of Canadian Parents for French's actions was that these parents believed that French immersion was the best option for their children, and they were determined to fight for the creation and expansion of these programs.

French immersion was piloted in the context of Quiet Revolution-era Quebec, where English-speaking parents began to realize that their children would be at a serious disadvantage in the Quebec economy if they were unable to communicate effectively in French. Under the guidance of Wallace Lambert, initial pilot projects were launched in the St. Lambert school board in 1965 and the Protestant School Board of Greater Montreal in 1967. Early evaluations of the program were favourable and the program was quickly replicated throughout the province (Lambert and Tucker 1972). At the same time as these pilot projects were being launched, the federal and New Brunswick governments were moving towards a policy of official bilingualism for government services, responding to the recommendations of the Royal Commission on Bilingualism and Biculturalism. Official languages legislation was passed by both governments in 1969, mandating that government services had to be offered in both official languages, a policy that also aimed to correct the under-representation of francophones in the civil service.

To supplement the *Official Languages Act*, Secretary of State Gérard Pelletier launched the Official Languages in Education Program (OLEP) in 1970. This program paid a percentage of the cost of educating students enrolled in minority language education programs and their second language programs. Primarily intended to support minority language education, which was funded at a higher rate than second language instruction, the Ontario government asked to have its French immersion programs (the first one piloted in Ottawa-Carleton in 1971) deemed eligible for the minority-language education funding level. The federal government agreed, paving the way for other provinces to seek additional financial assistance for their French immersion programs from Ottawa (Hayday 2001). This funding proved to be a major impetus for the provinces to begin creating French immersion programs, copying the St. Lambert model.

The first Commissioner of Official Languages, Keith Spicer, was also a major advocate for personal bilingualism among Canadians. His annual reports routinely decried the low levels of individual bilingualism in Canadians and lambasted Canadian universities for dropping their language requirements. In 1977, Spicer's last year in office, the Commissioner brought together parents from across the country for a conference on French-as-a-second-language acquisition. By this point, many provinces had created at least a few pilot French immersion programs. None, however, were governed by a province-wide policy that called for the mandatory creation of French immersion classes where demand existed. Rather, French immersion was treated as a boutique program, which could be cut in a situation of financial constraint.

Canadian Parents for French was born out of this 1977 conference as a national organization with a mandate to a) assist in ensuring that each Canadian child have the opportunity to acquire as great a knowledge of the French language and culture as he or she is willing and able to attain; b) promote the best possible types of French-language learning opportunities; and c) establish and maintain effective communication between interested parents and educational and government authorities concerned with the provision of French language learning opportunities. The organization received the bulk of its initial funding from the federal department of Secretary of State (now Canadian Heritage) and quickly established branches in every province. Initial membership fees were set at $5 per family, the bulk of which would be put at the disposal of local chapters where these were created. By February 1979, Canadian Parents for French claimed a membership of 3,901 families, of which 195 were in the province of New Brunswick.

Although CPF was interested in all aspects of French second language acquisition opportunities, its early years tended to emphasize the promotion of French immersion. Among its earliest initiatives were the creation of a national directory of French immersion programs, the development of the parental handbook *So You Want Your Child to Learn French!* (Mlacak and Isabelle 1979) and the compilation of bibliographies of the latest research on language acquisition. CPF published both national and provincial newsletters to communicate with its member parents. One of its earliest major advocacy activities was acting as a self-appointed intermediary between the federal and provincial governments, which were squabbling over the anticipated 1979 renewal of the OLEP (Poyen 1989). CPF was perhaps most active in Western Canada and certainly attracted the most attention for its activities in provinces that were not known for being supportive of French language rights.

In New Brunswick, French immersion had also taken off rapidly. By 1977, French immersion was governed by Policy 501 which gave school boards permission to create new French immersion classes if a minimum level of parental interest was expressed. The program was extremely popular in the major urban centres of Fredericton and Moncton, where parents realized that their children would have better access to government jobs if they were bilingual. By the fall of 1980, 5500 students were enrolled in French immersion in New Brunswick, out of a total student population of about 100,000 students. Enrolment jumped to 7,060 by the following year and continued to grow as schools added additional classes. A standard process for creating French immersion was to start with an initial grade one class and then add additional years to the program as the cohort progressed through the school system.

THE SACKVILLE CASE STUDY

In the late-1970s, the community of Sackville, New Brunswick, had a population of approximately 5,000 people. The town's population swelled annually to 7,000 during Mount Allison University's academic term. Sackville was part of the District 14 school board in New Brunswick, which also encompassed the neighbouring communities of Port Elgin and Dorchester. Sackville was served by two elementary schools, which merged into a new facility in the early 1980s, one middle school and the regional high school. As a result of the university, Sackville has a relatively high concentration of university-educated parents and other professionals. Moreover, as with many such communities, a town-and-gown dynamic existed, with the accompanying tensions between the university community and the rest of the population.

There was a current of anti-French sentiment in the community, as also existed elsewhere in the province. The process of implementing New Brunswick's official languages policy had not proceeded completely smoothly. Many Acadians chafed at what they felt was a slow implementation of the policy, while anglophones expressed discontent at a program they believed favoured the Acadian population. Loyalist associations, for example, often complained about the imposition of bilingualism. Indeed, in September 1973, when the first grade one French immersion class opened in Sackville, there was no story about this run in the local paper, the *Sackville Tribune-Post*. There was, however, a story about a newly founded anti-bilingualism party called the Dominion of Canada Party (*Sackville Tribune-Post* (hereafter *STP*) September 12 ,1973: 1).

It is also important to note that the baby bust had hit New Brunswick hard. Throughout the 1970s, New Brunswick was faced with a declining school-age population. This meant that many teachers were worried about the stability of their positions. The New Brunswick Teachers' Association considered the preservation of its members' jobs to be its highest priority.

The Sackville chapter of Canadian Parents for French was created in November 1978 with forty initial members (*CPF New Brunswick Newsletter* April 1979). Among its original members were two members of the provincial executive: alternate director Margaret Whitla, one of the original delegates to the 1977 Ottawa conference, and secretary-treasurer Phyliss Stopps (*CPF NB Newsletter* November 1979). When the local chapter was founded, a French immersion program existed at Central and Salem elementary schools, with the grade one to six classes split between the two schools, with a total enrolment of 147 children.[1] A grade seven class opened at the Marshview middle school in the fall of 1979.

The rationale for creating a local chapter for Sackville was that part of the membership fees ($5 per family) from local chapters were remitted back to local chapters and could thus be invested in local activities. Chapter status also made the community group eligible for project funding from the Secretary of State Department. The Sackville chapter proved to be very active. In addition to its lobbying activities with the school board, the chapter organized information meetings for parents, collected and donated French books to the local school libraries, helped to organize and fund class trips for the immersion students to visit francophone communities, organized an annual winter carnival event, set up French immersion summer camps and brought francophone authors, films and plays into the schools.

The political activism of CPF Sackville would also prove to be quite prodigious over its first decade. Among its varied activities, it would sponsor the Atlantic regional conference for French immersion parents, lobby the school board to increase the level of French instruction in the middle school grades, engage in debates with the school board and the local parents over the merits of a late-immersion program (with a grade seven start) in Port Elgin, become embroiled in disputes over bussing students in from Dorchester and raise concerns with the provincial government over split grades in immersion classes. Three of the most active members of the local executive — Susan Purdy, Berkeley Fleming and Margaret Whitla — went on to assume senior positions in both the provincial and national executives of the organization.

The most dramatic example of the impact of CPF Sackville is evident from a case study of the battle over accessibility to French immersion that was waged in 1980. This conflict came immediately after a period of intense activity for the local chapter. Sackville played host to the Atlantic regional CPF conference in February 1980, a conference that brought in governmental and pedagogical experts, including representatives of the Secretary of State Department and the provincial department of education, French immersion experts such as Jim Cummins and the former commissioner of official languages, Keith Spicer.[2]

Sackville's French immersion program had grown steadily from 1973 to 1979, with one new class being added per year and a grade eight class slated to be added in the fall of 1980. Perhaps encouraged by the local conference on French immersion, a record fifty parents indicated that they wanted their children to attend French immersion in the fall. The class had a capacity of twenty-eight, and the District 14 school board indicated that it did not intend to create a second grade one French immersion class.

Membership in Sackville CPF swelled, growing from its initial forty members to ninety-two, as parents who feared that their children might not get access to French immersion in the fall joined the organization. Many parents who already had children in the immersion program feared that their younger siblings — some of whom were attending a French immersion kindergarten — would not be able to join their older brothers and sisters (Barbara Jardine and Vanessa Bass interviews). In May, the parents circulated a petition around the community, calling for an end to the school board's policy of restricting access to French immersion. The petition, which bore 280 signatures, was presented to the school board at its May meeting by a group of fifty parents (STP May 28, 1980: 1). The parents raised three key arguments in their petition and accompanying brief outlining why open access to immersion was needed: 1) that New Brunswick is a bilingual province in a bilingual country; 2) that the education of students in French costs no more than education in English once the initial class has been established; and 3) that parents were convinced of the necessity that their children speak French fluently in order to find jobs anywhere in Canada.[3]

A number of other concerns were raised at the May school board meeting. In addition to the parents' concerns for their children, which echoed the results of a 1979 study of parents' motivations for sending their children to French immersion,[4] concerns were raised that the hiring of a second grade one immersion teacher could mean that an anglophone teacher might be laid off in the future. Indeed, the question of job security for teachers was a central preoccupation throughout the province. New Brunswick's French immersion programs tended to be staffed by francophone teachers, which created job security concerns among anglophone teachers who were members of the New Brunswick Teachers' Association (MacKinnon 1983; Williston 1983). The District 14 school board did have a few vacancies to fill in 1980, and the parents argued that one of these should be filled by a second grade one immersion teacher. The school board chair, Ove Samuelson, told the parents that a study was underway to see what could be done but did not make any promises to change the board's position. The parents, meanwhile, threatened to take their case directly to Premier Hatfield (*STP* May 28. 1980: 1).

The parents, eager for a positive resolution to their demands, attended the next school board meeting in early June. Board member Peter Mitchem put forth a motion at the meeting calling for the creation of a second grade one immersion class in Sackville, and a new grade one class in Port Elgin, where thirty-four parents had expressed interest in a new French immersion class. Before his motion could be voted on, Dorchester board member Bernie Bourgeois, who personally opposed French immersion, introduced an amendment to the motion that would oblige the board to also create a French immersion class in Dorchester if even a single parent requested it. Bourgeois' disingenuous motion passed by a margin of 7 to 5, with two abstentions. The amended motion was then defeated by a margin of 8 to 6 (*STP* June 11, 1980: 1). Board chair Samuelson indicated that he believed that the issue was closed and stated that there would be a public lottery later in the month at which the names of twenty-eight children would be drawn. Susan Purdy, speaking for the parents, made it clear that they were not finished with the issue and would be taking their case to the Premier.

Tensions continued throughout June, with many angry parents writing into the local newspaper. Barbara Jardine, who handled media relations for CPF Sackville, attempted to clarify the parents' position, pointing out that French immersion programs received more money from the province thanks to the federal granting programs. Moreover, a second grade one class would in fact increase the stability of the program, because enrolment in French immersion tended to decline in the senior grades as parents moved to other locations (the university community, in particular, tended to be transient) (*STP* June 18, 1980: 2, 5). Opponents of the program also raised their concerns in the paper, claiming that the program was elitist (*STP* June 25, 1980: 2). The board did proceed with the lottery, however, and sent out letters to the parents of the unlucky children on June 27, 1980 with the following message:

Dear [Parent],

As a result of the Lottery Draw, I hereby advise you that your child, [child's name], has not been selected for the total French Immersion Class to begin in September, 1980.

> We understand your disappointment at this time, but do wish to assure you that everything possible will be done to give your child a positive grade one experience.
>
> Sincerely,
>
> Mr. Stuart Burbine, Principal[5]

The question of a second French immersion class for Sackville was raised again at the board's late-June meeting, only to be defeated once more (STP July 2, 1980: 2, 6). Faced with intransigence at the local level, the parents decided to take their case to both Ottawa and Fredericton.

Barbara Jardine wrote to Premier Hatfield on June 30, 1980, calling on the premier to take action on the question of access to French immersion, and sent a copy of the letter to the regional representative of the commissioner of official languages. Jardine invoked the premier's commitment to bilingualism in her letter, noting that:

> Parents of children in Sackville NB desiring French immersion grade 1 in the fall of 1980 hold the honorable Mr. Hatfield, Premier of New Brunswick responsible for the failure of himself and his government to uphold and promote the bilingual nature of his province. It was under Mr. Hatfield that New Brunswick became the only officially bilingual province in Canada, and now while New Brunswick is still under his guidance English speaking children desiring to learn French are being discriminated against.... It seems rather ludicrous to these parents that Mr. Hatfield is working so hard to achieve constitutional reform for Canada when he refuses now to uphold reforms that his own government has made. What can his credibility in such matters be when the actions of his government show that the bilingualism in New Brunswick is only token and not equally for French and English.[6]

The commissioner of official languages was unable to intervene directly in this conflict, as education is a provincial responsibility. Robert Pichette, the Atlantic representative for the Commissioner, did however note that this decision was "regrettable" and expressed support for CPF's goals, noting: "Not only does this program seem to have become popular among a great many Canadian parents, but there is every indication that it is a most effective method for the learning of a second language."[7]

The parents also organized a trip to Fredericton. A group of parents gathered in the home of Vanessa Harpur and created placards for their protest. A small convoy of parents, mostly mothers of children who were denied access to the French immersion program, then headed to Fredericton, where they marched around the legislative building. It is worth noting that several of these parents had a history of activism in Sackville. Many of them were wives of Mount Allison University faculty members who had worked together on a number of campaigns for daycare and family planning services at the university, and thus had a history of working together (Vanessa Bass interview).

Before leaving for Fredericton, Susan Purdy had notified the media, Tantramar MLA Lloyd Folkins and the premier that the parents would be coming. After an hour of picketing the Legislative Assembly, the media arrived to film the protestors, who bore signs such as "Education — A Mickey Mouse Affair?" Shortly thereafter, Folkins emerged from the building to invite a small delegation in to meet with the premier. Purdy, Harpur and a few others then met with Premier Hatfield to discuss their concerns, and the parents "were served tea from the silver tea service" (Vanessa Bass interview). The premier did not make any firm promises, but attempted to mollify the parents, promising to look into their concerns. A smaller delegation met on a separate occasion with Minister of Education Charles Gallagher, with similar results.

Over the month of July, the *Sackville Tribune-Post* continued to receive numerous letters from angry parents, who copied their letters to the premier, the minister of education and the school board chair. Angry in tone, most were from parents whose children were unlucky in the lottery. The discourse of children's rights and children's comprehension of the issues at stake is a particularly interesting facet of this correspondence. Gerrit Moleman, invoking the children's song "Why Oh Why" by Anne Murray, posed his question to Ove Samuelson from the perspective of his six-year-old daughter, asking him to explain to his daughter, who had completed the immersion kindergarten program and whose mother taught in the French immersion program, why she could not attend the same program in grade one (*STP* July 2, 1980: 5). Colin Grant wryly noted, with reference to the board members who had voted against a second grade one class: "I am sure they [the 10] can show how they were motivated by concern for the children, and dispel the impression that they were prompted by parochialism, bigotry and vested interest" (*STP* July 9, 1980: 2). James Purdy asked how he was to explain to his child that he could not attend French immersion, when his friends and siblings could, while calling on the board to put the interests of the children first, and those of the community (including the teachers) second, since the children are the future of the community (*STP* July 9, 1980: 2).

Other parents eschewed this child-centred rhetoric, and instead went straight into political threats. Sally Booth claimed that Richard Hatfield was affecting virtues on the national unity front that he did not possess with regards to bilingualism in his own province. She then went on to note that Tantramar was a swing constituency, and that fifty students equaled 100 parents — a considerable number of people in a riding that the Conservatives barely won in the last election (*STP* July 16, 1980: 8). As it turned out, local MLA Lloyd Folkins did not run for re-election in 1982, and his successor was defeated by the NDP candidate.

These varied interventions by individual parents and Canadian Parents for French bore their first substantial results in mid-July. CPF member Barbara Jardine spoke with Deputy Minister of Education Harvey Malmberg on July 15 and 18. Over the course of those conversations, Malmberg made a partial concession to the parents. The nineteen unlucky children would not be eligible for grade one French immersion in September. However, he did promise that they would be placed in a separate class at Central School, and that the minister of education would personally guarantee that the children would be enrolled in a second grade two class in the fall of 1981. Moreover, while he indicated that it was too late for the province to revise its policies on immersion for the 1980–81 school year, it was considering placing immersion under departmental control in the future (*STP* July 23, 1980: 1).

Letters bearing the signature of Charles Gallagher were sent out to parents of the unlucky children on July 25, 1980, promising that they would be placed in French immersion in grade two and that a major effort would be made to ensure that these children would have as much French instruction as possible in their grade one year.[8] The same day, Gallagher announced his decision to the media: "It is our intention over the next year to change the policy so that school districts shall implement immersion classes where numbers warrant. Thought will have to be given to extra costs involved" (*STP* July 31, 1980: 1).

Although this was a partial victory for the parents, they were not completely satisfied. Barbara Jardine noted that there was a discussion among the nineteen parents about the possibility of creating a private grade one immersion class, withdrawing their children from the District 14 school board for the bridging year (*STP* July 23, 1980: 1). Berkeley Fleming accused Hatfield of implicitly rebuking the District 14 school board but still putting the need to mollify the school board ahead of the needs of the immersion children, and of putting his traditional conservative constituency's concerns first. Fleming, an NDP supporter, further noted that "provided we work hard, you may well lose this seat in the next provincial election" (*STP* August 6, 1980: 2).

Communication between the government, the school board and the parents broke down over the month of August. The parents of the nineteen excluded children prepared a brief to present to the school board at its late-August meeting, asking for an enriched program of ninety minutes per day of French instruction for their children, instead of the regular twenty minutes. However, before the brief could be discussed, the board went into an *in camera* session, then lost quorum when three board members left, leaving the parents without any resolution of their request. One of the members who walked out, Wylie McMullin, observed that the deputy minister had been "less than fair" with the school board and expressed his discontent that the board was being cut out of the loop by the provincial government, which had promised the grade two class without consulting the board. Of the remaining members, Karen Trueman noted that the Department of Education had been telling parents things without informing the board, while Ove Samuelson summed up the board sentiment that they were being "left floundering and flustered" (*STP* September 3, 1980: 1).

Classes began in September with eighteen of the nineteen unlucky students in a separate English-language class at Central school (one parent opted to transfer their child to the regular stream). Few could have predicted the stunning turn of events that would occur at the next school board meeting, held on September 11, 1980. Citing Minister Gallagher's decision to guarantee a second grade two class in for the fall of 1981, the District 14 board voted on a resolution to create a second grade one class, effective immediately, for the children covered by Gallagher's promise. Immediately following the resolution, Board Chair Ove Samuleson resigned, followed by another nine of the thirteen board members present that evening.

The mass resignation of the school board was accompanied by statements indicating the frustration of the board. Samuelson was particularly (yet indirectly) critical of Canadian Parents for French, stating: "While I'm not blaming anyone, we mustn't lose sight of the fact that we were dealing with a special interest group with one priority in mind." He complained that the parents had gone above the board's head to the minister and the CBC, when it was the board that would ultimately have to make the decision. He also raised the spectre of eventual job losses for anglophone teachers, claiming: "I'm not a bigot, but this is a fact. This year we have almost 50 percent of the students entering French immersion in grade 1 and I see this as a major change in the system and I wonder what social effects it will cause." He described the board feeling of "hopelessness and frustration" as they became spectators watching the minister dealing with parents (*STP* September 17, 1980: 1).

While expressing sorrow that the board members felt so strongly about their decision that they opted to resign, CPF member Sue Purdy was still pleased at the ultimate outcome. She noted: "It all boiled down to a matter of who has the ultimate authority and I guess it must be the minister of education — which would appear to be understandable in a democracy" (*STP* September 17, 1980: 1). Asked for comment, Charles Gallagher noted that a direct appeal from parents to his department was not unusual and that the request was only granted after careful consideration of their brief. Gallagher further observed that education is directly funded by the province, as opposed to the local board (a change instituted in the 1960s by the

Robichaud government), and that the province is not required to have board approval to make such decisions. Faced with the resignation of the District 14 board, District Superintendent Dale Aitken was given authority to run the schools until such time as new board members could be appointed. The parents, meanwhile, received letters from the school principal, R.H. Hanson, informing them of the school board's decision, and a second class was established on September 22, 1980.[9]

For the Sackville parents, the 1980 decision of the District 14 school board to grant their children access to French immersion was a victory that had direct resonance for their community and their children. The implications of their campaign were much broader. The New Brunswick parents managed to create a province-wide policy shift on access to French immersion. The policy change promised by Charles Gallagher came into effect on July 1, 1981, when the New Brunswick Department of Education Policy 501 was revised to read: "A school district shall implement an immersion program when there is sufficient interest to ensure that immersion classes are of comparable size to other classes in the district at that level of instruction" (CPF May 1981).

New Brunswick's parents were able to accomplish an objective that the national CPF organization was hoping would be realized nation-wide. Amidst the constitutional negotiations that led to the Charter of Rights and Freedoms, which contained minority language rights guarantees, CPF passed a resolution in November 1980, calling for the right of all Canadian parents to educate their children in either or both official languages.[10] Ultimately, this national objective would not to be achieved. Indeed, even the right to French immersion in New Brunswick would be circumscribed by mother-tongue status under the 1984 decision of Justice Richard to limit access to French immersion to non-francophone children. But for anglophone parents in New Brunswick, the actions of the Sackville chapter of Canadian Parents for French had implications that resonated province-wide. Although the questions of deadlines for parental expression of interest and board capacity to create classes remained the subject of controversies, parents in communities such as Chatham and Grand Falls were quick to demand access to French immersion for their children under the new policy (Everett 1981).

CONCLUSIONS AND ANALYSIS

Canadian Parents for French Sackville was able not only to achieve its limited goal of obtaining access to grade one French immersion for their children but also accomplished a province-wide policy change of mandatory immersion where sufficient numbers existed. How did this group of parents, which numbered a maximum of ninety-two paid members at the peak of their campaign, manage to succeed? Factors such as strategy, class and opportunities in the federal governance structure all played roles in terms of how CPF was received by its target audiences at each level of government.

CPF had some success in convincing the federal government to support its campaign. This is perhaps least surprising, as the organization received the bulk of its funding through the Secretary of State Department and was founded at the urging of the commissioner of official languages. The latter office provided moral support to the parents during their lobbying activities with the local school board and the provincial government but was ultimately unable to intervene directly in the provincial jurisdiction of education. The Secretary of State Department, while not pressuring the provincial minister of education directly, did however offer financial incentives that made the shift to a much broader access to immersion more palatable to the province. Parents were well aware of the OLEP funding programs and routinely brought up the federal grants in their arguments that immersion classes would not entail an additional financial burden on either the province or the District 14 board. Yet decision-making responsibility for curriculum did not rest with the federal government, and so there was only a limited amount that this level of government could do to support CPF in its campaign.

The District 14 school board was a very different case. For the first seven years of the French immersion program's existence in Sackville, interested parents and the local chapter of CPF were able to convince the board to follow their recommendations. A number of strategies proved to be useful in this respect. On a financial level, the parents made the board aware of the funding that Fredericton received from the federal government for immersion, which could trickle down to the board level to create new programs. Pedagogical arguments also proved effective. The national office of Canadian Parents for French distributed to its members bibliographies of the latest research on the effectiveness of early French immersion, which proved to be an effective tool in convincing school board members to create these classes. On a strategic level, members of CPF also noted that they made a major effort to meet individually with members of the local school board to build personal relationships with them, a factor which might have been particularly important in a small community.

In other respects, Canadian Parents for French found the school board resistant to its arguments. The board did have to operate within the financial constraints set out by the provincial government, and it feared that French immersion might prove to have indirect costs. In particular, there were fears that the expansion of French immersion might force the board to lay off teachers in the regular English-language program, which was something that many board members refused to countenance.

The perception of French immersion as an elitist program was also a major problem. While educational experts churned out many reports indicating that French immersion could be followed by all students, including those with learning disabilities, the program continued to be perceived as one designed for the children of upper-middle-class parents. This perception was particularly acute in District 14. French immersion was initially offered only in Sackville, home to the university community. Moreover, several of the leaders of CPF were either university faculty or their spouses. Other key CPF members included teachers, lawyers, a veterinarian and other university-educated professionals, which reinforced this image, despite the fact that of the 1980 cohort of students, only a minority were actually children of parents associated with Mount Allison University (interviews with Fleming, Bass, and Jardine). The town-and-gown dynamic of Sackville created pockets of opposition to a program that was believed to benefit only the elite of the community.

There were also only limited avenues for levying political pressure on the school board. Only a minority of its members were elected in competitive elections; many members were provincial appointees. Moreover, the board was serving three communities, only one of which was directly benefitting from French immersion in the 1970s and early 1980s. As a result, there was little reason for board members from Port Elgin or Dorchester to support a program that did not appear to benefit their constituents directly.

The provincial government of Richard Hatfield did prove to be receptive to the pressures levied by CPF Sackville, which indicates that the multiple-crack hypothesis has some validity. The concerned parents were able to appeal to a higher authority to have their demands met. Why was the Hatfield government responsive to CPF when the local jurisdiction had been resistant?

There were certainly political and ideological factors at play in the Hatfield government's decision to meet the parents' demands. Over the course of the 1970s, the Progressive Conservative Party, under Hatfield's leadership, had been revamping its traditional coalition and increasingly relied on a coalition of moderate anglophones and Acadians that supported its official languages policies to remain in power (Cormier and Michaud 1992: 132–38). In the late-1970s, Hatfield was feeling pressure both from more radical elements of the Acadian community, which had formed the Parti Acadien, and from anglophone leaders such as CPF members, who wanted to ensure that the province's official languages policy would not hurt their economic prospects. Indeed, Sackville fell within a vulnerable constituency for the Hatfield government, as Tantramar was a swing riding.

The Sackville immersion crisis was also conveniently timed, coinciding with the early months of the 1980–82 patriation of the Canadian constitution, a process in which Richard Hatfield was supporting Pierre Trudeau and was pushing to have New Brunswick's official languages policy entrenched in the constitution. Hatfield had to live up to his image as a promoter of the virtues of bilingualism or risk embarrassment in the media. Indeed, Susan Purdy's decision to contact CBC television for the Fredericton protest proved to be an astute one, as the protestors were quickly ushered into the Legislature.

The fact that New Brunswick is a fairly small province in terms of population doubtless facilitated CPF's relatively easy access to the Premier, as well as to the deputy minister and minister of education. However, not all groups that demonstrate in front of the Legislative Assembly are invited in to sit down for a civilized cup of tea with the premier. The rapidity of the government's response to these parents and the civilized manner in which exchanges between the provincial government and CPF took place reflects on the moderate, middle-class nature of the parents group.

Unlike many social movements, Canadian Parents for French was not proposing radical change to the political order of the province but was rather operating within conventional political channels to advocate significant, but nevertheless incremental, change to existing policies. The tactics deployed by the organization — developing formal policy briefs, writing letters to newspapers and government officials and meeting one-on-one with officials — were fairly conventional lobbying tactics, and the organization only resorted to picketing as a last resort. And yet, its vocal support for the New Brunswick government's official languages policy also made it possible for the organization to be perceived as a potential ally for the government. Indeed, the middle-class nature of the group and its largely university-educated composition, factors that made its goals suspect in the eyes of the District 14 board members (many of whom believed that French immersion would primarily benefit the university community and not the children of other town residents) and opponents of bilingualism, may have facilitated CPF's access to the provincial government.

The case of the movement for French immersion in New Brunswick appears to support the multiple-crack hypothesis for social movement action in federal systems, while also lending support to institutional theories of how states reply to social movements. It appears that the Hatfield government was not merely swayed by the pedagogical arguments of Canadian Parents for French over the resistance of anti-bilingualism advocates or the job-related concerns of the New Brunswick Teachers' Association. Rather, the Hatfield government was actively pursuing a pro-official languages policy and had a vested interest in supporting the growth of individual bilingualism in its citizenry, both for political support and to cultivate a new generation of bilingual civil servants. Moreover, it was committed on the national constitutional front to a policy of two official languages. These factors made the provincial government the key "crack" for the Canadian Parents for French to target when its efforts at the municipal level were frustrated. Support from the federal government both to CPF for its institutional activities and to the provincial government for official languages education also proved to be an effective way of advancing its official languages agenda in a policy sector that it could not directly control. Thus, while social movements with more radical agendas may have more difficulty in affecting government policies, the case of Canadian Parents for French indicates that it was possible for a parents' movement to work with the state to transform its policies and that funding from another level of government did not compromise its freedom of action.

PRIMARY SOURCES AND NEWSPAPER ARTICLES

CPF (Canadian Parents for French). 1979–1982. *New Brunswick Newsletter.*
Everett, Jon. 1981. "French immersion snowballs. But so do the hassles." *Atlantic Insight* (December).
MacKinnon, Jack. 1983. "The French Immersion Phenomenon." *NBTA News* xxv, 8 (January 24).
Sackville Tribune-Post. 1973. "One Official Language Said Cornerstone of New Party." September 12.
_____. 1980. "Appears Core Program Will Be Improved." July 2.
_____. 1980. "Ask School Board to Stop Restricting No. in French Program." May 28.
_____. 1980. "Department of Education Steps Into Immersion Controversy." July 23.
_____. 1980. "District 14 Rejects French Immersion." June 11.
_____. 1980. "French Immersion Policy Change." July 31.
_____. 1980. "Frustrated By French Immersion Debate." September 3.
_____. 1980. "Letters to the Editor." July 2.
_____. 1980. "Letters to the Editor." July 9.
_____. 1980. "Letters to the Editor." August 6.
_____. 1980. "Letters to the Editor." July 16.
_____. 1980. "Letters to the Editor." June 18.
_____. 1980. "Letters to the Editor." June 25.
_____. 1980. "School Board Left With Five Members Following Resignations." September 17.
Williston, Bob. 1983. "Immersion." *NBTA News* xxv (March)

NOTES

1. Canadian Parents for French fonds. 1976–1994. 2. CPF New Brunswick Branch records. 1977–1993. 2/5/1. New Brunswick Director reports to the National Board of Directors with draft copies and appended notes, 1986–1988. 1987–88 Provincial Summary — French Immersion.
2. Canadian Parents for French fonds. 1976–1994. 2. CPF New Brunswick Branch records. 1977–1993. 2/10/2. CPF Atlantic Conference, Mount Allison University, February 1980.
3. Personal files of Berkeley Fleming, past president of Sackville CPF. Canadian Parents for French brief to the Board of Education — District 14. 1980.
4. Canadian Parents for French fonds. 1976–1994. 1. CPF Sackville Chapter, Sackville, NB, records. 1976–1990. 1/1. NB School District, no. 14, Immersion Program. 1979–1983. Results of Parent Questionnaires — District #14.
5. Personal files of Berkeley Fleming, past President of Sackville CPF. Letter from Stuart Burbine to Berkeley Fleming.
6. Canadian Parents for French fonds. 1976–1994. 1. CPF Sackville Chapter, Sackville,

NB, records. 1976–1990. 1/3. CPF Sackville Chapter. 1979–1982. Letter from Barbara Jardine, CPF, to Richard Hatfield, June 30, 1980.

7.   Canadian Parents for French fonds. 1976–1994. 1. CPF Sackville Chapter, Sackville, NB, records. 1976–1990. 1/3. CPF Sackville Chapter. 1979–1982. Letter from Robert Pichette to Barbara Jardine, June 17, 1980.

8.   Personal files of Berkeley Fleming, past president of Sackville CPF. Letter from Charles Gallagher to Berkeley Fleming, July 25, 1980.

9.   Personal files of Berkeley Fleming, past president of Sackville CPF. Letter from R.H. Hanson, Principal of Central School, to Berkeley Fleming.

10. Archives du centre acadien, Université Ste-Anne, MG8 Fonds Fédération acadienne de la Nouvelle-Écosse, Vol. 5, B. 3b, Fiche 2: Canadian Parents for French, CPF News Release. "Governments criticized by parents' group" January 20, 1981.

CHAPTER EIGHT

"MANY CLOSET SUPPORTERS WILL COME FORWARD"
NEW BRUNSWICK'S CONFEDERATION OF REGIONS PARTY

Matthew James J. Baglole

In 1989, while addressing a New Brunswick audience, the founder of the Confederation of Regions (COR) Party spoke of widespread and virulent opposition to official bilingualism in Canada. In deadly earnest he warned that:

> Unless we stop the turmoil this bilingualism causes, there will be blood in the streets. Out west at our meetings, there are people who have said "Let's get the guns out." That's what we're trying to prevent. (Jones 1989)

Despite his warning and a national survey released in the early 1980s suggesting that, outside of Quebec, fully 55 percent of Canadians opposed official bilingualism, COR rose as a political force only in New Brunswick and then only for a brief time (Bibby 1982: 2). From 1991 to 1995, the Confederation of Regions-New Brunswick (COR–NB) sat as the official opposition in Canada's only officially bilingual province. That a "new right" party born in the Canadian west rose to prominence in the east did not necessarily strike witnesses as foreseeable. Retrospective electoral analysis reveals a significant block of clandestine COR–NB supporters undetectable by public opinion polls and suggests that anti-bilingualism forces in New Brunswick failed as a social movement but succeeded as a political party based on the modalities of Canada's electoral system. Publicly, New Brunswickers were unwilling to support an anti-bilingualism social movement organization but, given the privacy of a voting booth, the electorate proved willing to privately register its discontent.

If Maurice Pinard's theory tells us anything about how this occurred, it suggests that a period of economic strain and one-party dominance contributed to COR's rise in New Brunswick (Pinard 1971). According to Pinard such a period increases the likelihood that Canadian "third parties" will rise. Economic strain, when a portion of the electorate perceives a decline in its economic status, creates a salient grievance among a cross-section of voters. In turn, one-party dominance — characterized as a period during which opposition parties retain less than one-third of the popular vote and therefore fail to challenge the dominant party during elections or while sitting as official opposition — leaves opposition partisans without, or with an effectively muted, political voice (Pinard 1971: 64). Frustrated by a seeming inability to air political grievance those voters unwilling to support the dominant political party may look elsewhere to register their discontent. According to Pinard, third parties are most likely to rise in this atmosphere of grievance and broken partisan loyalty. By 1991, these conditions took root in New Brunswick as a recession gripped a perennially weak economy, the provincial Progressive Conservative Party collapsed, Liberals won every seat in the Legislature and an unassailable political consensus regarding official bilingualism substituted for one-party dominance.

Geoffrey Martin argued as much in 1998 when he traced the rise of COR–NB from a social movement through its reconstitution as a political party and to its destruction due to partisan infighting (Martin 1998). What Martin neglected to examine was the extent to which COR–NB was the latest expression of frustrated anti-bilingualism forces and how, as a political party, anti-bilingualism forces capitalized upon the clandestine supporters whose unwillingness to publicly support an anti-rights movement hampered their influence as a social movement. The electoral success of COR–NB offers a glimpse into the common frustrations uniting party loyalists and activists unable to effectively voice their opposition to official bilingualism and how the anonymity of an electoral booth allowed New Brunswickers of every partisan allegiance to express their discontent. Canada's official anti-bilingualism party thereby becomes a study in the nature of social movement and political party power and how one may succeed even where the other failed. A study of COR–NB also sheds light on right-wing social movements: an area of study overshadowed by studies of movements operating from leftist sensibilities.

FROM WEST TO EAST AND FROM SOCIAL MOVEMENT TO POLITICAL PARTY

In the early 1980s, Albertan tractor dealer and long-standing western-alienation activist, Elmer Knutson, launched the Confederation of Regions Party in response to the politics of bilingualism and the perceived centralization of political power in Ontario and Quebec. By the late 1980s, Preston Manning promoted —and the electorate embraced— the Reform Party as the clear western voice. Faced with its limited success during its first federal contest in 1984 and its displacement by Reform during the 1988 election, COR sought support elsewhere.[1] Having run candidates in Ontario and New Brunswick during the 1988 federal contest COR's executive targeted the province in which the party won its greatest province-wide support: New Brunswick.[2]

Given their dream of dismantling official bilingualism in Canada, the Party executive further hoped that New Brunswick, as the only officially bilingual province, might function as a "window to the nation" (*The New Brunswick Telegraph-Journal*, March 17, 1990: 3).

In 1989, the Confederation of Regions-New Brunswick Party was launched under the same headwind driving a social movement organization known as the Association of English Speaking Canadians of New Brunswick, or the English Speaking Association (ESA). The impetus for the ESA's formation was the Report of New Brunswick's Task Force on Official Languages, commonly known as the Poirier-Bastarache Report, which recommended further measures to ensure Acadian language rights in areas of provincial jurisdiction. Those banded together under the ESA banner believed that New Brunswick had already gone too far in entrenching rights for the province's Acadian minority. Yet, although the Poirier-Bastarache Report dealt with a potentially contentious issue, within the Legislature opposition was muted. In New Brunswick, official bilingualism had, under the stewardship of Louis Robichaud (Liberal, 1960 to 1970) and Richard Hatfield (Progressive Conservative, 1970 to 1987), become a non-partisan issue (Martin 1998: 28).[3] For those whose pet issue was official bilingualism, muted opposition to official bilingualism approximated an essential element of Maurice Pinard's theory of the rise of third-parties: a period of one-party dominance.

Len Poore, a former Fredericton city councillor and radical anti-bilingualism crusader, established the ESA in response to the expansion of provincial bilingualism. Nevertheless, the ESA was only the latest expression of a perennial Canadian issue: the nation's cultural and linguistic heritage. During the late 1960s, the Salisbury chapter of the Canadian Loyalist Society produced and distributed a pamphlet reading:

> The Canadian Loyalist Association wish to congratulate you on the masterful manner in which you [Louis Robichaud] have deceived the people of New Brunswick and Canada by leading them to believe that New Brunswick has two official languages.... Your senseless, degenerate and ruinous official languages act is one of the worst evils anyone ever tried to perpetuate on the citizens of this province. (Fitzpatrick 1972: 124)

Initially, the ESA drew upon a common social movement action repertoire based on traditional lobby tactics and public engagement (Tilly 1977: 131; Oliver and Myers 2003). As a social movement — here defined as citizens linked through a common grievance that girds a campaign for political reform and whose primary purpose is not to win political office, generate profit or engage in criminal activity — the ESA was officially non-partisan. Notwithstanding its public stance, most ESA members were alienated English-speaking Progressive Conservative (PC) partisans (Martin 1998:

29). Yet, many ESA members questioned their partisan loyalties when New Brunswick's PCs expanded bilingual programs. ESA activists, grown tired of the PC commitment to official bilingualism, voted for Frank McKenna's Liberals in the 1987 election. ESA assumptions that McKenna, as a new anglophone premier, would freeze language rights proved to be woefully inaccurate and the provincial consensus on legislated bilingualism continued (Martin 1998: 29).

With no opposition MLAs to pressure (McKenna's Liberals having won every seat in the 1987 election), some ESA members questioned the group's effectiveness. Len Poore's commitment to lobby tactics only further contributed to the fractures within the ESA. Future COR–NB leader Arch Pafford recalled the frustration of dissenting ESA members, stating:

> We brought our concerns to government but it just became frustrating because month after month we were bringing the same concerns, getting the same answers, and really not getting anywhere. (quoted in Martin 1998: 27)

Feeling stonewalled, ESA members readily accepted COR's 1988 invitation to attend its national conference. Upon their return, Delores Cook and James Webb suggested that ESA members might establish a provincial COR Party. The ESA split over the suggestion that they form a political party when some members refused to abandon their partisan loyalties. Those who formed COR–NB were already part of an existing, if fragmented, organizational structure dedicated to one of the party's main goals and, because of this, were readily mobilized (McAdam 1982: 44–48; Passy 2003: 21).

UNASSAILABLY BILINGUAL AND ECONOMICALLY TROUBLED

Between 1960 and 1987, a political consensus on official bilingualism muted the dialogue surrounding language policy and added to the limited sense of political efficacy among New Brunswick voters. Since at least 1969, when Robichaud introduced New Brunswick's *Official Languages Act*, provincial Liberals and Progressive Conservatives supported official bilingualism, passing linguistic initiatives with little debate (Aunger 1981: 159–78; Brownsey and Howlett 1992: 94). Faced with an in-Legislature consensus on matters of public policy it is perhaps not surprising that, by 1984 (two years after New Brunswick entrenched its bilingual identity in the constitution), feelings of political disaffection were highest among the electorate of New Brunswick (Ullman 1990: 176). For COR–NB, political disaffection delivered a number of voters and experienced politicians to the fledgling party. Former Hatfield cabinet minister Ed Allen left the Progressive Conservative Party because he disagreed with its language policies (Richardson 1991a: 3). According to Allen it was time to get "rid of terms like anglophone and francophone and be Canadians first, then New Brunswickers" (*The Daily Gleaner*,

August 10, 1990: 11). Yet, faced with a consensus on official bilingualism, Allen was left without a political home. A second former Hatfield cabinet minister, Dr. Everett Chalmers, also defected to COR–NB. Five of COR's eight Members of the Legislative Assembly were former card-carrying Progressive Conservative Party members.

Picking up erstwhile Conservatives in 1990, COR–NB's executive came to exemplify its social movement roots and political future. The membership elected ESA member Arch Pafford as leader while Ed Allen became party president. The defection of prominent Progressive Conservatives gave COR–NB a familiarity and degrees of political experience otherwise elusive to new political parties. Politicians brought riding and party member support as well. A Baseline Market Research survey revealed that COR–NB, as of late August 1991, received 52 percent of its support from former Tories (Richardson 1991a: 3). Former Liberals constituted 27 percent of the party's support and former NDP members 15 percent. Among those willing to publicly declare their COR–NB support, the party clearly drew most heavily on disaffected Conservatives.

COR–NB's growing membership revealed disquiet, centred on official bilingualism, within New Brunswick's electorate. In response, local politicians began to acknowledge language tensions. In 1990, Barbara Baird-Filliter, the leader of New Brunswick's Progressive Conservative Party pleaded with the Liberals and the electorate:

> The COR stands to win an election — but not the next one — if current language tensions are not eased.... New Brunswickers, especially those in rural areas, feel threatened by official bilingualism, and they also feel that the government isn't responding. (Meagher 1990a: 3)

If Baird-Filliter's comments underlined a growing reality, few people took the threat seriously, and she was haunted by her statement for a time. Yet, the national and provincial media reported similar tensions with growing frequency, and COR–NB embraced every opportunity to spotlight language issues (Cox 1991: 4).

Even as Pafford and his followers questioned language legislation frequently and drew support from the public on such issues, New Brunswick's traditional political parties refused to reconsider their support for the *Official Languages Act* and Bill 88 (An Act Regarding the Two Official Linguistic Communities of New Brunswick).[4] The latter provided both English and French communities with their own cultural and social institutions. The Liberals suggested a new scheme to implement the same language policies previously followed. Progressive Conservatives, under Baird-Filliter, promised to use consultation with the public while drafting their new scheme for implementing language and cultural policies, but remained committed to the spirit and word of the law. New Democrats sought further guarantees of language and cultural rights, including the constitutional entrenchment of Bill 88. Only COR–NB's public supporters raised a furore over official bilingualism and, in that regard, seemed to beat only one drum.

In 1991, when McKenna dissolved the Legislature for an election, economic strain and linguistic tensions simmered beneath the surface. New Brunswick's unemployment rate, in the double digits since the early 1970s, topped the national average for twenty-five years before COR–NB contested the 1991 election. Between 1987 and 1991, when COR–NB established itself, provincial unemployment ranged from 12.8 to 14.3 percent, which was between 2.4 and 4.7 higher than the national average. According to the 1991 Census, average family income in the New Brunswick was over $13,000, or 26 percent, below the national average (Statistics Canada 1991). In New Brunswick, the effects of the 1980s recessions were exacerbated by an increasing tax burden (following the introduction of the Goods and Services Tax) as well as Frank McKenna's spending cuts and imposition of civil service wage-freeze in contravention of their collective agreement (Martin 1998; Milne 1996). As New Brunswick's economic fortunes continued to lag behind national averages, politicians worked to bring the Acadian minority into the socioeconomic mainstream.

Steadily between 1964 and 1987, successive premiers introduced initiatives to equalize the opportunities available in New Brunswick's linguistic communities. Between 1964 and 1969, Robichaud introduced the Program for Equal Opportunity (1964) — a radical structuring of local government and taxation in New Brunswick in an effort to equalize the services available throughout the province — the *Human Rights Act* (1967) and the *Official Languages Act* (1969). Richard Hatfield, between 1970 and 1987, fleshed out the *Official Languages Act*, constitutionally entrenched New Brunswick's status as Canada's only bilingual province, and introduced Bill 88. As Pinard demonstrates, it is not economic hardship alone but perceived economic reversals among the electorate that fuels the rise of third parties (Pinard 1971: 370). In New Brunswick, economic hardship combined with a policy of official bilingualism to convince ESA members and COR–NB supporters that their province was "robbing Peter to pay Pierre" (Aunger 1981: 178). Moreover, following the Liberals' electoral sweep in 1987, malcontents had no opposition party to pressure in the Legislature.[5]

COR-NB: A UNIQUE VOICE IN THE 1991 ELECTION

It is scarcely surprising, then, that COR–NB would use such tensions to its benefit as the parties went to work on their electoral platforms. Conversely, New Brunswick's traditional parties remained generally unwavering in their support for the *Official Languages Act*, and most publications were reluctant to enter debates on language issues. In so far as COR–NB highlighted language issues and, in turn, were attacked for such views, certainly part of their reputation for being a "'one issue" party stemmed from interaction with mainstream parties. No great reversals were effected as a result of such exchanges, however, and each party adhered to its traditional support for official bilingualism. While cor–nb may not have exercised much influence on language policy, their influence was evident in other policy fields, as was the attraction of those policies for certain voters.

Unable to recover from a series of personal scandals surrounding Richard Hatfield, their former leader, and the 1987 Liberal sweep of New Brunswick's Legislature, provincial Conservatives appeared rudderless in 1991 (Calhoun 1992: 9; Dyck 1996: 185–86). In the four years between their defeat and the 1991 election, New Brunswick's pcs elected three leaders. Dennis Cochrane led the Conservatives into the election but offered little in the way of new direction. Rather than launch a broad assault on its rivals, the pcs differentiated their platform from those of other parties through a series of relatively narrow issues, one of which was wage disparity in the profession of teaching. Specifically, the pcs advocated an increase in pay for kindergarten teachers. The party further committed itself to solving the "bureaucratic nightmare" the education system had become (Belliveau 1991: 3). The Liberals met the challenge by making their own commitment to review both the problem of bureaucracy in the education system and the salary paid to kindergarten teachers. McKenna further vowed to control the deficit while improving social programs. The Premier warned, however, that he was limited by rampant political mismanagement before him (Dyck 1996: 187). Both the Conservatives and the Liberals also vowed to review health care across the province with the goal of ensuring equal and adequate coverage for all.

The New Democrats continued to champion the working class, poor and socially marginalized. Although the Party addressed the issues raised by provincial Liberals and Conservatives, ndp candidates also emphasized social programs and the need to entrench Bill 88. The New Democrats further committed themselves to gay rights in the area of housing, employment and medical benefits as well as an environmental bill of rights for New Brunswick. Consequently, voters concerned over official bilingualism, economic strain or the political consensus on language issues were not likely to find a viable alternative in New Brunswick's New Democrats.

cor–nb, on the other hand, built its platform around a series of issues not at all related to the issues animating mainstream parties. The policies on display in the 1991 election did not stray far from those already drafted by Pafford and Allen. Although often painted as a single-issue Party, cor–nb included many issues in its official campaign platform (Hoyt 1991: 3). Among them was a plan to combat the effects of the gst by reducing the provincial sales tax by 2 percent. Nevertheless, it is also true that cor–nb's anti-bilingualism framed most of its thinking. As a result, most policies related, either directly or indirectly, to official bilingualism — such as its plan to eliminate the provincial debt and repeal the Provincial Sales Tax (PST). Were the *Official Languages Act* and Bill 88 repealed, party litera-ture argued, the excess money could be used to reduce the public debt by $300,000,000 over four years. Future debt was to be eliminated through a balanced budget law and, if the public debt were eliminated, the need for a PST would disappear.

In the area of political reform COR–NB emphasized initiatives that would give government back to "'the people." Continuing in a populist fashion, the party dedicated itself to recall, referendum and initiative measures. The party also advocated the privatization of government corporations. The cabinet was to be cut to twelve positions and the appropriate cuts to bureaucracy were to follow. COR–NB also promised that its cabinet ministers would take a 20 percent decrease in pay (Gowan 1991: 4). In timely fashion, given the death of the Meech Lake Accord (a constitutional reform package designed to secure Quebec's place in Canadian confederation), COR–NB pledged to deny any group seeking "distinct society" status. Pafford went as far as to proclaim that a majority COR–NB government would serve as a referendum on the future of bilingualism in the province. The party, if elected, would immediately repeal all statutes addressing language and/or culture. In order to make COR's diverse policies more widely known the party produced ten television and thirty ra-dio advertisements, far more than any other party, in an effort to "blitz" the province (Richardson 1991b: 12).

Naturally, these policies helped set COR apart from its competitors, but what is equally interesting about this "one issue" party is how often its policies would converge with more traditional parties' stances. On the issue of health care, both COR and the Liberals supported community-based care and the expansion of existing clinics around the province (Dunsmuir 1991a: 5). Each of the COR, PC, and Liberal parties desired the improvement of rural roads and the twinning of the Trans Canada Highway through New Brunswick; each similarly arguing that Ottawa should fund the latter project. On the issue of the public servants' wage freeze, the COR and NDP were in agreement that it should be repealed immediately. Moreover, both believed that corporations were not shouldering their fair share of provincial taxation. In light of such convergence, Pafford accused McKenna of stealing COR's policies (Richardson 1991c: 10). Equally probable is that COR–NB did some borrowing of its own. By straddling PC, Liberal, and NDP policies in different areas, COR created the possibility that the party might draw from each traditional party's pool of voters.

During the leadership debate of September 12, 1991, COR–NB leader Arch Pafford — whose appearance was unique in that the party had never before won a seat in the Legislature but was permitted as no other party won a seat during the 1987 election — turned the discussion toward language issues.

Both Dennis Cochrane, the recently elected PC leader, and Premier McKenna suggested that, while they were in favour of entrenching Bill 88, their party's official position was not to entrench the Bill in its entirety as it would create "substantive rights." New Democratic Party leader Elizabeth Weir favoured entrenching the bill. McKenna attacked Pafford for fostering provincial disunity. Pafford retaliated by attacking McKenna's stance on the Meech Lake Accord. Pafford suggested that McKenna had not respected the wishes of New Brunswickers. In response, McKenna accused Pafford of confusing the issues in an effort to win votes. Notwithstanding McKenna's allegations, Pafford set the debate's agenda, which rarely steered away from language issues of one kind or another. Moreover, despite McKenna's attacks, COR–NB's approval rating grew as the election approached (Dunsmuir 1991b: 5).

The COR Party's message was more attuned to the electorate's concerns than many suspected. Over a year before the 1991 election, when Baseline Market Research released an opinion poll on February 13, 1990, COR–NB commanded only 12 percent of the popular vote (Meagher 1990b: 1). Notwithstanding its last-place standing, Baseline favourably reported that, aside from mother tongue, COR–NB supporters could not be singled out on the basis of age, gender, religion, income or education. As the election approached, issues favourable to COR–NB's success coalesced in the minds of voters. A poll released on August 23, 1991, by the Canadian Broadcasting Corporation revealed that official bilingualism, taxation and the economy were the chief concerns of New Brunswickers (Gowan 1991: 8). A few weeks later, Baseline Market Research released a poll in which Linda Dyer argued that, "the COR vote is not just an old vote. It's an angry vote and that's an emotion not restricted to the old" (Richardson 1991b: 4). Anger — variously related to perceived economic reversals, language policy and issues of representation — may not have been restricted to the old but neither was it restricted to any one party's electoral pool, nor centred on any one issue, and it had the potential to throw the Liberals from office.

OFFICIAL OPPOSITION TO OFFICIAL BILINGUALISM

In 1991, COR–NB won eight seats in the Legislature and became New Brunswick's official opposition. Authors Sydney Sharpe and Don Braid correlated the party's success with the events occurring in the west with the Reform Party.

> The Confederation of Regions Party won eight seats with twenty percent of the popular vote, showing clearly that some Maritimers are just as discontented as westerners and Ontarians. Many COR attitudes, especially annoyance at official bilingualism, echo precisely the feelings of Reformers. (Sharpe and Braid, 1992: 13)

Having won official opposition status after only two years as a provincial party, COR–NB could be proud of its achievement. Questions remain, however, regarding the cohort of discontented Maritime voters, the source of their discontent and why many had not previously registered their discontent.

Traditional analysis of the 1991 election suggests that COR–NB's success turned on the support of the elderly, former Progressive Conservatives and the middle-class and was rooted in the party's opposition to official languages.[6] However, an examination of its platform in conjunction with the issues and events surrounding the 1991 New Brunswick provincial election offers suggestive evidence of a picture that is somewhat more complex. First, the party won 21.04 percent of the popular vote when polling estimates gave the party no more than 13 percent leading into the election. Certainly, clandestine COR support existed. Second, the party drew from all established parties, not merely the PCs, and likely not for a single reason. A study of voting behaviour, riding profiles and campaign issues during the 1991 election offers insight into who supported COR–NB and whether electoral support came from those voters expected to support the party.[7]

COR–NB ran candidates in forty-eight of the fifty-eight ridings and won seats in eight ridings: Albert, Southwest-Miramichi, Oromocto, Fredericton-North, Riverview, Sunbury, York North and York South. Five of eight COR–NB MLAs were former Conservative Party members. The ten ridings in which COR failed to run candidates contained the largest number of Acadians. That the party could not find viable candidates for many of the francophone ridings was the most enduring pattern during the election. In the ridings won by COR, uncovering trends among voting patterns proved more difficult.

As polling stations offer the most detailed record of voter support, stations from the ridings in which COR won were analysed. Sixty-five polling stations representing the clearest COR polling station victories were selected. Shifts in voter support were then tracked through the 1982–1991 elections in an effort to discover the source of the COR support. Voter turnout had little or no effect on the results for any riding. In York North, when one considers the results from Douglas#25, where, between 1982 and 1991, voter turnout increased by over 13 percent, and Esteys Bridge#32, where voter turnout decreased by almost 4 percent, there was only slightly more than a 3 percent variation in the popular votes received by COR. In Esteys Bridge, where voter turnout decreased, COR garnered 61.7 percent of the vote, while in Douglas, where a marked increase in voter turnout occurred, the party won only 58.4 percent. In Mouth of Keswick, where voter turnout increased by less than 3 percent between 1982 and 1991, COR–NB captured 70.7 percent of the popular vote. In Sunbury, COR–NB's best result came from a polling district where voter turnout increased by less than 1 percent, and its second best result was found in a polling station where turnout decreased by less than 1 percent. In York North and Sunbury, as elsewhere, there was no correlation between turnout and COR's success. Clearly, New Brunswick voters did not flock to the polls, either to support or to defeat the COR Party. Had New Brunswickers felt strongly about electing or defeating the party one would expect to find a high correlation between increased voter turnout and the local support for COR. Instead, the party fared well both when more voters cast ballots as well as when fewer citizens participated. As its success did not depend on increases in voter turnout, the results suggest that COR–NB did not draw its support from previously disengaged voters but capitalized on actively engaged flexible partisans.

Two clear patterns emerge from the election results. First, with the exception of the NDP, in twelve of the sixty-five polling stations (or 18.5 percent) reviewed, each of the traditional parties lost electoral ground in 1991 when compared to the results of the 1987 election. The average gain made by the NDP in the twelve anomalous districts was 1.3 percent and the range spanned from .055 percent in Millerton/Derby to 4.9 percent in South Esk. Seven of the twelve ridings posted NDP gains of less than 1 percent. In contrast, COR–NB benefitted from the support lost among each traditional party. Having earlier swept all the ridings in the province, the Liberals lost the most support but also had the most to lose.

During New Brunswick's 1987 election, after scandal and absenteeism led to the collapse of the PC party, a large number of voters abandoned the PCs to support the Liberals. Consequently, the latter won every seat in the province. However, following COR–NB's emergence, flexible partisans left the Liberals to support the fledgling party (Forbes 1990: 6; Clarke et al. 1996: 16–50).[8] In each polling station examined for the 1991 election, the Liberals suffered losses from not only their 1987 results but, in fifty-five polling stations, they suffered net losses from their 1982 numbers. Nor did those voters return to the PC Party, which also suffered net losses from its 1982 and 1987 election results. That the Progressive Conservatives elected three leaders in the two years leading into the election likely convinced voters that the party had not recovered. Other than COR, only the NDP improved its electoral standing between 1987 and 1991, but, as previously noted, these gains were minimal and then only in a small minority of stations.

Following the collapse of the PC Party in 1987, a large number of flexible partisans were spun loose from the organization to which they had traditionally lent their support. In 1987, many voted for the Liberals and a few for the NDP. In 1991, however, COR–NB's emergence allowed those voters harbouring deeply rooted discontent to express their frustrations at the polls. All told, the PCs lost the most ground but each party suffered at the hands of COR–NB, whose success turned on a large number of "swing voters" and net losses posted by the three traditional parties.

Polling numbers cannot by themselves explain the issues fuelling COR–NB's electoral victories. By promising reduced taxes, the elimination of deficits, debt reduction, improved social services and political responsibility,

COR–NB promised the stuff of which Canadian dreams are made. Further, language issues, economic strain and issues of political representation drove voters from their partisan voting patterns or temporary allegiances. However, New Brunswick voters are not naïve, but rather, like other Canadian voters, demonstrate high levels of skepticism. New Brunswickers did not believe that COR–NB was the solution to all their problems. To clarify the picture and identify some common characteristics among COR–NB supporters, an examination of the specific ridings where COR–NB elected MLAS —considering their demographic make-up and the prevalent electoral issues— might reveal the source of discontent.

An examination of the ridings in which COR won seats reveals some similarities. Each riding that COR–NB won was predominantly English speaking with a relatively small bilingual populace. This naturally set up tensions over official bilingualism, which represented increased taxes, decreased levels of a variety of government services and lost job opportunities to the residents.[9] Moreover, to those who believed they had been ignored by the political consensus around language rights, official bilingualism was a manifestation of poor political representation. Individuals voted on issues of representation feeling, as Max White noted in the Sunbury campaign, that their opinions on official bilingualism were not yet given a voice in the provincial government (Dunsmuir 1991b: 8). Issues of representation were broader than simple bilingualism, however, and touched on incumbents' absenteeism (*The Daily Gleaner*, September 13, 1990: 11; Vaughan 1991: 8). Finally, issues of representation naturally arose at a time when the Liberals sat unopposed in the provincial Legislature. These themes found expression in most of the ridings that elected a COR candidate. Moreover, many of these predominantly English ridings (Albert, Riverview, Sunbury, Oromocto, York South and York North) were in close proximity to either the Acadian or bilingual centres of Moncton and Fredericton. Certainly, this proximity heightened language tensions.

Popular opinion often suggested that COR supporters were poorly educated and therefore bigoted; however, census data does not bear this out. Neither education levels nor economic wellbeing played a role in the ridings analyzed. Contrary to the image conjured by the derisive name "Confederation of Old Rednecks," the educational profiles of the ridings won by COR–NB compared favourably to provincial and national averages (possible exceptions include Sunbury and South West Miramichi). Moreover, most counties compared favourably with the national employment average and were, in fact, more economically vigorous than the New Brunswick average. In 1991 Canadians generally were feeling the effects of a recessionary economy as well as the recently introduced GST. In a peripheral economy such as New Brunswick, this was certainly true. So while economic considerations such as jobs, taxes and — for some voters — language issues played a role in COR–NB's rise, there is no reason to believe that the votes cast reflected those of the unemployed of uneducated voters. The average voter in these ridings was far more likely to be employed and to earn higher wages than their provincial counterparts.

Finally, local issues played a part in each candidate's success. In Albert County, Beverley Brine spent the campaign dealing almost exclusively with local issues (*The New Brunswick Telegraph Journal*, September 18, 1991: 3). In Fredericton North, a former Progressive Conservative cabinet minister, Ed Allen, highlighted issues of representation. He was also the only candidate to publicly declare that clandestine COR support existed (*The Daily Gleaner*, September 19, 1991: 5). In Sunbury, Max White balanced issues of representation (a province-wide plank for COR but the dominant issue in Sunbury) with local concerns, including the development of coal fields on the edge of the riding (Dunsmuir 1991b: 8). In Oromocto and York North, constituents concerned with economic and representation issues elected COR–NB candidates who used such discontent to highlight language issues, taxation and job creation (Wood 1991: 11; Shanks 1991: 12; Hanton 1991: 5; *The New Brunswick Telegraph-Journal*, September 19, 1991: 4). Danny Cameron, in York South, spoke often on the multiple grievances resulting from official bilingualism. In most ridings won, COR–NB used language issues as a lens through which local and provincial issues were framed (see the appendix to this chapter).

A SOCIAL MOVEMENT'S FAILURE AND A POLITICAL PARTY'S SUCCESS

To suggest that COR–NB was a single-issue party whose elected members rode to victory on a platform of opposition to official bilingualism is too simplistic. Using official bilingualism as a frame, COR–NB candidates touched on a wide-range of issues. In Albert County and Riverview, Beverly Brine and Gordon Whilden rarely touched directly on language issues, while in South West Miramichi and Oromocto, the Progressive Conservative candidates sounded more COR than the COR candidates. In each of these two ridings, as well as Sunbury, while there was talk of language policy, the campaigns run by COR candidates were diverse and local in nature. While in York North and South and Fredericton North, much of the campaign dealt with language, Hargrove, Cameron and Allen all situated the debate in larger contexts, such as representation in the case of Cameron and Allen and economics in the case of Hargrove (*The New Brunswick Telegraph-Journal*, September 18, 1991: 11; Shanks 1991: 12).

To contend that the party was almost entirely supported by former Progressive Conservatives, the elderly, "rednecks" and the economically disadvantaged presents an incomplete picture. Such arguments neglect the evidence suggesting that an oppositional current existed in New Brunswick based on a multitude of personal or political reasons (similarly ignoring that the majority of Canadians opposed official bilingualism as late as the early 1980s). And yet, if wide-ranging discontent existed it seems curious that malcontents had not previously expressed their displeasure. One might rightly point to support for the English Speaker's Association, or the occasional public outburst, as evidence of discontent.[10] The ESA — COR–NB's social movement foundation — did not, however, enjoy the public support necessary to force a public debate on official bilingualism. Social opprobrium and its effect on social movement and political party support offers a compelling explanation for why malcontents did not public support the ESA, why some ESA members embraced the political party alternative and why voters lent clandestine support to COR–NB.

Following decades of hard-won rights campaigns and the stabilization of a positive rights discourse in Canada, anything perceived as "anti-rights" faced criticism and ridicule. It is not coincidental, for example, that coverage of COR–NB events associated the party with an earlier era: one before greater secularization and the plethora of rights initiatives introduced throughout the 1960s, 1970s and early 1980s. Typical was an article in *The New Maritimes*, reporting:

> It is 1992, although it could be four decades earlier: in COR's world, men are gentlemen, wives keep the home fires burning, family values are the rock on which towns are built, and everybody — both French and English — gets along... Jesus is referred to frequently.... There are few visible minorities here, few people (other than the media) who speak French, and of course, no homosexuals or lesbians.[11]

In order to influence public policy, the ESA required a degree of political access. Political access, in turn, depended on political perceptions of a group's representation as indicated by public support. As several studies of social movements suggest, Canadian politicians are more receptive to those organizations representative of large constituencies (see Pross 1992: 101; 201–2; Young and Everitt 2004: 60–68). While the anti-bilingualism forces in New Brunswick were organized as a social movement they sought to break the mainstream political consensus surrounding official bilingualism and thereby influence language policy. However, consensus in New Brunswick's Legislature extended beyond the political realm. Social opprobrium had the effect of silencing potential language critics. The jokes about COR–NB supporters were a casual extension of the accusations levelled against anti-bilingualism forces on provincial editorial pages. Moreover, anti-COR–NB jokes and editorials underlined what, before the party's emergence, remained a tacit acceptance of official bilingualism.[12]

In New Brunswick, social opprobrium girded the political consensus surrounding official bilingualism. As anti-COR jokes and editorials suggest, provincial derision of anti-bilingualism forces did not abate. Socially, the party would continue to be referred to as the Confederation of Old Rednecks, and, between 1989 and 1995, the answer to the popular New Brunswick question, "what has 80 legs, 80 arms and 17 teeth?" was "the first two rows of a COR meeting."[13] More serious was the outrage and threat on display on New Brunswick's editorial pages very shortly after COR–NB's arrival.[14] Typical was Larry Hatt, who demanded that COR clarify its policies and warned that: "if it is indeed the type of party bent on destroying what has been accomplished on 'linguistic harmony,' it will show itself for the party the politicians of both major parties indicate it is: 'a bunch of red-necks and bigots'" (*The Daily Gleaner*, December 21, 1989: 4).[15]

Without visible support, social movement representation remains in doubt. Because opposition to official bilingualism was equated with anti-French sentiments and therefore bigotry, the ESA found both its appeal and political influence hobbled by citizens apprehensive of being associated with such an unpopular cause. Nor did the outrageous statement of various ESA members help assuage such fear. Founder Len Poore, for example, was widely known to have declared that a fence should be built around the Acadian peninsula to "keep those French bastards out."[16] Without a broadly supportive public the ESA suffered from limited political influence. A small social movement threatened only limited repercussions to politicians unwilling to accede to ESA demands. In this context, it is scarcely surprising that Arch Pafford recalled the frustration of political inaction. After years of political stonewalling some ESA members saw a political party as a viable alternative to their social movement approach.

Political parties similarly depend on a core membership in order to administer the organization. However, the essential power of political parties lies in the number of votes won. Unlike the ESA, those opposed to official bilingualism could support COR–NB at the polls without attracting unwanted attention or scorn. Once reconstituted as a political party, anti-bilingualism forces drew on the support of disgruntled New Brunswickers through the secret ballot. So great was individual apprehension to publicly support the anti-bilingualism movement that even opinion polls continuously failed to accurately predict the support COR–NB enjoyed. Voting for the party, however, was not such a public act. As a result, election results proved Allen correct in his prediction that "closet supporters" would emerge.

Although the party failed to form the government — and its time in government was short-lived — the secret ballot allowed those unable to publicly support the ESA or COR–NB to register their displeasure. As a political party, anti-bilingualism forces created a vigorous and perhaps cathartic public debate on official bilingualism for the first time since it took shape in the 1960s. As one political science professor working at the University of New Brunswick commented in 1992, New Brunswick's political parities "walked a tightrope when it came to language, essentially agreeing not to disagree."[17] Unable to provoke a debate on language issues as a social movement, anti-bilingualism advocates organized a political party with the hopes that they could reverse the tide of linguistic rights won throughout the 1960s, 1970s and 1980s. As social movement scholars and historical evidence suggest, backlashes are a common reaction to social movement activism (McAdam 1982, 1999; McAdam, Tarrow and Tilly 2001). The history of COR–NB suggests that, if stifled, such reactionary movements may — given the proper conditions — find alternate means to pursue their goals. One wonders if, while they sat in the Legislature together, McKenna's Liberals apprehended the irony of a political stonewall raised against an unpopular social movement that, in direct response its limited political influence, remobilized as a political party.

If stonewalling led the ESA to reconstitute itself as a political party, it was nevertheless the secret ballot and a very particular set of circumstances that allowed anti-bilingualism forces to assume seats in the provincial Legislature and force further debate on language issues. The success of COR–NB, whose success depended on the fantastic and fortuitous convergence of numerous factors, would not be easily replicated. A national survey released in the early 1980s reported that, outside of Quebec, 55 percent of Canadians opposed official bilingualism (Bibby 1982: 2). For the residents of unilingual provinces, however, bilingualism was largely a federal issue — one that Canadians ranked seventeenth among twenty-three social problems identified as concerns in the early 1980s (Bibby 1982: 5). It is scarcely surprising, then, that the Confederation of Regions Party met with little success in the federal arena or as a provincial party on the Canadian prairies. Conversely, in Canada's only officially bilingual province — where the issue was both a provincial and federal matter — official bilingualism emerged as a more salient issue among the electorate. In addition to the heightened relevance of language issues, economic and representation issues (both of which could be framed as language issues) girded whatever opposition to official bilingualism had previously existed. The confluence of perceived economic reversals and one-party dominance (or its approximation) in a province where official bilingualism assumed local dimensions was a unique moment in Canadian politics and one not easily replicated. Yet, even in an atmosphere conducive to its rise, COR–NB's overall effect on provincial politics was limited.

The linguistic rights won and programs introduced in New Brunswick between 1964 and 1987 were not repealed, slowed or significantly reformed because of COR–NB's interventions. Since John Diefenbaker introduced Canada's Bill of Rights in 1960 Canadian politicians have recognized that, once passed, the repeal or dilution of rights promised grave political consequences. In 1960, Prime Minister Diefenbaker argued that a statutory bill of rights would function just as well as a constitutionally entrenched amendment as no subsequent government would so "recklessly court public wrath" as to repeal a freedom statute (Newman 1963: 224; Diefenbaker 1976: 27; Smith 1995: 346). In the four years they sat as New Brunswick's official opposition, COR–NB could not alter the course of New Brunswick's linguistic policies.

Following the 1991 election, COR–NB failed to elect a single MLA. Nevertheless, in a study of social movements and political parties, Mildred A. Schwartz argues that regardless of their duration third parties "affect the content and range of political discourse and ultimately public policy, by raising issues and options that the two major parties have ignored" (Schwartz 2006: 10).

Between 1989 and 1995, New Brunswick's anti-bilingualism forces launched a six-year public debate on linguistic issues. Although no significant policy directions resulted from their foray into formal politics, they broke the silence and presumed consensus surrounding official bilingualism in New Brunswick. Ultimately, the positive discourse surrounding linguistic rights was rebuilt following a public dialogue that was, at times, painful for New Brunswickers. Likely to the relief of New Brunswick's traditional political parties, the Acadian minority and many anglophones, COR–NB imploded over the course of its four years as New Brunswick's official opposition. Since that time, the party and language issues have fallen off the political radar in New Brunswick, allowing linguistic rights — forged in the heyday of rights activism — to continue untroubled by potentially divisive representation and cost issues simmering beneath the surface.

PRIMARY SOURCES AND NEWSPAPER ARTICLES CITED

Belliveau, Marc. 1991. "Shippigan-Les Liberals Acclaim Landry." *The New Brunswick Telegraph-Journal*, September 2.

Calhoun, Sue. 1992. "Getting to the Core of COR: The New Brunswick Opposition: A Special Report." *The New Maritimes* XI, 2 (November/December).

Confederation of Regions Party. 1991. *A Fair Deal for New Brunswickers: Election Platform, 1991*. Fredericton: Party Publication.

Cox, Kevin. 1990. "With No Opposition Ruling New Brunswick Liberals Lead a Charmed Life." *Globe and Mail*, March 19.

_____. 1991. "Liberals Take N.B. As COR Surprises." *Globe and Mail*, September 24.

Dunsmuir, Heather. 1991a. "List of Campaign Promises by Party." *The Daily Gleaner*, September 21.

_____. 1991b. "Sunbury Riding Profile." *The Daily Gleaner*, September 13.

Gowan, Derwin. 1991. "COR Cabinet Ministers Would Take a 20 Percent Pay Cut: Pafford." *The New Brunswick Telegraph-Journal*, September 3.

Hanton, Elizabeth. 1991. "Language Issues Carries Hargrove to Victory in York North Riding." *The Daily Gleaner*, September 24.

Hoyt, Don. 1991. "COR Drops Many Veils but Can't Avoid Language Theme." *The New Brunswick Telegraph-Journal*, September 5.

Jones, Robert. 1989. "Anti-bilingualism convention expected to be largest ever in N.B." *Globe and Mail*, September 9: A4.

Meagher, David. 1990a. "'We're Using the Best Process Available': COR: Draft Policies May Change." *The Daily Gleaner*, January 15.

_____. 1990b. "Poll: Liberals Overwhelming Favourites." *The Daily Gleaner*, February 13.

Office of the New Brunswick Chief Electoral Officer. 1982. *Results of the Thirtieth General Election*. Fredericton: Government of New Brunswick.

_____. 1987. *Results of the Thirty-First General Election*. Fredericton: Government of New Brunswick.

_____. 1991. *Results of the Thirty-Second General Election*. Fredericton: Government of New Brunswick.

Pond, Sharon. 1991. "Coal Remains a Hot Issue in Queen's North." *The New Brunswick Telegraph-Journal*, September 18.

Richardson, Don. 1991a. "COR Supporters Vary from Popular View." *The New Brunswick Telegraph-Journal*, September 4.

_____. 1991b. "Poll Shows Liberals Heading for Another Big Win." *The New Brunswick Telegraph-Journal*, September 4.

_____. 1991c. "Another Liberal Sweep's A Possibility: Pollster." *The New Brunswick Telegraph-Journal*, September 17.

Shanks, Connie. 1991. "Oromocto Riding Profiles." *The Daily Gleaner*, September 18.

Task Force on Official Languages. 1982. *Toward equality of the official languages in New Brunswick: Report on New Brunswick*. Fredericton: Government of New Brunswick.

The Daily Gleaner. 1989. Letter to the Editor. December 17.

_____. 1989. Letter to the Editor. December 20.

_____. 1989. Letter to the Editor. December 21.

_____. 1989. Letter to the Editor. December 27.

_____. 1989. Letter to the Editor. December 28.

_____. 1989. Letter to the Editor. December 30.

_____. 1991. "Poll Shows COR Support Growing." September 19.

The New Brunswick Telegraph-Journal. 1990. "An Improved Legislature." March 17.

_____. 1991. "Main Albert Issues Include Tourism." September 19.

Vaughan, Allyson. 1991. "COR Wins York South Riding by 778 Votes." *The Daily Gleaner*, September 24.

Wood, Jane. 1991. "Miramichi Newcastle Hopefuls See Jobs as Key Election Issue." *The Telegraph-Journal*, September 18.

APPENDIX

Demographic/Political Characteristics of Ridings Won by COR–NB, 1991

Riding	Language/Ethnic Identification/ Religion	Educational Achievement	Average Family Income	Partisan Allegiance	Key Issues in 1991 Campaign
Albert	English/ British/ Protestant	Above provincial and national figures (with exception of university completion)	Above provincial average and comparable to national figures ($600 less per annum)	Conservative (1952 to 1982); Liberals (1987)	Highways Schools Healthcare Tourism Representation
Riverview (established as separate riding in 1974).	English/ British/ Protestant	Above provincial and national figures (with slightly lower of university completion)	Well above provincial and national figures (13,000 and 5,000 respectively)	Conservative (1974–1982); Liberal (1987)	Amalgamation Local services Highways Representation
South-West Miramichi (est. 1974; no related census division)	Predominantly English/ Unknown/ Unknown	Unknown/ predominantly rural	Unknown: Resource/ tourism based economy	Liberal (Conservatives in 1974)	Bilingualism Gaming Laws Tourism Jobs Taxes

York North/ York South	English/ British/ Protestant	Above provincial and national figures	Above provincial average and slightly lower than national figures ($1,600 less annually)	Conservative; 1987 election of Liberal candidates in both ridings	North: Bilingualism Agriculture Economy/Taxes Representation South: Representation Development
Fredericton North	English/ British/ Protestant	Above provincial and national figures	Above provincial average and slightly lower than national figures ($1,300 less annually)	Conservative (1967 to 1982); 1987 Liberal	Bilingualism Education Representation
Oromocto	English/ British/ Mixed (Catholic and Protestant)	Slightly lower than provincial and national figures	Above provincial average and slightly lower than national figures ($1,800 less annually)	Mixed (alternating mandates)	Economy/Taxes Military Cuts Bilingualism Healthcare Roads/Bridges
Sunbury	English/ British/ Protestant	Below provincial and national averages	Above provincial average but below national figures ($5,500 less annually)	Mixed (alternating mandates)	Bilingualism Representation Jobs/Taxes Health/Education Roads

*for more thorough analysis see: Matthew James J. Baglole, "Some of the People, Some of the Time: The Confederation of Regions Party in New Brunswick, 1989–1991," MA thesis, University of New Brunswick, 2002.

NOTES

1. On electoral support for COR, see Christopher Adams, "The COR and Reform Parties: Locations of Canadian Protest Party Support," Paper presented to the Annual Canadian Political Science Association conference, 1991.

2. New Brunswick awarded COR 4.34 percent of the province-wide vote. During the 1984 federal election Manitobans gave the COR 6.69 percent of its popular support but by 1988 had rescinded enough of that support to make New Brunswick the most supportive province.

3. Martin largely excludes Robichaud's part in the consensus because he neglects the lingual aspects of the Program for Equal Opportunity, instead concentrating on the *Official Languages Act*, which only passed the house at the end of Robichaud's tenure in 1969. For more on New Brunswick reforms, see Della Stanley, "The 1960s: The Illusions and Realities of Progress," E.R. Forbes and D.A. Muise, eds. *The Atlantic Provinces in Confederation* (Toronto: U of T Press and Fredericton: Acadiensis Press, 1993); Keith Brownsey, *The Provincial State: Politics in Canada's Provinces and Territories* (Toronto: Copp, Clarke, Pitman Ltd., 1992); and Rand Dyck, *Provincial Politics in Canada* (Scarborough, ON: Prentice-Hall, 1996).

4. For evidence of support see *The Daily Gleaner* or *The Telegraph Journal* editorial pages from 1989–1991. Although less frequent, for an opposing point of view see *L'Acadie Nouvelle*'s editorial page from the same era.

5. For a more thorough analysis of economic and linguistic tensions in New Brunswick, see Matthew James J. Baglole, "Some of the People, Some of the Time: The Confederation of Regions Party in New Brunswick, 1987–1991." M.A. thesis, University of New Brunswick, 2002.

6. Occasional deviation from the common view did surface during the campaign, often led by the party in response to polls released (e.g., February 13, 1990), as when Arch Pafford countered figures posted by Baseline Market Research. Only infrequently, however, would journalists acknowledge as much, though one staff writer for *The Daily Gleaner*, on September 17, 1991 wrote, in an article on the coming election, that "there is a growing awareness... that the anti-bilingualism vote could be a much bigger factor than first believed." While this suggests that many no longer dismissed COR–NB's ability to attract numbers, it by no means deviates from the traditional view of the source of its support.

7. For a more thorough analysis, see Matthew James J. Baglole, "Some of the People, Some of the Time: The Confederation of Regions Party in New Brunswick, 1987–1991" M.A. thesis, University of New Brunswick, 2002.

8. While most Canadians think of themselves as supporters of a single party, that support is most often contingent or limited. As a result, polling data consistently show that as many as three-fifths or three-quarters of Canadian voters are in fact "flexible partisans" — those able and willing to vote for a party other than that with which they traditionally identify.

9. Demographic characteristics are based upon the 1991 Canadian census. For the root data, see Statistics Canada, *Results of the National Census* (Ottawa: Government of Canada, 1991).

10. Among those outbursts was a very public spat over whether the Acadian flag should fly over the Legislature and an incident that saw audience members hurl insults and eggs at members of a public panel on official bilingualism in New Brunswick. On these incidents, see Dyck, *Provincial Politics*; and Aunger, *Political Stability*.

11. Sue Calhoun, "Getting to the Core of cor: The New Brunswick Opposition: A Special Report," *The New Maritimes* XI, 2 (November/December 1992), 8.

12. *The Daily Gleaner*, editorial page, 1989–1991, passim; *The Telegraph-Journal*, editorial page, 1989–1991, passim, and *L'Acadie Nouvelle*, editorial page, 1989–1991, passim.

13. For a variant of this joke, see: Don Richardson, "cor Supporters Vary From Popular View," *The New Brunswick Telegraph-Journal*, September 4, 1991, 3.

14. *The Daily Gleaner*, editorial page, 1989–1991, passim; *The Telegraph-Journal*, editorial page, 1989–1991, passim, and *L'Acadie Nouvelle*, editorial page, 1989–1991, passim.

15. For more examples, see the editorial page of *The Daily Gleaner* on December 17, 1989, December 20, 1989; December 21, 1989; December 27, 1989; December 28, 1989; and December 30, 1989. Although the pace would vary, the battle between pro and anti-cor–nb forces continued as the election approached.

16. Sue Calhoun, "Getting to the Core of cor: The New Brunswick Opposition: A Special Report," *The New Maritimes* XI, 2 (November/December 1992), 9.

17. Qt. Conde Grodin, in Sue Calhoun, "Getting to the Core of cor: The New Brunswick Opposition: A Special Report," *The New Maritimes* XI, 2 (November/December 1992), 10.

CHAPTER 9

SOCIAL MOVEMENT LEARNING
A CATALYST FOR ACTION

Donna M. Chovanec, Elizabeth A. Lange and Lee C. Ellis

> Some of the most powerful learning occurs as people struggle against oppression, as they struggle to make sense of what is happening to them and to work out ways of doing something about it. (Foley 1999: 1–2)

Social movements are sites where knowledge is contested and constructed, where identities and subjectivities (both individual and collective) are defined and redefined, where citizens are formed and where oppression is named. We know that these activities within social movements are educational and social learning processes. However,

> while systematic education does occur in some social movement sites and actions, learning in such situations is largely informal and often incidental — it is tacit, embedded in action and is often not recognised as learning. The learning is therefore often potential, or only half realized. (Foley 1999: 3)

In this chapter, we draw upon our own experiences as researchers and activists in three social movement contexts (global justice, environment and women's movements) to bring attention to the taken-for-granted yet understudied dimension of learning in social movements. Following a brief discussion of the connection between learning and social movements and an overview of our empirical work, we argue the following:

- Learning and action are dialectical and iterative processes.
- Learning in social movements is multidimensional (e.g., spiritual, cognitive, ethical, emotional, physical, psychological, socioeconomic, political and cultural).
- When a reflective educational dimension is *intentionally and explicitly* integrated into a social movement, the membership is more effectively mobilized to action, particularly across generations.
- Learning within social movements can be assessed by its catalytic valid-

ity, that is, its ability to transform frameworks of thinking and action.

Our research is situated at the theoretical intersection of social movements and adult education, an area that has become known as "social movement learning." Adult education has a strong historical relationship to social movements.

> Adult education and its relationship with social movements may be thought of at three levels of generality.... Firstly, all social movements, to some extent, have an adult educational dimension. Secondly, some adult education initiatives were or are social movements. Thirdly, to some activists, all of adult education, as they define it, is a social movement. (Hall and Clover 2005: 589)

According to Spencer (1998), "adult education (or at least a substantial part of it) has always been associated with social change, social action, social movements, community development, and participatory democracy" (62). Within the labour, feminist, peace, human rights and environmental movements are numerous examples of educational activities, from awareness-raising and skill-building workshops to the highly informal learning of action-reflection cycles. Hall (2006) "makes the case that it is precisely the learning and knowledge-generating capacities of social movements that account for much of the power claimed by these movements" (230). However, learning and education receive little direct attention. As Foley (1999) observes, "informal learning in social action... is an aspect of learning that has been paid too little attention by adult educators; it is a dimension of political action that has often been ignored by political activists" (39). Yet, "reflection on the tacit skills being learned by social movement activists is of critical use for strengthening and extending the power and reach of social movements today" (Hall and Clover 2005: 587).

A recent state-of-the-field report on "social movement learning" (Hall and Turay 2006) confirms that social movements are "powerful instruments" of change (5), that learning and education necessarily occur in informal and formal ways by virtue of the "stimulation and requirements" of the social movement (6), that the construct of social movement learning is "under-conceptualized" (12) and that "in-depth empirical studies of learning in and because of social movements are scarce" (6). The most promising theorizing to date is connected to various transformative or critical learning theories (e.g., Allman 2001b; Brookfield 2005; Foley 1999; Holford 1995; Lange 2004; Welton 1995). Hall and Turay (2006) argue for a "much more precise study of the linked phenomena of learning and social movements" (7).

Because this specific field of study is in its early stages, social movement learning is not yet clearly defined. A preliminary definition is presented by Canadian adult educators Hall and Clover (2005):

> Social movement learning refers to: a) learning by persons who are part of any social movement; and b) learning by persons outside of a social movement as a result of the actions taken or simply by the existence of social movements. Learning by persons who are part of a social movement may occur in an informal way because of the stimulation and requirements of participation in a movement... [or] as a result of intentional educational activities organized within the movement itself. Learning for those outside a social movement happens both in informal and intentional ways. The study of social movement learning recognizes that whatever else social movements are or do, they are exceedingly rich learning environments. (584)

While social movement learning is in its theoretical infancy, particular theoretical traditions and frameworks guide current conceptualizing. Hall and Turay (2006) contend that critical social theories (e.g., Marx, Gramsci, Habermas) and Freire's critical pedagogy (Freire 1970/1990) are among the dominant theories employed by adult educators studying social movement learning. For example, Allman's (2001a, 2001b) theory of critical consciousness and Welton's (1995) emphasis on the lifeworld originate from these foundational theories. Holst (2002) identifies several examples of a useful, albeit underdeveloped, socialist analysis of adult education literature related to social movements. Foley (1999) argues "for the analytical strength and political utility of holistic and materialist analyses of learning in particular sites and struggles, maintaining that a critique of capitalism must lie at the heart of emancipatory adult education theory and practice" (6). Emancipatory, liberatory, radical or critical adult education (terminology used interchangeably in the field) is a form of adult education that is generally a response *against* repression, poverty, oppression and injustice and a struggle *for* justice and equality. Critical learning attempts to foster an individual's consciousness of himself or herself as situated within larger political and economic forces and to act upon those forces for social change.

Our own theoretical framework is situated within this critical scholarly tradition and radical community-based adult education practices. A critique of capitalism and a vision of social justice lie at the heart of such a framework. Of particular note is the work of Brazilian adult educator and activist, Paulo Freire. Freire is most well known for *Pedagogy of the Oppressed* (1970/1990), a book that has had considerable influence on the field of adult education around the world. Freire asserted that education is never neutral, but always political, because learning is positioned within power structures either in a domesticating way or in a liberating way. He proposed that the fundamental purpose for education is the task of humanization, i.e., to become critical and creative producers of the conditions of existence, our societies, ourselves and our destinies. Freire coined the term "conscientization" (*conscientização*), which he defines as "learning to perceive economic, political, and social contradictions and take action to change oppressive elements of reality" (Freire 1970/1990: 19). Our practice and our theorizing are also indebted to post-structural critiques that bring a more nuanced and complex understanding of the intersection among multiple oppressions and between oppression and privilege (hooks 1990; Luke and Gore 1992).

OUR EMPIRICAL WORK: ACTIVISM AND RESEARCH

The empirical data for our arguments are drawn from our experiences as activists and researchers in three social movements: a Canadian ecumenical coalition that is part of the global justice movement (Ellis 2002, 2006), an adult education course on sustainability at the University of Alberta designed to make deliberate linkages to the environmental movement (Lange 2001, 2004), and two women's social movements — abused women turned anti-violence advocates/activists in Canada (Chovanec 1994) and the Chilean women's movement (Chovanec 2004a, 2004b, 2006). In each case, the purpose of the study was to explicitly investigate and expose the learning dimension of the social action and/or social movement as well as the learning experience of the social activists.

Until his untimely death in April 2007, Lee Ellis was a longtime and committed activist. His early exposure to the social gospel movement, which animated much of the nineteenth- and twentieth-century agrarian social movements in western Canada, was instrumental in developing in him the framework for a social justice orientation. His early work in an ecumenical coalition informed his research as well as his continued activism in a variety of global social justice movements. The research reported here is drawn from his examination of critical transformative learning, critical revolutionary praxis and critical consciousness in a Canadian adult education program based on the pedagogical principles of Paulo Freire. The program, Ten Days for Global Justice (Ten Days), was an initiative of the Canadian PLURA churches (Presbyterian, Lutheran, United, Roman Catholic and Anglican) between 1973 and 2002. It was a Canadian model of an adult education initiative with a global social responsibility agenda and, until recently, an "institutional" social movement aimed at critical evaluation and focused action related to global socioeconomic, political and cultural issues. For this research, Ellis conducted document analysis and interviews with six long-term, committed Alberta members of the program, asking for their views on a range of issues related to critical global adult education and how well Ten Days responded to pressing issues of social justice through their educational program.

Elizabeth Lange is another long-time activist in several Canadian social movements. She was also a member of Ten Days in various provincial and national leadership capacities and is currently part of the sustainability movement as an educator-activist. She was previously active in the global education movement within the public education field, including organizing around various professional, social and educational issues. The action research study reported in this chapter is an example of her research related to the environmental sustainability movement. For the study, Lange designed and assessed an extension course on sustainability. She interviewed fourteen adults prior to the course about their knowledge and level of activity regarding issues related to social justice and the environment. The curriculum and pedagogical processes of the course were designed to engage the participants in a transformative learning process meant to introduce the concept and practices of sustainability related to workplace, household and lifestyle. For example, Lange incorporated community study tours and speakers to connect participants to the environmental sustainability movement. Near the end of the course, she also engaged the participants in action planning to encourage short- and long-term changes in living and working that would free up time and energy for active citizenship engagement. Throughout the course, Lange used a "double spiral action research" process with the fourteen participants, which included ongoing group reflection/action, interviews and journal-writing. The initial findings of this study are reported in Lange (2004). Further collection and analysis of longitudinal data that will assist in assessing the long-term impact of the educational intervention is ongoing.

Donna Chovanec has participated in diverse social advocacy and activism efforts including those for quality childcare and for the integration and inclusion of children with disabilities. For almost twenty years, her activist and research focus has been on various aspects of the women's movement, including women who are abused and women who use substances. Personal relationships with anti-dictatorship activists from Chile led her into solidarity and research with women's movements in Latin America. In both studies of women's movements reported here — among abused women in Canada and with the Chilean women's movement — she explores the central importance of critical consciousness and how it develops (more on this in a later section). In the first, Chovanec conducted participant-observation and individual and group interviews with four formerly abused women attending a drop-in centre and support program for abused women. All of these women were committed to anti-violence activism. For the second study, Chovanec engaged in nine months of ethnographic fieldwork in Arica, a small city in northern Chile. Methods included cultural immersion, document review and group and/or individual interviews with sixty women who had been active in the women's movement at some point over the previous thirty years; most had been involved in anti-dictatorship activism in the 1980s.

In the remainder of the chapter, we explore four conclusions drawn from our collective analysis of learning across all of these social movement studies.

DIALECTICAL LEARNING IN ACTION

We assert that learning and action are dialectical and iterative processes. For adult educators, social movements themselves are *educational* projects. However, there were no professionally designated "adult educators" in the women's movement in Chile. Nor are there or have there been in most social movements, old or new.

> The majority of radical adult education before and during the time that adult education emerged as a field of study has occurred in settings not necessarily considered educational, and it has been practiced by people not necessarily considered... as educators. (Holst 2002: 5)

Indeed, as Kastner (1994) has pointed out in her study of Canadian social movements, professional adult educators are sometimes viewed with suspicion. Nonetheless, adult education and adult educators abound in social movements whether designated as such or not. Freire (cited in Holst 2002) spells this out clearly.

> When we're in the process of mobilizing or organizing it begins to be seen also as an educational problem.... Education is *before*, is *during* and is *after*.... It's impossible to organize without educating and *being* educated by the very process of organizing. (80)

If one concurs with this premise, it becomes apparent that the educational endeavour is integral and inherent in social movement organizing. Not only is everyone a philosopher as Gramsci (1971) maintains, so too is everyone an adult educator.

Chovanec's research with the women's movement in Chile exemplifies, what she calls, the "organic" educative and learning dimension of social movements. Radical adult education occurs through the organic presence of adult educators within social movements in a dialectical relationship with organizing. By organic, we mean that adult educators (whether identified as such or not) are an inherent part of social movements and that they are continuously embedded within the movement. Thus, adult education and learning is occurring all the time.

In Arica, Chile, learning and educational experiences are woven into the women's life paths as they are juxtaposed with the social movements in their community. The centrality of education is demonstrated by both its presence (the multiple ways in which the women learned in the women's movement) and its absence (the consequences resulting from lack of attention to a reflective component) in the women's movement. An organic approach to education is particularly apparent in the consciousness-raising role of parental teaching and the political party that was a key feature of the women's social environment. Most women were rooted in families and communities that espoused leftist philosophies through participation in leftist political parties and/or liberation theology, through the legacy of earlier workers' and women's struggles and through the political trajectory that ultimately led, in 1973, to an elected socialist government in Chile. But, even for those women whose environment was not explicitly leftist, seeds were sown in their early learning of values related to fairness, dignity and community. This early learning established a set of communitarian values, humanist/socialist philosophies and/or Marxist ideologies that provided the foundation upon which the women developed, often at very young age, their critical consciousness. This early socialization is recognized in many studies of social activists (e.g., della Porta 1992; Marx and McAdam 1994). In Chile, women "participated in a family dynamic where the political was part of the conversations.... Under those conditions, it wasn't strange that a particular worldview would be shaped in childhood" (Cortez Díaz and Villagra Parra 1999: 118). Gramsci (1971) provides further insight into this phenomenon: "The child's consciousness is not something 'individual' (still less individuated), it reflects the sector of civil society in which the child participates, and the social relations which are formed within his [sic] family, his neighbourhood, his village, etc." (35). Thus, acquiring consciousness is a somewhat passive and structurally determined learning process that organically occurs during the early years as we learn values and beliefs from the collective that makes up our social world.

While not wholly conscious at the time, these early experiences establish the predisposition for developing a more robust critical consciousness in the future when individual agency acts upon the predispositions and opportunities presented by the structural conditions. In Spanish it is more common to use the word "*tomar*" (taking) when referring to consciousness. The idea of "taking" critical consciousness implies an intentional commitment made by women whose own lived experiences resonate with their already acquired consciousness. As they entered their youth, many women in the study made deliberate choices to act upon their consciousness. Thus, women became party militants themselves or they affiliated themselves with party militants. Some actively participated in the Catholic Church, which, at that time, professed a theology of liberation. Prior to the coup, the older participants had worked for Allende's campaigns, participated in community organizations and established their homes through land takeovers. So that, in living out their "potential consciousness," it was deepened and expanded into a "real consciousness" (Goldman, cited in Freire 1970/1990: 105). It was brought to a level of awareness and integration that is only possible through action. As Allman (2001a) states, ideas or thoughts can "become part of our consciousness when we receive them from an external source... [but] reception depends upon our active engagement with them" (165–66). Once engaged, this consciousness becomes internalized and subjectified — it is *taken* into oneself — and acted upon.

However, Allman (2001b) reasons that "authentic social transformation is never a sudden event. It is a process through which people change not only their circumstances but themselves. Consequently it must be an educational process that involves the simultaneous transformation of educational relations" (1). This was the explicit intent of Lange's study. Educational and learning processes were at the forefront of her intention to catalyze involvement in the environmental sustainability movement. These processes began with participants examining cultural and ideological barriers. She used the central concept of sustainability to link individual wellbeing to ecological wellbeing and to global wellbeing. When people examined their freneticness and lack of meaning, they concluded that they needed to rethink their definitions of financial security, success, working hard, stability, status and comfort. At a social level, they needed to analyze the impact that the changes in technology, culture, money and work have on their daily lives and their local communities. Only when they realized how the ideas and material realities were creating their unhealthy, stressful ways of living, were they able to engage in a global socioeconomic critique. From this analysis, they began to craft changes that would enhance the wellbeing of their individual lives and also free up time and energy for societal involvement. Learning about the interlocking nature of cultural messages, for example that money and position are indicators of success and that we use consumption and "style" to portray this success, created a desire for change. As people moved through the change process, they often needed to revisit these messages in an iterative fashion, continually giving voice to the conflicts between these messages and their own values, and further redefining their own cultural scripts toward more meaningful criteria for their work, their lifestyle and consumption, and their relationships. As they listened to speakers from the environmental movement who espoused different values and lifestyles, they began to change how they worked and lived in ways that would free up time for more citizen and/or activist involvement.

Ten Days also used this explicit approach to education by using learning activities designed to engage participants in national action strategies, then to reflect on the impact of the strategies that would, in turn, inform further actions. Drawing from the praxis of Latin Americans like Freire and the liberation theologians, the animating questions for such ecumenical justice coalitions were: "How could the Canadian churches be prophetic in this time and place? What role could we play in the liberation process?" The starting point of their educational process then was the sociohistorical reality that linked Canada with the South. Profoundly influenced by voices from the South, particularly Christian voices from partner churches, priority was given to their stories of exploitation and oppression, to the social analyses they provided and to their requests for action (Beaudin 1994). This was considered an act of solidarity and a concrete manifestation of our "option for the poor." The justice coalitions took two approaches — one was to lobby government and corporations to achieve changes in public policies and business practices linked to structural justice and the other was to use an educational approach to hear the local and global stories, demystify the power structures behind them through collective social analysis and engage in theological reflection culminating in social action. This process very clearly manifested a dialectical approach to learning and social action.

LEARNING IN SOCIAL MOVEMENTS IS MULTIDIMENSIONAL

Various schema are used to categorize, analyze and interpret learning in social movements. For example, when social movement research studies from other disciplines are analyzed from a learning perspective, as Foley (1999) has done in his book on learning in social action, various political learnings become apparent. Some adult education researchers reveal types of learning that reflect a rational Habermasian typology: instrumental, interpretive and critical (e.g., Schmidt-Boshnick's 1996 study of a women's collective in a marginalized urban area). Numerous adult education studies have been conducted that consider transformative learning in social action. These studies might emphasize cognitive transformations based on Mezirow's (1991) theory of transformative learning, the psychological transformation explored from a depth psychology perspective (e.g., Scott 1992) and/or critical social transformation more typical of Freirian or feminist analyses (e.g., Hart 1992).

Each of these learning dimensions is also revealed in our own research. However, we recognize the limitations of uni-dimensional analyses of social movement learning. Instead, we acknowledge that learning in social movements has spiritual, cognitive, ethical, emotional, physical, psychological, socioeconomic, political and cultural dimensions. Moreover, we contend that all dimensions of social movement learning must be simultaneously considered in effective mobilization and engagement of activists. However, social movement literature across disciplines has revealed that some dimensions are less well considered or theorized. From our own work, we highlight the lack of attention to socioeconomic, emotional and spiritual dimensions of learning in social movements.

The Ten Days approach to multidimensional learning began with a faith-based approach to education and action for social justice, thus incorporating a spiritual dimension. Some elements within the Canadian churches sought a more critical social analysis reflective of the influence of liberation theology in Freire's work in Latin America. Freire insisted on the centrality of class struggle and maintained that most of what we think about how the world works is conditioned by our actual or perceived position on the socioeconomic ladder. However, class analysis was not a central focus of Ten Days. The abandonment or neglect of a central part of Freire's teachings meant that it became difficult, if not impossible, to address the root causes of the many injustices identified by Ten Days participants and researchers, global partners and others. In concert with much of so-called Freirean pedagogy in North America, the message was "domesticated" for consumption by a concerned, but largely conservative or liberal, Canadian audience. Thus, elements of the socioeconomic learning and educational elements were largely lost, particularly after a new umbrella organization, KAIROS, was formed to replace Ten Days.

Learning in the women's movement in Chile was mainly shaped by political learning and action that was informed, to one degree or another, by socialism and feminism. Alongside, political learning, however, Chovanec found that emotions of all kinds ran high among the women. Emotions swung from the exhilaration of adventure and invincibility to the compassion of solidarity to the terror of the unknown and the known; from the passion of commitment to the disillusionment of reality. Anger, passion, love, fear, pain, anguish, hope, deception and suspicion were present in large doses and at elevated levels, especially among the younger activists. For example, learning to manage the profound and ever present element of fear was essential to survival and to activism. The women demonstrated the same fear management mechanisms as those described by others, such as intimate social networks, communal gatherings and strong movement identification (e.g., Goodwin and Pfaff 2001). The women also talked about deep friendships, connectedness and solidarity that can lead to an intense and exclusive collective identity, the loss of which is grieved in later years (DeVries 1996). Conversely, "emotions help to explain not only the origin and spread of social movements but also their decline" (Goodwin, Jasper and Polletta 2001: 21). Exhaustion, frustration, and disappointment "can generate also negative, profoundly disempowering learning" (Foley 1999: 142).

Despite the emotionally charged nature of social movement experience, the emotional dimension of social movement learning is rarely considered. Recent social movement theorizing suggests that the "explanatory variables" of the current theories are inaccurate or incomplete without the addition of complex emotional realities. Based on our research, we concur with Goodwin, Jasper and Polletta (2001), who argue that "emotions are important in all phases of political action, by all types of political actors, across a variety of institutional areas" (16).

It was Lange's explicit intent to integrate the spiritual into the multi-dimensional approach she used in the environmental sustainability study. As participants moved through the course, the embedded sociocultural analysis often bred a sense of fear of change as well as anxiety, which had the potential to block change. However, tapping spiritual sources through use of archetypes, visualization or mindfulness activities, and recording dreams as well as physically reconnecting to the natural world and at a deep emotional level with other participants, the participants began to transform this fear and anxiety into energy for change. The impact was that their sense of self began to expand beyond ego boundaries. A deliberate aspect of the pedagogy was to offer activities and reflections that would facilitate these organic (i.e., natural world) and spiritual connections. Inner spiritual connections led the participants to engage with the restorative properties and the living models of the natural world. Participants commonly observed that their sense of balance was restored when they were outside in a wild, natural area. The solitude and quiet offered a natural reflective circumstance and the chance to hone a mindfulness of one's surroundings. It also helped to identify their deepest yearnings. These connections to spiritual energies helped to maintain their commitment in disorienting times and in the face of detractors, especially among their own friends and families. Most important, recovering suppressed values and ethics transformed their worldview, habits of mind and social relations. This transformative process in all of these dimensions restored their ethics and energy which lifted their sights away from the daily personal sphere and ego self onto broader ecological and global human concerns.

INTENTIONAL LEARNING IN SOCIAL MOVEMENTS

It is well recognized that social movement learning is often informal and unintentional. However we contend that, when a reflective educational dimension is intentionally and explicitly integrated within social movements, the membership is more effectively mobilized to action.

In a departure from typical social movements, education was a deliberate function in most social change initiatives presented in this chapter, i.e., Ten Days, the sustainability course and the abused women's support groups. Ten Days is "a focused education-and-action program designed to encourage grassroots support for constructive social change. It is dedicated to helping people discover, examine, reflect and act on the ways global and domestic structures and policies promote and perpetuate poverty and injustice for the majority of the world's people" (Howlett 1996: 33). The abused women's support group was a structured program for battered women that combined social-emotional support with education. The educational component included a sociohistorical understanding of abuse (thinking), personal development (feeling) and change (doing). The accompanying drop-in centre provided crisis support and encouraged advocacy. Through a series of educational interventions and a critical pedagogical process, the sustainability course was specifically designed for adults to analyze their lives and find ways to transform their working and living toward more sustainable forms.

With respect to the intentional integration of education into a social movement, it is important to grasp the crucial significance of a critical revolutionary *praxis*, the essential, yet elusive, dialectic that privileges neither action nor reflection, as well as the continual challenge of finding the dialectical equilibrium between the two. Both action and reflection are crucial to effective engagement and mobilization in social movements and we see some evidence of this in the aims of the activities described in the previous paragraph.

Yet, we frequently find a tendency to privilege one over the other. Lange and Ellis, working and researching within middle-class North American contexts, observe the privileged propensity to think, talk and study issues at length. The women in Chile, on the other hand, argued for the urgency of action during their anti-dictatorship activism. Those that advocated for the simultaneous engagement in a reflective or "study" component that would introduce a sociopolitical critique and analysis to movement activity were marginalized and ridiculed. This particularly affected the younger women, whose introduction to politics was through campus strikes, neighbour-hood barricades and street demonstrations. The purposive elucidation of a coherent ideology was lost in the frenzy of anti-dictatorship mobilizations that privileged action over reflection and left the women without a clear critique of capitalism or a vision for the future. The idealism and energy of their youth was channelled into a grueling schedule of anti-dictatorship activities without the "ideological education" that the older women had experienced. Similar concerns arose in other Latin American studies (e.g., Moyano 1992; Olavarría 2003).

The lack of attention to ongoing nurturance of critical consciousness had repercussions for the women's movement as a whole in Arica. Consciousness is not a static phenomenon. It is fragmentary, contradictory and constantly in the process of becoming. New situations, particularly those as traumati-cally disjunctive from the past as happened with the coup in Chile, demand that a critical consciousness be constructed and re-constructed through an ongoing and deliberate educational process. The women's prior (in the case of the older women) or nascent (in the case of the younger women) critical consciousness was not fully realized due to inadequate attention to its central importance in a critical revolutionary praxis.

However, the reverse is also true. If Canadian social movements tend toward analysis they can also experience paralysis or, what Freire calls "al-ienating subjectivism." "In other words, reflection is only real when it sends us back, as Sartre insists, to the given situation in which we act" (Freire 1984: 528). In the following quote, Freire (1970/1990) demonstrates the fundamental relationship of action and reflection by drawing attention to the potential consequences of de-linking the two.

When a word is deprived of its dimension of action, reflection automatically suffers as well; and the word is changed into idle chatter, into *verbalism*.... On the other hand, if action is emphasized exclusively, to the detriment of reflection, the word is converted into *activism*. The latter — action for action's sake — negates the true praxis and makes dialogue impossible. (75–76)

We generally use the term "activism" to signify the totality of social movement work, implying perhaps that we are typically guilty of Freire's accusation. Like Freire, we argue instead for a purposeful dialectical relationship between learning and action in social movements.

MOBILIZING ACTION THROUGH LEARNING

Finally, we propose that the learning that occurs in or related to social movements has what Patti Lather (1991) terms "catalytic validity" (68) and that it can be assessed by its ability to transform participants' frameworks of thinking and action. Lather links catalytic validity directly with Freire's notion of conscientization, not only through the recognition that praxis-oriented learning has a reality-altering impact but "in the desire to consciously channel this impact so that respondents gain self-understanding and, ultimately, self-determination..." (68).

In the study that engaged learners in knowledge and action related to sustainability, Lange deliberately fostered catalytic capacity by engaging participants in a study tour that allowed them to meet community members who had significantly transformed how they lived and worked. One goal for participants was to understand how individuals had made choices to live out their principles of personal, community and ecological sustainability. A second goal was to bring the participants into contact with these individuals as leaders of local social movements who were accorded a significant degree of legitimacy in their communities. Exposing participants to social movement leaders illustrated the diversity and dynamism of the thinking and living alternatives that already exist in society. In contrast to their initial feelings of futility and cynicism that individual actions could have a lasting and meaningful impact, revealing this underside of mainstream living and working offered them a sign of hope that life could be lived in a way that prefigured a more just and environmentally respectful society. It also held the possibility of generating a network of supportive mentors that could engage with the participants well beyond their course involvement.

As was expected, these exemplars created a natural bridge to social movements. As one participant said, "I found the study tour to be very 'eye opening.' I felt like I was in another world. The study tour presented many principles that I would like to add to my work life.... It broadened my scope of thinking and made me feel like I can have an impact in my community and the environment by the way(s) I choose to live and work." Another participant concurred: "I found the visits to be very inspiring, both from the point of listening to the commitment, integrity, and choices made by these people.... [I] was touched by the courage they each displayed.... I found myself impressed with the dramatic lifestyle choices I encountered and immediately felt strengthened to look at the small steps in my life." This sentiment is in stark contrast to the general belief at the start of the course that spaces for citizen engagement were not effective or "respectable" because social movement activists (as portrayed in the media) were strident, exclusionary and confrontational. Instead, they saw the heart of committed citizenship and the courage to act on beliefs to create a sustainable, just future.

After the course, many of the participants volunteered in various social movements. For instance, one woman became active in her labour union to support exploited teacher aides, another joined the Sierra Club to do workshops on urban sprawl, one joined the gay and lesbian movement, and several others joined local environmental organizations. They volunteered for political parties, in one case to support one of their mentors in an election bid, and they became involved in a host of other community organizations. Over half of the participants stayed together and started the Fireweed Institute, an organization committed to sustainability education and community action, so that they could offer this learning to others, including family and friends. They were very active for three years offering a host of courses, workshops, speakers and sponsoring various action projects. For example, one project involved transforming urban yards dominated by lawn into yards awash with native species of plants, shrubs and trees that would increase the local habitat for other species, or into organic vegetable gardens so that urbanites could produce some of their own food. The Institute's activist-educators maintained their contact within the environmental movements and some moved into paid work related to various movements — from a climate change consortium to sustainable architecture. The Institute has been in hibernation for over a year but, because members have lately realized the crucial importance of links to others in the environmental movement, there is talk of revitalizing its activities.

In a similar vein, one effective educational technique used in the Ten Days' experience was to have speaking tours, lectures and discussion groups with spokespersons from partner organizations in "Third World" countries. Eloquent, knowledgeable individuals speaking from personal experience about intolerable injustices in their homelands, injustices which many in the rich, industrialized nations of the world have the power to prevent, can influence frameworks of thinking and action. For example, for the annual theme of "freedom from debt" in 1992, two visitors from the Freedom from Debt Coalition in the Philippines were invited to travel across Canada to discuss the origins of the issue, their social movement and the role of activists in Canada (see Moffat 1994 for an excellent description of this activism).

While the speakers provided background information regarding the key annual theme, the network across the country was encouraged to carry out directed social actions based on these informants. "The visitor program has always been a key component of Ten Days," reported one participant, "It allows for a face-to-face interaction which is part of the pedagogy." Another participant provided a concrete example.

> A visitor was speaking about the garment industry program, the sweatshop campaign, in the high schools. As the kids were listening to this woman speak, I could see them all looking around at one another, looking at the clothes they were wearing. That's a very clear connection. When she was talking about the conditions that the people work under making these clothes, these kids are all of a sudden feeling themselves as part of this woman's life and problems.... Our government is starting to listen in initiating a task force on sweatshop abuses because they were pushed and pressured by the people. Programs such as Ten Days alert people to these things.

Church influence was consistently acknowledged by parliamentarians, royal commissions and standing committees, and the views of Southern visitors were reflected in final documents. Ten Days' campaigns contributed to modest changes in public policy (see Lind and Mihevc 1994 for more on the impact of church coalitions on public policy). For example,

- improving Canada's acceptance and treatment of refugees;
- curbing government and corporate investment in South Africa during the apartheid regime;
- influencing the creation of an exploratory commission to Central America that impacted Canadian policy in the region;
- obtaining greater transparency of the international reporting of the banks about how the debts of Southern countries are calculated and pressuring for a "jubilee year" where debts of the poorest nations are forgiven (as happened in 2000);
- ending the dumping of molybdenum mine tailings which threatened the lives of the Nisga'a First Nation's peoples; and
- pressuring for corporate codes of practice for transnational corporations and higher compliance standards for sulphur emissions and lead content in gasoline.

Although the Freirean impulse towards a more radical egalitarianism has been suppressed in the successor organization, KAIROS, Ten Days participants inspired by Freirian ideals have found ways to continue with that work, through KAIROS or through other movements and organizations in the global justice movement.

Similar to most social movements, learning in the women's movement in Chile was incidental and informal. Because direct action was the primary form of movement activity during the anti-dictatorship struggle, learning was directed to determining safer and more effective action strategies for both open demonstrations and for clandestine activities. It is well documented that the participation of women in Chilean social movements was a powerful presence in the eventual downfall of the dictatorship and the transition process (Cañadell 1993; Chuchryk 1989; Valdés and Weinstein 1993; Valenzuela 1991; Waylen 1993). However, as Chovanec argues in the previous section, the absence of a deliberate focus on learning reduced the long-term catalytic validity of the movement so that the women were unable to coalesce around new goals and strategies to combat neoliberalism in the so-called transition to democracy. One woman lamented, "We went out into the streets as women. So, we didn't prepare ourselves politically, we didn't educate ourselves as women. We forgot this part of ourselves because we didn't see any ambitions for the future. We saw nothing more than that this country was weighed down with pain." Another woman added, "we women weren't prepared to be involved…. There was no work to say how we were going to maintain democracy and maintain it in good form."

Nonetheless, all the women maintain a strong sense of themselves as political actors and citizens with a critical social consciousness and an astute socioeconomic critique. Two social movement "abeyance structures" (Taylor 1989) remain in place almost twenty years post dictatorship: a small feminist-socialist women's organization active since 1983 (Centro de Encuentro de la Mujer) and an annual event (Mujeres de Luto), inaugurated in 1984 and held every year since on the anniversary of the coup, wherein women stand in black and in silence on the steps of the cathedral to bring attention to the human rights abuses of the dictatorship.[1]

Thus, it is clear that learning can be deliberately catalytic and that such learning is vital to the growth and sustenance of social movements. First, learning can familiarize participants with the work and perspectives within social movements that undercut stereotypical and sensationalized media coverage through which most public views are shaped. Second, learning can be a bridge into social movements where people, once familiar with activists, feel welcome, knowledgeable, and able to contribute to the work. Third, ongoing deliberative learning can maintain commitment and nourish personal growth within the social movements. Fourth, learning can foster a sense of community that is vital when people are deliberately trying to live and work against the grain of society that can easily create burnout. In sum, the stimulation of learning, a sense of community, and the realization that their activism can make a difference in the future direction of society can bring people into social movements and keep them mobilized and engaged.

NOTES

We dedicate this chapter to the memory of our friend and colleague, Lee Ellis, who died unexpectedly after presenting an earlier version of this paper on our collective behalf at the Social Movements in Canada Conference. We thank the editors for their encouragement to submit this chapter, allowing us space to draw attention to the learning dimension in the study of social movements. Donna Chovanec is grateful to the many women worldwide who are dedicated to the struggle for justice and especially to those who shared their lives and their stories through the course of her research projects. She also acknowledges the generous financial support for the doctoral research cited here (including the International Development Research Centre Doctoral Research Award, Izaak Walton Killam Memorial Scholarship, Organization of American States PRA Fellowship and the Social Sciences and Humanities Research Council Doctoral Fellowship). Elizabeth Lange thanks the participants in the course "Transforming Working and Living" for their ongoing patience with the longitudinal study and their willingness to continue to share the developments in their lives. For their inspiration and exemplary practice, she also expresses appreciation to the many colleagues that she and Lee Ellis worked alongside in Ten Days for Global Justice.

1. This event precedes the establishment of the international network called Women in Black that was started in Israel in 1988 and that acknowledges other international women's movements that had previously engaged in a similar mode of protest. See Berkowitz 2003 for a recent analysis of Women in Black, including an excellent reference list.

SECTION III – THE ACTIVIST'S PERSPECTIVE

CHAPTER TEN

EQUAL MARRIAGE FOR SAME-SEX COUPLES

Laurie Arron

I have been asked to discuss the struggle for equal marriage for same-sex couples in Canada. I want to say that I'm so incredibly thankful that I've had the opportunity to participate in this campaign for this historic advancement in equality. I think of the long years that I spent in the closet in quiet desperation, from the age of thirteen, when I realized I was gay, to the age of twenty-seven, when I finally came out. Now I'm forty-four and I can look back at the last thirteen years of activism with tremendous pride and with gratitude that I was able to get past my doubts and fears and to have been lucky enough to land in the eye of the storm. And equal marriage really was a storm.

I knew the campaign for equal marriage was going to be big. But I had no idea how long and winding a road it would be, ultimately taking us through courts in eight provinces and the Yukon, across the country with the Justice Committee, to Parliament, to the Supreme Court, and through two elections and three prime ministers.

Even before it started, I knew it was going to be big because every step along the way, opponents of our equality pointed to marriage. In 1995, when we first got some protection against hate crimes, they said "don't do it, it will lead to gay marriage." In 1996, when the government amended the Canadian *Human Rights Act* to prohibit discrimination based on sexual orientation, they said it was going to lead to gay marriage. In 2000, when the government amended federal law to recognize same-sex common-law relationships, they said it was going to lead to gay marriage. So I knew that the idea of two men or two women getting legally married struck fear in the hearts of those who view homosexuality as threatening, perverted or just plain wrong.

I also knew that the impact of this legal recognition would be huge. Regardless of what you think of the institution of marriage, the fact remains that it is the most prominent way in which our society recognizes committed romantic relationships, and so inclusion or exclusion sends a powerful signal about our place in society. Sometimes I like to imagine a future in which one's gender identity or sexual orientation isn't an issue at all. But I know that such a world cannot be if we are excluded from such a central social and legal institution as marriage.

I also know that inclusion in marriage is especially important to young people. A letter from a young man to the *National Post*, published in the midst of Parliament's deliberations about equal marriage, highlights this importance:

> Re: Speaking of Man and Wife, Father Raymond de Souza, March 5
>
> I wonder if those fighting so hard against same-sex marriage ever consider how much it means to gays. They don't know what it's like to be a teenager — when the pressure to conform is so great — and you experience the horror of realizing that you are gay. They can't understand what it's like to listen to your friends talk about how they hate queers and how they wish they were dead. You consider suicide, because you never want anyone to find out the truth about yourself; your shame is too great to bear.
>
> And these people can't understand the hope that filled my soul when I first found out that Canada was considering allowing same-sex marriage. This legislation goes so far beyond marriage. It is a symbol. It represents the hopes and dreams of gays for a better world. Now that I'm 18, I can finally admit to myself that I am gay and no longer feel the shame that almost drew me to suicide. At least now I have hope. What I can't understand is how people like Father de Souza, who are supposed to be in the business of giving people hope, are so determined to crush it.
>
> Jason Reede, Toronto (March 8, 2005)

I lived for years hating the fact I was gay. The reason I think achieving equal marriage is so important is because of the impact it will have on kids struggling with their sexual orientation and their gender identity. I was often questioned, especially in the early years, as to why I wanted anything to do with such an oppressive institution as marriage. I was often told that we didn't need it, and that we didn't need the acceptance of others. But struggling teenagers do need the acceptance of others. In fact, we all do. We live in the world. We are not separate from it. We cannot help but be built up or taken down by what others think, say and do.

This leads me to another observation. I noted earlier how the thought of equal marriage struck fear in the hearts of those who think homosexuality is threatening, harmful or just plain wrong. It's important to take this fear into consideration and to have understanding and compassion for everyone. It's important to do everything in our power to not lose sight of what the struggle for equality and inclusion is all about. It's about the idea that we are all human beings, equally worthy of consideration and respect. I know very well how difficult it can be to maintain consideration and respect for those who speak ill of you or whose words and actions cause you harm. But if we seek consideration and respect, then we must also extend this same consideration and respect to others.

To those who say, "well, I don't really care about these people," my answer is that your personal opinions of those people don't matter. Consideration and respect is not only good for them, it's good for the cause. If people are afraid of you, then the best way to reduce that fear is to be as non-threatening as you can. That doesn't mean you don't go forward with your court challenges and your political activism. It means you do it in such a way as to always consider the impact of your actions on those who oppose you. You try to understand them, and you try to lessen their difficulty.

It's also important because those in the middle will judge both you and those opposed to you based in large part on how you come across. If you come across as angry and insensitive, that won't help your case. But if you come across as reasonable and respectful, people will go out of their way to try and understand your perspective.

I'd like to turn now to some of the nuts and bolts of our campaign that you may find useful in your own struggles. To distinguish briefly between the two organizations I was a member of, Egale Canada is Canada's national group advancing equality and justice for LGBT people, while Canadians for Equal Marriage (CEM) was the temporary umbrella campaign set up to see equal marriage through Parliament and then later re-established to defend it when the federal legislation granting equal marriage was challenged. Canadians for Equal Marriage was set up and resourced largely by Egale Canada, with a large number of partner groups like the Canadian Federation of Students, the Canadian Labour Congress, the Canadian Psychological Association, the Canadian Association of University Teachers and PFLAG Canada, among others. Following the defeat of the fall 2006 vote to re-open the equal marriage debate, Canadians for Equal Marriage has closed up shop, but Egale Canada continues its work for equality and justice.

There were some elements of the equal marriage campaign that did not work as well as we might have hoped. Two elements stand out in particular — our ad campaign and the call for strategic voting in the 2004 election. The ad campaign proved to be costly, with little return for our precious financial resources. A major ad agency had offered to create a free campaign for CEM, promising that it would be possible to generate free public service placements and publicity for the ads. To generate interest, our campaign spent a few thousand dollars on disbursements. Unfortunately, the ads got very little airtime and no publicity.

More problematic in a political sense was a decision made in the heat of the 2004 election campaign. In the 2004 election, we were really scared that Stephen Harper's Conservative Party would win, effectively killing the chance for positive parliamentary action on equal marriage. One member of our organization made a statement calling for strategic voting to defeat Conservatives. This approach backfired, as its main impact was to tick off the NDP, our staunchest allies in Parliament and the source of some really top level volunteers. This call for strategic voting was interpreted by the NDP as a call to vote Liberal. It is not an approach that I would recommend in the future, particularly in light of new election financing laws that give each party money for every vote they receive. Even if a supportive party's candidate is ultimately defeated in their riding, the party will still receive funding for each vote received by that candidate, which in term can help the party's work to support key strategic issues — so there is no such thing as a wasted vote!

Fortunately, several factors worked in our favour and helped us to accomplish our goals. Certainly the Canadian Charter of Rights and Freedoms, passed in 1982, was essential. This legislation, unlike earlier human rights codes, has real teeth. If a law violates the Charter, then courts are required to strike down that law.

Even with the Charter, we still had to get past the "puke test." This term was coined by a famous American judge, Oliver Wendell Holmes, who said that judges start by following the established legal analysis, but if the result makes them puke, then they re-do the analysis. The first equal marriage Charter challenge, the 1992 *Layland* case, didn't get past the puke test, as is clear from the court's circuitous reasoning. The Ontario Divisional Court held two to one that excluding same-sex couples from marriage was not discrimination because everyone had the right to marry — they just had to marry someone of the opposite sex!

In the first of the most recent series of court challenges, the 2001 decision by the B.C. Supreme Court, we also didn't get past the puke test. There, the single judge did find discrimination. However, he argued that another part of the Constitution, the division of powers section, froze the definition of marriage in time to the 1867 definition. This was amazing considering that the division of powers contained no definition of marriage, it just used the word. Moreover, this ruling also cast aside the longstanding legal principle that our Constitution is a "living tree" and its interpretation must evolve with changes in society.

Every subsequent court decision did get past the puke test. Each followed the established legal analysis and found that excluding same-sex couples from civil marriage is discrimination. The courts also found that there was not one shred of evidence that including same-sex couples in the definition of marriage harmed anyone. If it were not for the courts, there is no way that Parliament would have extended equal marriage to same-sex couples. This route through the courts and the Charter was definitely something that worked.

However, I believe that our two-pronged strategy, combining political advocacy with legal advocacy, is something that was important, since the two reinforce each other. This political advocacy succeeded as a result of many different strategic factors. Careful use of language was critical, which was one reason why we settled on the phrase "equal marriage." The alternative phrase used frequently in the media, "same-sex marriage," sounds like something different than marriage — contrasting "marriage" against "same-sex marriage." In fact, many opponents of equal marriage actually said that they supported same-sex marriage, as long as it wasn't called marriage. But that is a civil union, which is segregation by another name. It's not marriage. The phrase "same-sex marriage" is a slippery term, whereas the phrase "equal marriage" makes it clear that we want inclusion in marriage itself. It proved to be difficult to argue with "equal." Even Bruce Clemenger, President of the Evangelical Fellowship of Canada, one of the staunchest and most active opponents of equal marriage, protested to me that he found it hard to argue against something called "equal marriage"! Eventually, our opponents would find their own term of choice and argued for the preservation of "traditional marriage." Ultimately though, equality trumped tradition.

This was part of a broader strategy of appealing to universal values, rather than focusing on the specific issue of equal marriage. People tended to need to relate the issue to their own experience and to things that matter to them. For this reason, we always talked about universal values like equality, inclusion and respect for difference, often in combination with Canada's record as a world leader in human rights. These are things that mattered to a broad group of people and extended the importance of our issue beyond the community of same-sex couples who were seeking equal inclusion in Canada's marriage laws.

It also paid to be persistent. Over time, and thanks to many personal discussions, we saw people change their hearts and minds. We saw support for equal marriage climb from the high 40s to almost 60 percent of the Canadian population. By the fall of 2006, over two-thirds of Canadians were against re-opening the debate. We saw the positions of many MPs "evolve," including people like Bill Casey and Judy Sgro, who voted against equal marriage in 2005. Even supporters like Jean Chrétien, Paul Martin and Andy Scott were once opposed to equal marriage. So don't give up, keep talking, be nice to people even if they oppose your equality, and eventually, hopefully, they'll come to see it your way.

An effective media strategy was needed. One general rule was to not make the perfect the enemy of the good — in other words, put the emphasis on quick responses to events, rather than agonizing over the perfect wording and/or process. Much of our media coverage came from reaction to outside events, driven by the actions of politicians and judges. We found that by responding fast and always being available to the media, we were more likely to get coverage and to be the first group called for reaction. Had we delayed our response, we may have got our wording just right, but nobody would have been listening to our reaction.

It also paid to generate our own news stories. Once, we called around the country to get statistics on the number of married gay and lesbian couples, then put out a press release. This not only got immediate coverage, but our statistic also was quoted in almost every subsequent article about equal marriage.

Another self-made news story came about during the 2004 election, when we decided to go after Mr. Harper. On June 1, he was asked about whether he would invoke the notwithstanding clause to block equal marriage. He obfuscated, refusing to say whether he'd use it to take away our Charter rights. On June 2, I got in his face. I couldn't get near Harper in the morning at the Hamilton airport, so I and a volunteer named Bob Smyth followed him to a rally in a Guelph Legion hall.

Getting inside was no problem, but at one point, Bob turned to me and said he was awfully nervous being there, that it looked like an unfriendly bunch. We waited almost an hour for Harper to appear. There were no microphones set up to ask questions, and I began to think this would be a complete waste of time. I wondered if I could just shout out a question at some point. Finally, Mr. Harper came out and began speaking. When he talked about being "mainstream and moderate," I screamed out my question — the one I'd been practising and practising — "When are you going to come clean on using the notwithstanding clause to take away our Charter rights?"

I didn't get two words into my question before the place went nuts! People started screaming at us to sit down, those around us used their signs to try and force us to sit down. I was totally focused on Mr. Harper, while Bob shielded me from the onslaught of his supporters. One guy had his fists up and was threatening to punch Bob. Bob told him to calm down and then the guy punched Bob right in the chin. It wasn't much of a punch; the guy was about eighty years old and Bob said he hardly felt it. But it landed, and the Canadian Press reporter got a perfect shot of it.

The story made the cover pages of newspapers in Canada as well as the evening TV news and was even reported as far away as Australia. The image was particularly damaging to Stephen Harper. The Conservatives looked like intolerant bullies, and their "scary" image was reinforced. Ironically, the people in that legion hall had no idea we were gay. The place went nuts after I got out only one or two words, and so they were all shouting "Sit down Liberal!" But there you have it, all those years of law school and my biggest contribution to equality was heckling Stephen Harper in a legion hall in Guelph!

The Internet was another key tool for both Egale Canada and Canadians for Equal Marriage, which helped us to fundraise, to lobby, to empower people and more broadly, to get our message out. In particular, Canadians for Equal Marriage's website was a very effective advocacy tool. The website was structured to guide visitors through four action steps.

Step One, "MP Action," was aimed at getting people to find out more about their individual MP. These pages contained contact info for every Canadian MP, as well as the latest information on where they stood in the equal marriage debate — firmly in favour, firmly opposed, undecided or leaning one way or the other. Hyperlinks allowed visitors to easily send a standard email either directly to their own MP, or to send a mass email to all MPs.

Step Two, "Petition," was intended to empower people. Visitors could sign an electronic petition to Parliament, which served as both as a lobbying tool and also as a means of collecting email addresses from supporters, who could let CEM know if they wanted to be kept informed of new developments. This petition collected over 50,000 names and email addresses, and was key both to getting CEM's message out and for fundraising purposes.

Step Three, "Donate," was a direct appeal for fundraising, which allowed supporters of equal marriage to provide financial support for our lobbying efforts. Finally, Step Four, "Invite Friends," was a networking tool. Visitors to this section of the website could provide email addresses for up to five people. The site would generate a standard email that would invite these people to visit the site and take action, thus raising awareness of the campaign.

Based on my experiences with Egale Canada and Canadians for Equal Marriage, I would reiterate the following key strategies for other activists: 1) Find a message with broad appeal; 2) Frame the issue to your perspective; 3) Stick to your message, and repeat it over and over; 4) Respond quickly to get in the media; 5) Make your own news; 6) Do your best to speak kindly of those who oppose you, try to understand them and to respect their views, no matter how difficult that may be.

To conclude, there is one thing I can say with certainty. Equal marriage is here to stay. I am so proud of this country. Despite the overwhelming resources and tenacity of those who fear equal marriage, they were unable to convince Canadians to exclude same-sex couples from civil marriage. Most Canadians have come to understand that equal marriage is not a threat to marriage; it is a strengthening of the institution and a strengthening of society. They understand that you need an awfully good reason to exclude people, and that there is no good reason to exclude same-sex couples from civil marriage. Even Stephen Harper, who has fought LGBT equality every step of the way, could not roll back the clock on equality. His attempt to do so failed miserably, and even he had to admit that the issue is settled. I still have concern about what a Harper majority government might do on so many social justice issues. But I think that even a Harper majority would not try to re-open the equal marriage debate.

NOTE

This chapter was adapted from a speech delivered at Mount Allison University, March 9, 2007.

CHAPTER ELEVEN

WHY US? THE CAMPAIGN AGAINST WAGE CONTROLS IN SAINT JOHN, NEW BRUNSWICK, 1975-76

David Frank

On October 14, 1976, more than one million Canadian workers stayed off work in protest against the government-imposed program of wage controls announced a year earlier by the prime minister. Although it was officially called a Day of Protest, the event is also recognized as the first Canada-wide general strike in Canadian history. More than thirty years later, this episode is beginning to attract historical attention. This is so partly because it was one of the more controversial episodes in the public career of the late Prime Minister Pierre Elliott Trudeau. As in the famous events of the 1959 loggers' strike in Newfoundland, when Premier Joe Smallwood lost his reputation as an ally of the labour movement, Trudeau's decision to impose wage controls similarly undermined his reputation as a defender of collective bargaining rights. In his influential book on the Asbestos Strike of 1949, Trudeau had warned:

> If the right to strike is suppressed, or seriously limited, the trade un-
> ion movement becomes nothing more than one institution among
> many in the service of capitalism: a convenient organization for
> disciplining the workers, occupying their leisure time, and ensuring
> their profitability for business. (Trudeau 1974: 336)

The 2007 Supreme Court decision that identifies collective bargaining as a right protected under the Charter of Rights and Freedoms adds further interest to this theme, as the institution of the Charter in 1982 was one of Trudeau's major political achievements. Although the Supreme Court accepted the constitutionality of his wage controls package in 1976, it was a divided decision at that time, and it is not so clear there would be the same outcome today (Russell 1977).

The academic literature on the wage and price controls program of 1975-78 has tended to focus on relatively narrow administrative and econometric concerns (Maslove and Swimmer 1980). One interesting exception, from the point of view of a free-market economist, was Richard G. Lipsey's critique, under the title "Wage-Price Controls: How To Do a Lot of Harm by Trying To Do a Little Good" (Lipsey 1977); there have also been broader critiques more sympathetic to the philosophical aims of the union movement and its preference for distributive justice and social democracy (Weldon 1991). However, from the standpoint of themes such as "Mobilizations and Engagements" and "Social Movements," the wage controls experience is most significant as a chapter in Canadian labour history. It was a time when workers and their organizations defined and then defended their interests through a campaign of resistance against what they saw as a government program that favoured the interests of business at the expense of workers. In the contemporary era the welcome multiplication of new social movements has sometimes eclipsed the importance of labour activism as a source of an ongoing practical critique of capitalist economic priorities. The divide between "old" and "new" social movements is sometimes exaggerated, for it is important to recognize that there has always been a diversity of resistance within capitalist society. Moreover, it has long been clear that social movements based in the working class offer a tradition of activism and a relevant body of experience in questioning the dominant social order (Carroll and Ratner 1995; Vahabzadeh 2007).

In this context the following pages may be understood as an account of the articulation of local protest and its place within a larger movement. It tells us how a shared experience of subordination was transformed into a demonstration of solidarity that claimed space both in the discourse of the times and in the public places of the community. The site of the discussion is one of Canada's oldest industrial towns, Saint John, New Brunswick, which is known in Canadian labour history as one of the early birthplaces of trade unionism in the nineteenth century. Although the city has experienced considerable deindustrialization in recent decades, in the 1970s and since it has remained one of those working-class communities where organized labour plays a significant part in public life. The focus in this discussion is on the first-person narrative of one participant, which was originally drafted for limited circulation but which has now become in book form a useful contribution to an historical understanding of the wage controls experience. The account by George Vair is not primarily "about" him as an historical subject, but it has particular interest as a narrative because it is told from the subject-position of a working-class activist and because it captures the details of a local movement for which general accounts and archival sources are inadequate (Vair 2006).

In 1975 George Vair and other younger workers of his generation were beginning to emerge as leaders within the local labour movement in Saint John. Vair had left the Saint John Vocational School in grade ten in order to join the Royal Canadian Navy, where he served for five years as a signalman. When he returned to work at an industrial job at Canada Wire and

Cable in Saint John, he was soon raising a young family with his spouse Carol and also becoming involved in the union movement. As older labour activists retired from the scene, Vair and others were being pushed forward into positions of leadership. By 1969 he was president of Local 2094 of the International Brotherhood of Electrical Workers and later Local 1905 of the United Auto Workers. Most importantly, at a critical moment in 1976 the thirty-five-year-old Vair became president of the Saint John District Labour Council.

A few notes here about the larger context of the 1970s may be helpful. At the beginning of the 1970s, organized labour in Canada seemed to be gaining ground. The 1960s had been a time of social unrest. This unrest included many working-class Canadians who fought to extend the meaning of social justice and economic democracy within Canadian society through a variety of social movements, including the revitalization and expansion of the labour movement. In one major breakthrough, workers in the public sector had won the right to collective bargaining. More than one million new members joined unions in the 1970s, and the overall rate of union membership was rising sharply. In 1972 a new Canada Labour Code proclaimed a growing consensus around the place of unions in Canadian society when it stated, for the first time in Canadian law, that collective bargaining was a constructive social force. Noting that Canada had ratified the International Labour Organization Convention No. 87 on Freedom of Association and Protection of the Right to Organize, the preamble stated that Parliament "deems the development of good industrial relations to be in the best interests of Canada in ensuring a just share of the fruits of progress to all."[1]

Yet ten years later, at the start of the 1980s, the situation was changing again. There was a new constitution, proclaimed in 1982, that included a Charter of Rights and Freedoms; but apart from a statement regarding freedom of association in Section 2, it contained no specific protections for workplace rights, union membership or collective bargaining. In the making of the Constitution there was much necessary attention to the rights of women and Aboriginal peoples, but a proposal to include the right to union organization and collective bargaining was voted down by the Special Joint Committee on the Constitution (Savage 2001). Later that same year Parliament placed federal employees under a two-year regimen in which their bargaining rights were suspended; the provinces were not slow to take the cue, imposing rollbacks, suspensions and back-to-work orders. The change has been described as a transition from "consent" to "coercion," which has gradually become a state of "permanent exceptionalism" in which the "normal" rules of collective bargaining and industrial relations established in the 1940s have been suspended with increasing frequency (Panitch and Swartz 2003).

Interestingly, both the 1972 Canada Labour Code and the 1982

Constitution Act were enacted by the same prime minister, who had long regarded himself as a friend of the unions and, as noted earlier, had specifically identified the right to free collective bargaining as an essential element in the functioning of a democratic society. Trudeau's shift from endorsement to exceptionalism during the course of the decade was visible on the Thanksgiving Weekend in 1975. Wearing a somber face, the Prime Minister went on television and announced his intention to fight inflation through the enforcement of a three-year program of wage and price controls, a strategy he had ridiculed in the previous year's federal election campaign. Such measures had been undertaken before in Canadian history, but only in the context of wartime economic management and, in the case of the Second World War, the controls were accompanied by explicit promises for new labour rights and social security as part of a postwar settlement. The constitutionality of the Anti-Inflation Program itself was debatable, as it was based on a loose interpretation of the federal government's peacetime emergency powers, a position cautiously accepted by the Supreme Court of Canada (Russell 1977). In 1975 Bill C-73 went on the statute books as the *Anti-Inflation Act*, but as Vair points out, it also became known as the "Wage Measures Act." This was a name that captured the punitive spirit of the *War Measures Act*, an emergency measure that had been invoked by the same prime minister five years earlier in the October Crisis of 1970 (Vair 2006: 30, 48).

General textbooks tend to regard the 1970s mainly as a time of debates over such matters as economic nationalism and Canadian unity, yet these were also the years when the real incomes of working people ceased to grow and unemployment rates rose higher than they had at any time since the end of the Great Depression. Much of this had to do with factors such as escalating international oil prices and corporate profit-taking strategies that were beyond the control of the Canadian government (Gonick 1975). As usually happens in times of economic crisis, workers would be the first to pay for the failures of the economic system. In retrospect the 1970s were the end of the long postwar boom for North American capitalism and the beginning of a new period in which the struggle over the rewards of economic life became increasingly intense. Older assumptions about distributive justice and Keynesian economics were being abandoned, and inflation was increasingly targeted as the most important issue for the Canadian economy. Meanwhile, the so-called philosopher-king who had helped to raise expectations was now determined to reduce them. For many Canadians who had hoped that the 1970s would be a decade of forward advance towards the Just Society promised by Trudeau, the events of 1975 represented a sudden stop.

The announcement of wage controls in October 1975 was the beginning of a long year of confrontation between organized labour and the government. It raised the age-old questions about the place of labour unions and workers' rights in Canadian society. The public debate that followed in Saint

John and across the country culminated in the Day of Protest on October 14, 1976. As Vair points out, the event officially had a slightly euphemistic name as a "National Day of Protest." Yet it fits the definition of a general strike because it was a mobilization that brought workers off the job and into the streets all across the country on the same day around a common cause. This has not happened often in Canadian history, and when such appeals do succeed, at least in part, it is worth trying to understand why and how this happens (Heron 1998).

Vair's detailed account allows us to follow the response to wage controls in a city where the measures had a large impact and there was an especially forceful response. The process of mobilization and engagement reminds us especially of the significance of labour councils as sites of working-class activism (Basque 1992). The labour council in Saint John traced its origins back to the late nineteenth century, some dozen years before it received a charter of affiliation from the Trades and Labour Congress of Canada in 1903. In the early twentieth century it was a leading force in campaigns for social reforms such as limitations on child labour and the enactment of workers' compensation laws and the recognition of union rights. In the 1970s, the labour council stationery still carried a classic nineteenth century endorse-ment: "'Labour Unions are the bulwark of modern democracy' — Gladstone." Files on the activities of the Saint John District Labour Council in 1974–76 show the council concerned about a wide range of issues, including support for a cardiac alert program and the public library. As an executive member in 1974 George Vair was proposing a new per capita tax system in order to meet "higher costs, resulting from trying to get involved in community programs."[2]

When the controls were announced in the fall of 1975, more than a dozen unions in Saint John were at some stage of the collective bargaining process. No situation was more important than the one at the Irving Pulp and Paper Mill, where the company in November concluded agreements with the Canadian Paperworkers' Union and the International Brotherhood of Electrical Workers. The CPU in particular expected to use the Irving settlement as a pattern for settlements in other mills in New Brunswick, and New Brunswick in turn would set the pattern for Eastern Canada. In a fascinating scenario, the unions and the company collaborated in evading the regulations and appealing rollbacks all the way up to the federal cabinet (Vair 2006: 36–41).

Meanwhile, it was becoming clear that the issue of wage controls was important well beyond the ranks of any single union. Local activists were turning out in large numbers to the meetings of the Saint John District Labour Council, and on January 2, 1976, Vair was elected — in absentia, because the development coincided with his mother's death — as the new president of the Council. Almost immediately they established a Wage

Control Committee, which grew to fifteen members, a largely male group (only two of the delegates were women) that included workers from the Canadian Paperworkers' Union, the Canadian Union of Public Employees, the Canadian Union of Postal Workers, the International Longshoremen's Association, the International Brotherhood of Electrical Workers, the National Association of Broadcast Employees and Technicians and the United Auto Workers. As Vair notes, "With the exception of one or two members, our committee was young — between twenty-five and thirty-five years of age. We had lots of energy, were not afraid to take risks, were idealistic and somewhat naïve" (Vair 2006: 46). These were the people who provided the essential leadership. They met every week at the Carpenters' Hall or the Longshoremen's Hall, and from there they organized information meetings and published newsletters, directing their attention first to union activists and then to the wider public.

By the late winter the Canadian Labour Congress had stirred into action and organized a large protest on Parliament Hill on March 22. About 35,000 people participated, and this memorable event is sometimes confused with the actual Day of Protest in October. Back in Saint John — where the sugar refinery workers had just seen their wage agreement rolled back — the Labour Council was holding a major public meeting at the Saint Malachy's High School auditorium. It was standing room only, and although there were high profile visiting speakers — including Bob White of the United Auto Workers and Shirley Carr, vice-president of the Canadian Labour Congress (CLC) — it was Vair himself who made headlines. In an unexpected intervention, the leader of the provincial Liberal Party came forward to assure the crowd that he would convey their concerns to the Prime Minister. When the speaker was finished, Vair invited him to leave the stage, telling him: "There's no purpose of you being here any longer, we've had enough of you to last a lifetime. Why don't you just leave?" These were not intended as public comments, but Vair's remarks were picked up on a live microphone, and for much of the media, those comments became the big story. At subsequent labour council meetings Vair expected to hear reprimands for careless behaviour, but instead he received support. For Vair, one of the most meaningful expressions of support came from Fred Hodges, a respected senior activist, a railway worker who was a former labour council president and a founder of the New Brunswick Association for the Advancement of Coloured People, who said: "You're dreaming if you expect labour will ever get fair coverage from the capitalist Irving-owned media" (Vair 2006: 57–64).

The mobilization continued to accelerate over the course of the next several months. By May, there were protest marches in the provincial capital. At the meetings of the Canadian Labour Congress in Quebec City that spring there was talk of a general strike. New Brunswicker Lofty MacMillan, Director of Organizing for the Canadian Union of Public Employees and a former president of the Saint John Labour Council and the New Brunswick Federation of Labour, stood as an opposition candidate for CLC president against the incumbent Joe Morris. Vair obviously counted himself a militant among the delegates in attendance, yet he helps demonstrate the complexity of internal labour politics when he also explains why he did not support MacMillan's candidacy: "Although Joe Morris did not inspire me, I rationalized that the election of Lofty MacMillan would split the labour movement at a time when we needed unity" (Vair 2006: 69–70).

Back in Saint John, the situation was turning into what Vair calls "A Long Hot Summer." As the weeks rolled by, there were more rulings, more rollbacks and more strikes, including a week-long wildcat walkout at the sugar refinery in late July and early August. The New Brunswick Department of Labour advised workers that such strikes were in violation of the province's *Industrial Relations Act*, but this did not stem the discontent. Vair himself — who had during this time become business agent for the provincial Local 1065, Retail Wholesale and Department Store Union — was involved in a one-day walkout at Willett Fruit, where workers had been waiting since February for a ruling on their scheduled wage increases.

By August the CLC had launched plans for the National Day of Protest, and in September the labour council appointed a fulltime organizer for the Saint John event. A twenty-seven-year-old activist from the MacMillan-Rothesay paper mill, Larry Hanley shared George's views and was somewhat less low key than George about advancing them. Hanley did not hesitate to use the term "general strike," and he particularly objected to the CLC's "Why Me?" campaign slogan. As Vair puts it in his narrative,

> Some of us were never comfortable with the "Why Me?" theme. We thought maybe it should be "Why Us?" There is an obvious difference because unionism is all about solidarity, about working people all being in the same situation.... There is nothing wrong with being an individualist, but the "Why Me?" idea seemed a too limited kind of slogan for the kind of thinking we were trying to advocate. (Vair 2006: 29)

One highlight in the local campaign was a September visit to Saint John by the Prime Minister. While Trudeau spoke to a business lunch indoors, King's Square was filled with hundreds of demonstrators carrying placards spelling out their message of repudiation. The CLC had been nervous about this event and had urged organizers to cancel it, but there was no untoward incident to discredit the protest. However, before he left New Brunswick on that trip, Trudeau made one of his habitual off-the-cuff statements that stirred up rather than calmed resentments; when asked by a reporter what he thought about the labour protests, he replied: "Maybe I'll have to try bludgeoning them" (Vair 2006: 104).

By early October plans for the Day of Protest were fully underway, and it was clear that Saint John was well-organized. There would be no buses and no taxis; the waterfront would be closed; so too the paper mills, the oil and sugar refineries, the liquor stores and other public services; the nurses and firefighters and police all offered support while maintaining services. Dry dock workers walked out two days early when they received a rollback order from the Anti-Inflation Board.

On the eve of the strike, there was an interesting exchange between Vair and a senior officer of the CLC. They were sitting down at the Admiral Beatty Hotel and Vair was explaining the plans for the Day of Protest to Donald Montgomery, the CLC secretary-treasurer. As Vair explained the strategy, workers would assemble in the early morning hours at central locations in the four corners of the city. Then they would march into town through the streets, shutting down the main thoroughfares and converging on the downtown area for a program of speeches in front of City Hall. Montgomery was concerned:

> "How to hell did you get a parade permit for that?" When I told him we did not have one, he was not pleased. Montgomery told me that if we got in trouble for not having a parade permit, he hoped I didn't think that the Canadian Labour Congress was going to bail us out. (Vair 2006: 112)

The anecdote reveals the careful preparation of the local activists as well as underlining their reluctance to seek official sanction from authorities in Saint John or Ottawa.

As it turned out, the Day of Protest in Saint John in 1976 was among the most successful demonstrations of labour solidarity in the country.[3] Vair's account makes it clear that this did not happen by accident but that it was the outcome of months of intensive preparation. If there is a central lesson or argument about labour activism to be drawn from Vair's experience, it is about how such mobilizations are prepared. They depend on the prevailing circumstances and the particularities of the issues, but they also owe much to the individual character and solidarities of the people involved. In this case the campaign against wage controls did not originate with the leadership of any single union or its headquarters staff. Instead it was led by a core group of youthful activists in and around the labour council and the major industrial unions. They were the ones who engaged their membership and community in debates over the controls and carried their message to the wider public. Indeed it is also clear from Vair's account that the militancy of affiliates and activists in places such as Saint John helped push the Canadian Labour Congress towards endorsement of a larger campaign, to which it ultimately devoted substantial resources.

In analyzing the success of the mobilization, Vair suggests that the struggle had already succeeded by the time of the Day of Protest. This is because the wage controls had been targeted by a not always acknowledged campaign of civil disobedience. Unions had demonstrated non-compliance by insisting on bargaining as if the controls did not exist. They refused to sign substandard contracts and then regularly appealed and sometimes evaded adverse rulings against their agreements. These forms of resistance, sometimes abetted by employers who also resented the interference with the bargaining process, added enormously to the challenges of administration and enforcement facing the Anti-Inflation Board.

The controls were abandoned in 1978, and this too could be counted as a sign of victory. Indeed the prime minister who had introduced the program went down to electoral defeat in the 1979 election and prepared to go into retirement. Vair shows good historical judgement in concluding that the abandonment of controls was not the end of the story. He goes on to point out that this was the beginning of a new wave of struggles for organized labour, in which they faced renewed challenges from governments and employers in the context of the new neoliberal (sometimes called neoconservative) political and economic restructuring of the 1980s. In that sense the struggle against controls in the 1970s helped prepare organized labour in Canada to play a more active part in the 1980s, as organized labour sought out allies within other social movements in the local, provincial and Canadian contexts.

Indeed labour was also winning a few battles in the public discourse at this time. For instance, statements such as the Catholic bishops' "Ethical Reflections on the Economic Crisis" in 1983 reminded Canadians that the rights of labour were entitled to a certain moral priority in economic decision-making: "labour, not capital, must be given priority in the development of an economy based on justice"; the statement called for "the restoration of collective bargaining rights where they have been suspended" as well as "assurances that labour unions will have an effective role in developing economic policies" (Baum and Cameron 1984: 7, 10). As Steven High has recently argued in a book about resistance to plant shutdowns during this period, history and experience made Canadian unions strong defenders of the idea of community at local, regional and national levels. The participation of Canadian unions in that strategy reached a peak after the election of Brian Mulroney in 1984 and in the struggle against the Free Trade Agreement in the 1988 election (High 2003). Since then Canadian unions have continued to make common cause with other social movements in confronting the implications of globalization and of restructuring initiatives that threaten labour, environmental and human rights standards at home and abroad.

After 1976 George Vair went on to spend most of his working life in the service of organized labour.[4] Since his retirement in 2000 he has taken up several research and writing projects, including an historical calendar published by the Saint John and District Labour Council in 2003. In deciding to prepare his account of the campaign against wage controls in Saint John, Vair wanted to explain how local activists had contributed to the success of a Canada-wide campaign to defend union rights. His plan was that there would be several copies of his narrative available for circulation through the labour council, especially among younger activists who needed to have access to the memory of past struggles.

In due course his account went on to become a book, completed in collaboration with labour history researchers and published by the Canadian Committee on Labour History.[5] But the initiative began with Vair, whose engagement with history belongs to a tradition of adult learning and self-education that has deep roots in communities such as Saint John. Even in a time when history is increasingly professionalized, Vair recognized that he was in a position to make his own contribution to understanding the past. Like all good history, his account places events in context, gives them life and makes a claim on the public memory. Future studies of labour's response to the wage controls, and of larger themes such as the place of labour in Canadian society in the 1970s, will need to pay attention to Vair's evidence. It is also an instructive case study in the mobilization of local solidarities. As Bob White, former president of the Canadian Labour Congress, states in his foreword to the book, "This is a story that needs to be known all across the country" (Vair 2006: 10).

PRIMARY SOURCES

Labour History Project of NB (LHTNB). 2006. "Provincial Solidarities" and "Our Blog: Wage Controls." Available at <www.lhtnb.ca> (accessed on July 16, 2007).
Library and Archives Canada. MG28 I 103, Canadian Labour Congress Papers.
Provincial Archives of New Brunswick. MC1819, New Brunswick Federation of Labour Papers.

NOTES

1. Government of Canada. 1972. *Statutes of Canada.* "Canada Labour Code." c. 18.
2. Library and Archives Canada. MG28 1 103, vol. 447, file 9 and vol. 484, file 34, Canadian Labour Congress Papers.
3. The pattern of activism across the country on October 14, 1976, requires closer study; on this occasion, Ottawa was not the site of a major demonstration, and it is clear that some of the strongest manifestations of protest took place in small to medium-sized industrial centres such as Saint John. In New Brunswick there were additional public demonstrations in Moncton, Fredericton, Newcastle, Campbellton, Dalhousie and Edmundston.
4. He has represented workers before numerous boards and tribunals and has sat on arbitration and conciliation boards on scores of occasions. He served as a vice-president of the New Brunswick Federation of Labour in 1981–83 and as an employee representative on the New Brunswick Industrial Relations Board and

the New Brunswick Labour and Employment Board. Within the labour movement, Vair became a lifelong student, taking advantage of courses offered by the unions and also earning college credits. He has been active also in a variety of social justice causes, including Oxfam Canada's Sweat Shop Campaign. He and Carol have four grandchildren.

5.   This discussion arises from a labour historian's collaboration with a labour activist in preparing the book for publication. The author first met George Vair at labour education sessions sponsored by the Saint John District Labour Council. The editorial project that produced his book formed part of a larger Community-University Research Alliance entitled "Re-Connecting with the History of Labour in New Brunswick: Historical Perspectives on Contemporary Issues" (LHTNB 2006; Frank 2006). The book was officially launched in Saint John on 28 February 2007, at an event co-sponsored with the New Brunswick Museum and the Saint John and District Labour Council.

CHAPTER TWELVE

THE CANADIAN STUDENT MOVEMENT AND THE JANUARY 25, 1995, "NATIONAL DAY OF STRIKE AND ACTION"

Michael Temelini

As a doctoral student and executive member of the Post-Graduate Students' Society of McGill University, Michael Temelini was an active participant in the Canadian student movement throughout the 1990s. A member of the Canadian Federation of Students national executive committee from 1993 to 1998, he played a principal role organizing and participating in many of the events he describes in this chapter. Temelini helped to mobilize Montreal students, and was a founding member of the Quebec-based solidarity movement "Coalition X." At the Montreal January 25, 1995, rally Temelini was among the keynote speakers, sharing the podium with well-known Quebec icon, Madeleine Parent.

On January 25, 1995, an editorial of *The Globe and Mail* remarked:

> The National Student Day of Strike and Action is likely to sink with scarcely a ripple: a mark of the lack of support for the student unions in their hysterical campaign against plans by Human resources Minister Lloyd Axworthy to reform federal funding of higher education. (A20)

What is remarkable about the January 25, 1995, National Day of Strike and Action in fact is the degree to which this editorial was simply wrong. By means of a carefully planned and executed campaign involving the tactic of a general strike combined with a sophisticated media and public relations strategy the student movement earned remarkable support in its opposition to Human Resources Minister Lloyd Axworthy's plan to reform federal funding of higher education. This movement was successful in convincing a broad base of the general public that its goals were not hysterical but entirely reasonable. Because of these tactics the Canadian Federation of Students (CFS, or the federation) and its coalition partners were effectively able to stymie one of the central planks of Lloyd Axworthy's 1994 review of the social security system. In this sense at least, the January 25 National Day of Strike and Action was a highly successful example of an organized non-violent public mobilization. This chapter surveys the events that gave rise to the 1995 mobilization, considers the degree of its success and explores its significance as a Canadian social movement.

THE 1994–95 SOCIAL SECURITY REVIEW

With a solid majority following the October 25, 1993, general election, the government of Prime Minister Jean Chrétien launched Canada's 35th Parliament with a sweeping agenda of neoliberal structural adjustment. On January 31, 1994, Minister of Human Resources Development Lloyd Axworthy outlined a process for "social security reform" that included every social program constituted since 1942. Among those up for review were two programs directed at post-secondary education: the Canada Student Loans Program (CSLP) and Established Program Financing (EPF) — Post-Secondary Education (Canada 1994).

Axworthy also outlined a "consultation process" that included cross-Canada hearings. But from the outset it was obvious to student leaders that the government was not interested in genuine dialogue, nor did it have any intention of taking dissent and opposition seriously. It seemed to many students that the driving force of the social policy review was not an authentic desire to reform social programs according to principles of justice and fairness. Rather, the review appeared to be driven by the bleak fiscal context and the obsession of Finance Minister Paul Martin with deficit and debt reduction.

First announced during the 1993 election campaign in the so-called "Red Book" (Liberal Party of Canada 1993: 20) and then in the February 1994 budget, as well as subsequent economic updates, the Finance Minister set a deficit reduction target of 3 percent of gross domestic product (GDP) by 1996–97. Since he proposed neither tax increases, nor any large scale public investments to expand the economy, it was clear that this fiscal target would be attained by severe expenditure cuts, particularly to provincial transfers. In fact, Martin justified this approach and his fiscal target at a 1995 symposium in which he admitted that "a very long period of restraint would have to be endured to turn the debt momentum around" (Martin 1995: 205). These early indications pointed to a radical shift in policy direction regarding provincial transfers and student aid. Many were concerned that the government would cut the provincial cash transfers outlined in the EPF Act, and replace the CSLP with an income contingent loan repayment plan (ICRP).

THE INCOME CONTINGENT REPAYMENT PLAN

Introduced by Milton Friedman in 1955, the concept of an ICRP was promoted as a way to limit the government's role and increase that of private enterprise, in financing post-secondary education, thereby encouraging the "denationalization of education" (Friedman 1955: 129). By eliminating public subsidies, the aim of this plan was to preclude income redistribution and to assure that the costs of post-secondary education would be "borne by those who benefit most directly rather than by the population at large" (Friedman 1955: 144). Under the plan individual recipients would "bear the whole cost" of education by means of "equity capital" loans borrowed on condition that they agree to pay the lender "a specified fraction of... future earnings" (137–38, 144). With this, and because the loan payments could be combined with income tax payments, Friedman envisaged limited administrative expense "so as to make the whole project self-financing" (140).

For these reasons, the ICRP found favour with various individuals and organizations (Stager 1989; Smith 1991: 27; Duncan 1992: 4, 16–25) and particularly those on the ideological right because it simultaneously gave governments a way to increase revenues to post-secondary institutions, while at the same time reducing taxes to citizens not directly participating in the post-secondary system, and without increasing government debt (Ontario 1984: 53). While post-secondary education revenues would derive primarily from tuition fees (from the recipients of higher education) the plan is typically defended as flexible and fair because loan payments would be based on a percentage of income after graduation, which is to say income-contingent.

With the publication of its 1992 position paper *Compromising Access* (Duncan 1992) the CFS launched a campaign to expose the flaws in this ICRP logic. Several problems were initially raised, but the principal objection was that accessibility to education would be undermined because the plan would entail the deregulation and increase of tuition fees, the accumulation of lifelong debt and the abandonment of public education. The CFS argued that most proposed variations of the ICRP called for higher tuition fees which could be determined by individual universities and "no longer regulated by provincial governments" (Duncan 1992: 29). Furthermore, the CFS was concerned about a dramatic increase in student loan debt because of a combination of high tuition fees and due to high accumulated interest and length of repayment. The CFS pointed out that there would be no interest subsidy on ICRP loans as with CSLP. And in order to be self-financing the plan would need to compensate for unexpected administrative costs due to such factors as default or migration, so that repayment income thresholds would have to include low income earners, thereby undermining the very principle of income-contingency. These concerns were based on the actual experience of other jurisdictions, such as Sweden, whose student aid officials criticized their own version of ICRP because the debts were "too high," the incomes were "too low" and "in some cases the loan will never be repaid" (Duncan 1992: 26). Furthermore, the CFS raised other fundamental questions about the role of government in the financing of higher education. Many ICRP proponents favoured scrapping the CSLP and eliminating public funding altogether. The CFS vehemently objected, and rejected the ICRP based on the fact that it was neither a form of student assistance nor did it share the same mandate of the CSLP to improve access to higher education. Instead, as an Australian official said of that country's plan, the purpose of the ICRP was simply a way "to raise revenue from recipients" (Duncan 1992: 27).

With the 1994 Axworthy review the CFS was increasingly active in disseminating these concerns about ICRP, and particularly its inherently regressive and unfair aspects. For example, the federation argued that the plan would disadvantage low wage earners, who would have to repay their loans over a longer period of time at the cost of large sums of accumulated interest, compared to high wage earners who could repay more quickly and therefore pay less interest (Duncan 1994: 4). And the plan was additionally discriminatory against women, for whom repayment difficulties would be more pronounced since they earn on average less than men and because many are likely to temporarily interrupt waged employment due to pregnancy and childrearing (Duncan 1994: 5–6).

The CFS saw the ICRP as little other than a clever user-pay system promoting life-long individual debt and masquerading as student aid. And so it was described as a mechanism to shift responsibility for the cost of education from the state to the individual, and perhaps to the benefit of private financial institutions. In this sense it was understood as one aspect of a broader neoliberal public policy agenda to remove public control over education, to eliminate public subsidies and cut public expenditures on social programs, and to offload public fiscal obligations onto individuals. Because its aim was to shift responsibility from public to private, for the CFS the very idea of such a scheme was simply unacceptable. Based on its longstanding policy position that post-secondary education was a right and a public good, the CFS argued that a just and fair mechanism of financing was not user-fees and loans but progressive taxation and grants (Duncan 1992: 33–39).

Axworthy did not hide his preference for the ICRP. His public and private musings about its merits and feasibility triggered alarm bells among the leadership and the membership of the CFS. In a March 29, 1994, meeting for example, the Minister expressed his intention to finance ICRP pilot projects on the grounds that "people who can afford it should pay more" (CFS 1994a: 2). At its May 1994 meeting, the organization responded by adopting a resolution moved by delegates from two British Columbia-based community colleges directing the national executive to call a "national student strike" if the "federal government begins implementation of any reform that moves the education system towards further privatization of both post-secondary education funding and student aid." The resolution also directed the leadership to schedule an "action planning session" for the November 1994 meeting to draft such a nation-wide action. The sponsors of the motion were motivated by their concern that "such a move toward privatization would drastically minimize access to post-secondary education for any students other than those from an upper-middle class socioeconomic position" (CFS 1994b).

A week after its general meeting, a CFS delegation (including the national chairperson, several members of the national executive and staff) attended a conference of the Council of Ministers of Education, Canada (CMEC), held in Montreal, from May 26–29, 1994. It was an important opportunity to lobby influential public officials against the emerging consensus for an ICRP. Moreover, it was at this meeting that alarm bells were once again triggered when the Ontario Ministry of Education and Training announced a national symposium on ICRP scheduled for September. The province of Ontario had already experienced its own bitterly divisive reform of social programs, known as the "social contract," and its government, (particularly Premier Bob Rae) was seen as closely allied with the Axworthy review. Therefore many students suspected ulterior motives behind the symposium, and feared that its aim was not genuine dialogue but, rather, to create legitimacy for the federal government's position. Preparing for this conference therefore became a critical aspect of organizing (Caron 1994).

SUMMER ORGANIZING STRATEGY

Following its May national general meeting, at which a strike directive was adopted in the closing plenary and with the information learned at the CMEC meeting and through its regular contacts with government officials, the CFS national executive committee devoted its summer 1994 organizing efforts to oppose Axworthy's review. The strategy was to focus specifically on the income contingent loan repayment plan, which was rumoured to be the central aspect of the government's reform of student aid and post-secondary education financing (Carlisle 1994:1). The goal was to dispel the misconception about ICRP as a fair and progressive alternative to the status quo. So, the executive developed an "integrated approach" by promulgating the federation's research and by devoting all its human resources to coordinate communications, government relations, coalition work and media activities against the proposed reforms. Production of materials was initiated to raise membership awareness of the social security review and its implications for student aid and the financing of post-secondary education. For example, plans were undertaken to devote the fall 1994 edition of the federation's newspaper *The Student Advocate* entirely to Axworthy's proposed social program reforms. Federation members were encouraged to participate in any public consultations undertaken by the federal government. Student leaders were encouraged to hold campus information sessions about the ICRP.

In some cases, the CFS contacted and organized students from unions that were not CFS members, many of whom were requesting more information and assistance in organizing debates against ICRP supporters.

Throughout the summer, the CFS also prepared for the September 22–23, 1994, Symposium on Income Contingent Loans in Toronto. The aim of the two-day conference was to determine the feasibility of implementing the ICRP and to decide whether it would be an improvement over the existing system of public financing. But before the symposium even began, prominent policymakers (including Ontario Minister of Education and Training Dave Cooke) announced their support for the scheme (Council of Ontario Universities [COU] et al. 1995: 6). Many were therefore convinced that the symposium was part of the federal government's strategy, this time with the help of the Ontario government, to secure a consensus around Axworthy's reforms. The symposium gathered together 373 participants from every province and territory as well as international delegates. Close to half the participants were representatives of student unions, and the rest were college and university staff, representatives from the federal and provincial governments and representatives from other organizations such as labour unions, financial institutions and businesses.

Despite the wide divergence of views represented at the conference, the CFS delegation was able to focus its interventions to present a coherent and united front. Consequently, it was able to dominate discussion, particularly in the workshops, where its delegates were able to effectively challenge arguments in favour of ICRP. Three main arguments were mobilized. First, the ICRP was described as a mechanism to reduce the "financial and social policy role" of the federal government in post-secondary education ("it would be used as an excuse to further reduce government funding"). Second, ICRPs would result in "substantially higher tuition fees" and consequently "much higher student loan debts that will take 25–30 years to repay" (COU et al. 1995: 34). Finally, the ICRP was described as elitist and discriminatory, because it would reduce accessibility to education particularly for women, "who earn less than men" and "because people from low-income backgrounds are averse to incurring debt." On these grounds, CFS researcher Caryn Duncan denounced the very idea of an ICRP as immoral: "That any government would consider implementing a form of student assistance that systematically discriminates against individuals with lower lifetime earnings is unconscionable" (COU et al, 1995: 34).

For the CFS, the Toronto ICRP Symposium was a watershed moment. The federation used the opportunity as a two-day national seminar and training session for its membership and supporters. Moreover, the prominent and informed participation of national leadership and staff inspired students and labour activists in attendance, and so the conference helped build confidence and momentum for the continuing campaign. Just two weeks later, on

October 5, 1994, Axworthy released the federal government's long-awaited discussion paper, "Improving Social Security in Canada" (Canada HRD 1994a). The government also released a series of "supplementary papers," including one specifically devoted to post-secondary education. The details contained in these documents realized students' worst fears about the government's intentions. Citing the goal of reducing the deficit to 3 percent of GDP by 1996–97, the documents declared that "our challenge... is to bring our social programs into line with current... fiscal realities" (Canada HRD 1994b: 19). The papers reiterated a spending freeze first announced in the 1994 budget, followed by a proposal to reduce the "cash component" of EPF to zero (Canada HRD 1994b: 19, 25). Equally troubling was the admission that these measures would place "upward pressure on tuition fees" and this was excused as "a necessary price to pay" (Canada HRD 1994a: 63). To help students "cope" with rising fees, the papers proposed to reform the CSLP by considering "new approaches" to providing aid "such as income-contingent repayment" (Canada HRD 1994b: 22).

The proposals sparked a storm of protest across Canada. Following the release of the discussion paper, the Human Resources Development Standing Committee launched a five-week pan-Canadian "consultation" in twenty-two cities, from November 13 to December 16, 1994, from Whitehorse, Yukon, to Fredericton, New Brunswick. The *Globe and Mail* reported that students "vented their frustration... at every stop" of the Committee (Greenspon 1994: A3). The main focus of debate centred around the elimination of EPF cash transfers and the creation of the ICRP. In its brief to the committee, the federation reiterated the argument presented at the Toronto symposium correlating ICRPs with increased tuition fees and student debt. For this reason, the brief was mockingly entitled "Lifelong learning, or lifelong debt?" According to the federation, the phasing out of transfer payments "would likely set in motion" a chain of events in which the provinces would be forced to increase tuition fees or "deregulate fees entirely" by allowing universities and colleges to set their own in order to make up for the shortfall in operating revenue (CFS 1994c: 4). In lieu of the Axworthy proposals to eliminate cash transfers and introduce ICRP, the federation recommended ending the freeze on transfer payments, returning to the original EPF funding formula, introducing a system of national grants and convening a national symposium on the future of post-secondary education in Canada (CFS, 1994c: 10).

In defence of his proposals, Axworthy blamed the fiscal context and promoted the ICRP as a progressive and fair alternative. He also demonized his opponents as a selfish, irresponsible, "privileged" elite unwilling to assume its fair share of the costs of education (Greenspon 1994: A3). In response, students ridiculed this gross mischaracterization and exposed the flaws of his economic assumptions. Axworthy's position was based on the assumptions that with his proposals student loan debts would be relatively small and could be easily repaid after graduation because university and college graduates would have access to high-paid employment. Many students dismissed these assumptions, claiming that the Minister was ignorant of demographic statistics and prevailing political-economic realities. They argued that many post-secondary students lived in poverty, and upon graduation faced either unemployment, part-time employment or employment insecurity, rendering the loan debt an impossible life-long burden. As one student argued, "If the job is not there, how am I going to pay it back?" (Greenspon 1994: A3).

Dismissing the discussion paper as a "finance document clothed in bad social policy rhetoric," (Carrière 1994: 1), the CFS criticized the social security review as nothing but an elaborate exercise to create legitimacy for the sweeping neoliberal agenda promoted by the Finance Department. The stage was now set for large-scale public protest. In a widely reported October 12 press conference (for example, Ferguson 1994; Ward 1994: A2), CFS Chair Guy Caron suggested the possibility of strike action and denounced the Axworthy review. He raised several objections: he renounced the consultation process itself as fraudulent; he repudiated key neoliberal ideological assumptions underlying the review; and he corrected the mistaken economic assumptions underlying ICRPs.[1] Consequently, the CFS chair demanded that the government abandon its plans to cut the "social safety net" and "transfer payments to the provinces" and also called for a "national forum on the future of post-secondary education" (Caron 1994).

CFS NOVEMBER NATIONAL GENERAL MEETING

Despite the overwhelming support for the same resolution at its May 1994 national general meeting, a lively debate took place at the November national general meeting on a resolution for a general strike. Many delegates agreed that organizing against the social security reform proposals (and their move towards "the privatization of student loans and the funding of education") was the most important aspect of the meeting (Vila 1994: 1). They supported the idea of a multi-city pan-Canadian action on the grounds that striking and protesting are democratic rights and that students had a duty to oppose the massive cuts and to save social programs from the "devastating" restructuring (CFS 1994d). A small minority did not agree. Some suggested that the Axworthy reforms were a foregone conclusion, so protesting was futile. Others opposed the tactic of a strike, arguing that resources would be better allocated to lobbying. Still others proposed to compromise with Axworthy and to adopt certain versions of ICRP. All the objections were soundly rejected and following a long thorough debate the membership overwhelmingly adopted a resolution calling for a "national day of strike and action" for January 25, 1995, in a vote of thirty-six to ten, with eight abstentions. On November 15, at a press conference at the National Press Club, CFS Chair Caron announced the strike date. Caron explained that the CFS was not "a special interest group" but the authoritative voice of "thousands of students," and he issued an open invitation to all Canadians to join in protest. In justifying the action, Caron cited the decade-long "massive tuition fee increases" and soaring debt loads. He rejected the government's proposal to eliminate cash transfer payments to the provinces. He objected to the government's plan to introduce the ICRP and thereby shift its "burden of debt onto students' shoulders" which he claimed would "destroy Canada's public system of post-secondary education" (CFS 1994e). And Caron denounced the government for cutting social programs and "looking for scapegoats, such as students (who "have been depicted as spoiled brats bent on preserving our perks") as well as unemployed and welfare recipients "as if people who rely on the social safety net were really to blame for our country's debt" (CFS 1994e; CFS 1994f).

The following day, protests erupted across Canada. In Vancouver hundreds of demonstrators blocked Robson Street and forced their way into a hotel room where the Human Resources Committee was hearing submissions (*The Province*, November 17 1994: A22; McMartin 1994: A3). And in Ottawa, thousands of students from Ontario and Quebec demonstrated on Parliament Hill, pelting Axworthy with eggs and Kraft Dinner noodles when he made an appearance.[2] At the height of the demonstration Axworthy met the CFS chair and deputy chair during which he reiterated Canada's financial constraints, defended the merits of ICRP and excused the proposed cuts to provincial cash transfers (CFS 1995). When representatives of this growing pan-Canadian student protest movement met Axworthy five days later, they criticized his position and justified the November 16 demonstration on the grounds that his reforms would place upward pressure on tuition fees, and "simply transfer Canada's public debt to students," and this would negatively affect access to post-secondary education "especially for students from lower income backgrounds" (CFS 1994g). Still, Axworthy appeared to be uninterested in the student leaders' views, and it was obvious to them that the Chrétien government had no intention to reconsider its agenda. As a student leader from Quebec said, "If this is an exercise in consultation then this is a failure" (CFS 1994g).

In fact, from the moment the social security review was announced, the CFS leadership suspected that the government simply attempted at every step to manipulate the process and to manufacture consent among hand-picked supporters and sympathetic journalists, in lieu of holding a genuine public dialogue. When the government's expected consensus failed to materialize, and when its public relations strategy began to crumble, the government secretly worked to undermine its opponents, such as the Canadian Federation of Students, through deliberate political interference. This view is corroborated by Anthony Wilson-Smith and Edward Greenspon, who have explained that, when Axworthy learned that the federation was under pressure on many campuses, he exploited these internal divisions by contacting rival student unions and encouraged such groups to make their views known to the local media (Wilson-Smith and Greenspon 1996: 193).

The CFS was indeed under pressure, and these events were unfolding at a time when the organization was dealing with protracted and ongoing divisions and tensions within its own membership base, and was facing challenges from established and upstart rival organizations. For many years the federation experienced a vigorous and healthy internal debate among student union representatives largely driven by left-right ideological divisions that centred around three principal aspects: organizational structure, goals and tactics. Students promoting a broad left agenda sought popular control and greater democratic accountability over the permanent staff; and they promoted an innovative constitutional structure that accommodated on decision-making bodies special democratic representation for identity groups such as women, First Nations, students of colour, francophones, students with disabilities and gay/bisexual/transgendered students. Furthermore, the left majority successfully upheld longstanding policy goals such as the elimination of tuition fees as well as a broad host of domestic and international social policies addressing economic equality, peace and human rights. Many student union representatives defending a broad right agenda held opposing views. They defended CFS management against perceived political interference, they favoured a decision-making structure restricted to provincial representatives, they opposed the "zero-tuition" policy as unrealistic and they sought to exclude broad social policies and severely limit the federation's mandate to narrowly defined post-secondary education issues. Furthermore, the differences between the left and right centred around conflicting tactics. Many on the right advocated the quiet diplomatic strategy of lobbying public officials. Many on the left became increasingly disillusioned with that approach and wanted to complement lobbying with non-violent forms of civil disobedience such as rallies and public demonstrations. These ideological differences of opinion culminated in 1994, when at least a dozen student unions, principally from Ontario, Nova Scotia and New Brunswick, served notice to hold disaffiliation referenda in February and March 1995. Furthermore, executive members from several student unions, including dissident CFS locals, agreed to form a new rival organization called the Canadian Alliance of Student Associations, which was incorporated in 1995.

FALL ORGANIZING STRATEGY

These internal tensions and external challenges were an ongoing cause for concern, but they did not stop the momentum nor the resolve to organize. Throughout the fall months, the CFS stepped up its efforts in planning the day of protest. To mobilize public opinion the federation launched an intensive public relations initiative in which national executive members provided frequent interviews to both print and non-print media. Particular attention was given to the student press, which supplied a sympathetic weekly forum, but there was also much success with national public media.[3] And there were growing indications that this public relations campaign was working. For example, the CFS gained unexpected support from the Association of Universities and Colleges of Canada (AUCC), which represented university presidents. In their November 1994 submission to the Standing Committee on Human Resources Development the AUCC advocated creating an ICRP. But the organization agreed with CFS concerns over cuts to provincial transfer payments and criticized the Axworthy proposals for their potential "dramatic consequences for student debt, accessibility and overall fairness" (Fisher et al. 2005: 66).

In order to organize the membership awareness and media campaign most effectively, a toll-free 1-800 number was established and a full-time dedicated national strike coordinator was hired. The strike coordinator played a key organizational role by creating a contact list for every city and province in which there were member student unions of the federation, developing regular media and membership advisories and planning national media events. Part of the organizing strategy entailed sending a January 25 organizing kit to all member student unions, as well as to student clubs within the unions, such as women's centres and social justice groups. The kit included the fall 1994 edition of *The Student Advocate*, which was dedicated to the social security review; a national poster; small handbills for distribution on campuses;[4] volunteer recruitment sign-up sheets for use at campuses and high-schools; draft/model resolutions for use at meetings of coalition partners such as trade-unions and faculty associations. Since many students had little or no experience organizing a protest, the kit also provided detailed advice such as "four steps to a successful action."[5] In January the strike coordinator and other national staff produced a "Strike Bulletin" for organizers, listing "Strike and action committees currently up and running." As a result of these extensive preparations strike committees were ready to mobilize in every province. There were even strike committees in cities where there were no members of the CFS, such as Whitehorse and cities throughout Quebec.

SOLIDARITY: NON-MEMBERS, QUEBEC STUDENTS, CIVIL SOCIETY

With its dedicated staff, officers and volunteers, the CFS was able to develop a comprehensive strategy of building a broad-based coalition with other civil society organizations. It was also able to use the January 25 National Day of Strike and Action as an opportunity for membership development, both in recruitment and retention. One part of this strategy was to organize non-member student unions, to whom strike action kits were sent, as well as high-school students, for whom a flyer was produced.

Another critically important aspect of this strategy was to open the lines of communication with Quebec-based francophone student unions. The CFS had no members and no formal relationship with francophone Quebec post-secondary students, and the impending secession referendum complicated coalition building efforts. The Quebec student movement, for example, was dominated by two nationalist organizations comprising the majority of post-secondary student unions: the university-based Fédération étudiante universitaire du Québec (FEUQ) and the CEGEP-based Fédération étudiante collégiale du Québec (FECQ). Both federations resisted any formal alliance with student organizations outside Quebec and insisted on holding a separate Quebec-wide event for February 7, 1995.

This lack of support was problematic for CFS members who wanted pan-Canadian student solidarity. To avoid the embarrassing prospect of no participation among Quebec francophones, the CFS approached student unions either unaffiliated or disaffected by FEUQ and FECQ. And so the CFS's graduate student members at McGill University, as well as sympathetic organizers from Concordia University, contacted students at l'Université du Québec à Montréal (UQAM) as well as from various Montreal CEGEPs. The result was the creation of a January 25 solidarity movement called "Coalition X" — a loose coalition of Montreal-based student unions and student groups from the four universities and dozens of colleges, and primarily organized by the union of students in the social sciences and humanities at UQAM, and the student association at CEGEP de Saint-Laurent, and the Post-Graduate Students' Society of McGill University.

In addition to the cooperation and support received from Quebec students, an equally impressive aspect of the organizing campaign was the success in solidarity work undertaken with trade unions and other non-governmental organizations. An important part of the strike coordinator's work was to seek endorsements, donations and coalition agreements from various civil society organizations, such as the Action Canada Network, the Council of Canadians and the National Anti-Poverty Organization, as well as from trade unions with whom the federation had longstanding relations. Its denunciation of Axworthy's proposed cuts to social programs, as well as the other proposed reforms, resonated particularly with anti-poverty and labour groups, who were concerned about the proposal to reform the unemployment insurance system, as well as with the fact that skyrocketing costs would make post-secondary education inaccessible to all but the wealthy. Two aspects of labour solidarity are particularly worth noting. The Public Service Alliance of Canada (PSAC) agreed to print fifty thousand stickers advertising the January 25 day of action, and dozens of PSAC offices all over Canada offered to help with photocopying flyers and posters. Creative solidarity was also evident in the relationship with the Canadian Union of Public Employees (CUPE). The CFS learned of a potential obstacle to its alliance with CUPE because its member locals had no collective agreement protection for refusing to cross picket lines. In order to avoid an embarrassing scenario, the union suggested the production of stickers with the slogan "CUPE supports students on January 25" and requested that they be considered "strike passes" to cross pickets without hindrance.

By January 1995, the civil society support for the National Day of Strike and Action was truly widespread. On January 13, 1995, the federation held a press conference announcing a "solidarity pact" with all the national endorsing groups. Noting the looming national day of protest, and both the federation's success and Axworthy's failure at such coalition building, the *Globe and Mail* reported that "Axworthy's inability to build alliances... is making some of his government colleagues antsy" and "the alliance lined up against [Axworthy], however, is not going away" (Greenspon 1995a: A4). On the eve of the mobilization the CFS boasted some hundred official endorsements from various public officials and from a host of national, provincial and local social justice organizations including trade and professional unions, university faculty and teachers associations, healthcare workers, senior citizens groups, associations of citizens with disabilities, women's groups, anti-poverty organizations and organizations of the unemployed, as well as Newfoundland Liberal Member of Parliament, George Baker (Gander–Grand Falls).

THE DAY OF STRIKE AND ACTION

While there is some disagreement about the actual number of participants on January 25, 1995, what cannot be disputed is that students, as well as members of trade unions and community groups, organized an impressive and highly successful mobilization. In over fifty-two cities in every province and in the Yukon (Audet 1995: 3) from at least seventy university and college campuses outside Quebec, and from virtually every post-secondary institution across Quebec, and with participation from thousands of high-school students despite threats of discipline (Helm 1995: A1; *Vancouver Sun*, January 26, 1995: A2; Konschuk 1995; Tye 1995: 1) students boycotted class, marched, demonstrated, rallied, organized forums, leafleted, blocked highways and in some cases conducted full-fledged strikes (Caron 1995; Clairmont 1995; Nielson 1995; Fong 1995: A1). Eyewitness and media reports from cities such as Kamloops, Kelowna, Nanaimo, Nelson, Prince George, Vernon, Calgary, Edmonton, Regina, Saskatoon, Brandon, Guelph, Peterborough, Ottawa, Edmunston, Moncton and Shippagan described participation in the hundreds and in some cases over a thousand. Media and eyewitness reports from Victoria, Vancouver, Toronto, Corner Brook and St. John's described participation well into the thousands.[6]

The largest demonstration that day was probably in Montreal, where eyewitnesses estimated as many as 12,000 and 15,000 students (Roy 1995: B6; Helm 1995: A3; Moore 1995: A3), both francophone and anglophone (with huge contingents from the CEGEPs and with participants from McGill University), peacefully zigzagged through several blocks of the downtown core singing, banging drums, chanting, carrying banners and placards and shouting slogans in English and French denouncing neoliberalism, poverty and debt and ridiculing Axworthy's proposals to cut social programs. One of the chants declared: "On ne veut pas d'abris fiscaux, on veut des programmes sociaux!" ("we don't want tax shelters, we want social programs"). [7] One of the placards read "endiguons le néo-liberalism" ("Stop neoliberalism") and another announced "non à l'apauvrissement" ("no to povertization") (*Voir*, January 26–February 1, 1995). The magnitude of the demonstration impressed even the Montreal Urban Community's police spokesperson Raymond Labelle, who admitted that "it has been a long time since we have had such a large demonstration" (Moore 1995: A1). In the midst of the demonstration, in response to questions from reporters, Coalition X spokesperson Marie-Claude Ricard claimed that all of Quebec's post-secondary institutions were participating, and another spokesperson Pierre Tadros remarked: "J'ai des nouvelles pour vous: le mouvement étudiant est en marche!" [I have news for you: the student movement is mobilized!] (Roy 1995: B6). Michel Pelletier, a member of Solidarité Populaire Québec, expressed the anti-neoliberal political values of the mobilization when he stated that it was "unfair for the government to unload its debt upon the financially disadvantaged" and that "students, minorities and the poor in general will suffer as a result" of Axworthy's reforms. Another student remarked: "The tuition hikes will make the universities into elite institutions for the rich and I think this is immoral" (Milloy and Low 1995: 6–7).

The day's events were reported live on radio and television in local and regional reports all over Canada, and it was the lead story on several national television and radio flagship newscasts. The following day the event was widely reported in almost every daily newspaper in Canada. The student protests in some cases constituted the lead print editorial, they were featured as the first item on national television and radio news, and the issue of student debt and the high cost of education became the central focus of public debate. The national media, which a year earlier had dutifully reported a "consensus" between "the political left and right" over the Axworthy reforms (Philp 1994: A1–A4) woke up to the crisis in post-secondary education and documented an astonishing pan-Canadian student "résistance" (Monpetit 1995b: A1, A3).

ASSESSING THE DAY OF STRIKE AND ACTION

In assessing the pan-Canadian mobilization of students, it could be described as a success in some respects, while in other respects it was a failure. Among the achievements, the National Day of Strike and Action improved the public profile of the CFS and certainly conferred upon the federation respect within the community of non-governmental organizations. The CFS mobilization also likely increased the federation's lobbying influence among provincial governments. Perhaps it is no coincidence that in succeeding years, and with subsequent demonstrations, several provinces froze tuition fees. The mobilization was also effective in improving membership retention and recruitment and in capturing the imagination of a new generation of student activists who were deeply inspired by the event, and by an understanding of its limitations, to organize a more fundamental "culture of resistance" (for example, Hudson et al. 1997: 7–8).

Another favourable outcome was the establishment of civil society solidarity between anglophones and francophones within Quebec, and between Québécois and Canadians outside Quebec. Because Quebec-based groups were so successful in building alliances with non-governmental organizations in the rest of Canada, and against the federal government, this social solidarity was a critically important reason why the government of Canada abandoned its proposed reforms, including its most contentious aspect, the ICRP.[8] And stopping Axworthy's plan to implement the ICRP is perhaps the most important tangible outcome of the mobilization. On January 31, 1995, less than one week following the National Day of Strike and Action the lead headline of the *Globe and Mail* announced that "Social reforms take a back seat" and Axworthy conceded that "there is no consensus" for "his idea for income-contingent loans." Reporter Edward Greenspon noted that in the four months since Axworthy introduced his discussion paper "nothing has consumed as much time and political energy" as "his controversial scheme to overhaul post-secondary education funding." He continued: "Now, he is showing signs that the idea is all but dead, repeatedly referring to the proposal in the past tense…." Greenspon suggested that the idea's "death knell" may be partly attributed to "the resistance of university administrators, faculty and students" (Greenspon 1995b: A1, A3). A further testament to the success of the mobilization was *The Globe and Mail* editorial of May 17, 1995, which declared "the failure of Mr. Axworthy's comprehensive reforms" (*Globe and Mail*, May 17 1995: A20).

On the other hand, while the mobilization may have brought about some tangible success, it ultimately failed to hinder the Chrétien government's broader long-term neoliberal agenda, including the sweeping cuts to social programs. In the 1995 federal budget, the government scrapped the EPF and the Canada Assistance plan, replacing it with a new block funding regime known as the Canada Health and Social Transfer — a system in which

THE CANADIAN STUDENT MOVEMENT AND ... - 237 -

Ottawa would exercise no control over how the transfers would be spent. In doing so, the government implemented the much-anticipated cuts to post-secondary education, by $2.786 billion in 1996–97 and $1.8 billion in 1997–98, totalling $4.586 billion.

CONCLUSION: SOME LESSONS ABOUT COLLECTIVE ACTION

There are a number of important lessons about collective action that can be learned from the January 25 National Day of Strike and Action. One is that democratic and non-violent forms of civil disobedience, such as demonstrations with widespread public participation, can succeed in shaping public policy. The January 25, 1995, *Globe and Mail* editorial therefore misjudged the importance of the mobilization in the federal government's decision to unconditionally abandon key elements of Axworthy's reforms. In this respect, the significance of this example of non-violent civil disobedience should not be underestimated or neglected. The movement undermined the legitimacy and the authority of a powerful senior cabinet minister in the early mandate of a new majority government. In so doing, it thereby illustrated the legitimacy, utility and power of a mobilized independent civil society. Indeed, the National Day of Strike and Action heralded and helped spark a new resurgence of student activism and broader citizen engagement, given that many of the January 25 student and trade union participants went on to organize other major protests that were important political events in the final decade of the twentieth century. In this respect, the ramifications of the strike were remarkable. Less than eleven months later, the labour movement in Ontario launched a series of rotating city-wide strikes known as the Ontario Days of Action. In the fall of 1996 in Quebec CEGEP student activists organized widespread occupations and strikes. In 1997 in British Columbia, students organized the well-known protests against the Asia Pacific Economic Cooperation summit in Vancouver. Some January 25 protestors also actively participated in the famous November 1999 demonstrations against the World Trade Organization in Seattle. Many others went on to successfully organize demonstrations at the 2001 Quebec City Summit of the Americas opposing a Free Trade Area of the Americas.

Another lesson about collective action emerging from this protest movement relates to the conventional distinction between new and old social movements, or the distinction between struggles over distribution and struggles over recognition. Numerous explanations have been suggested for the rise in protest movements in advanced industrial states. Among the varieties of opinion, there is a well-known thesis about "post-materialism." In 1996, Neil Nevitte offered such an explanation for "surging interest group activism." In *The Decline of Deference* he claims that the "new forms of protest" of the post 1960s era are "qualitatively different" from earlier ones in three important respects: they involve "different kinds of issues," they attract "different kinds of actors" and they involve the use of "different strategies of political action" (Nevitte 1996: 84). Nevitte argued that new protests focus less on redistributing wealth and instead emphasize "quality of life" issues. Second, he argued that the ranks of new protest movements "are not filled with those who suffer from any personal deprivation" but "an educated new middle class who are typically well-off." Finally he claimed that unlike the spontaneous uprisings typical of old, new protests rely on a more deliberate array of political tactics, including media campaigns designed to mobilize public opinion, and the formation of new political parties. Nevitte's thesis is that the values of the "new politics" place less emphasis on "material-ism," which is to say physical and economic security and group solidarity. Instead, they place greater importance on "post-materialism" which means "individualization," "individual freedom," "quality of life," "self actualization," "inner goals" and "a humanistic critique of the prevailing system and the dominant culture" (85). Nevitte concludes that "those with post-materialist orientations" are "no longer preoccupied with material security and instead give priority to aesthetic and intellectual needs and the need for belonging (2).

It is necessary to clarify that Nevitte's study examined the period 1981–90, and he makes no reference whatsoever to student protests or the principles of the student movement. Rather, he considers how new social movements promote a variety of goals ranging from "environmental protec-tion, peace, human rights and women's issues to animal rights" (85). Nevitte's claim is that post-materialism is "the best single predictor of support for all these movements" (87) and this is particularly true among people under forty-five years old, whereas older people were more likely to be materialists. He concludes that by 1990 "a general value shift towards post-materialism took place in all the advanced industrial states, including Canada" and this value shift does "appear to be linked to intergenerational change" (32).

There are four reasons why Nevitte's form of analysis has very limited capacity in explaining the January 25 movement. First, if Nevitte's typology were the only available language of explanation we would have to conclude that January 25 resembles exclusively an old materialist movement, and not a post-materialist new one, primarily based on the issues articulated and actors involved. As I have explained in great detail, the issues cannot be character-ized as post-materialist. In denouncing the government's neoliberal agenda, its attempts to deregulate, privatize and cut social programs, the foundational values of this movement were the distinctly "old" politics of wealth redistri-bution, economic security and social solidarity. Furthermore, the actors did not resemble Nevitte's post-materialist typology. Lloyd Axworthy tried to portray his opponents all along as "pampered and privileged" (Greenspon 1994: A3) but students rejected this post-materialist description. The par-ticipants of this movement, and their supporters, rejected any suggestion whatsoever that they were elites or that they represented such interests. Like the "old protest movements" the ranks of the January 25 mobilization were filled not with a "new middle class who are typically well-off" as Nevitte's typology suggests, but in fact included organized labour, the unemployed, anti-poverty organizations, seniors and students who did in fact suffer from "personal deprivation." Moreover, many participants who did not suffer such deprivations expressed concern that the reforms would hurt the poor more than anyone else.

Second, because it obliges us to accept an historical transition from distribution to recognition, the post-materialist thesis would make sense only by either ignoring the particular distributive aspects of the January 25 protest or recasting these aspects in post-materialist terms. It would force us in other words to see the goals of the movement exclusively in terms of recognition rather than as a struggle for social and democratic rights. Third, Nevitte's more fundamental claim that post-materialism is the dominant value type among young people is rendered problematic when we consider the self-described goals and values championed by the participants of the January 25 mobilization.

Finally, the post-materialist thesis prevents us from understanding James Tully's observation that there is not an historical transition from distribution to recognition or *vice versa* because the two are internally related. He claims that issues of distribution and recognition should be seen as "aspects" of political struggles, rather than distinct types of struggle, "and thus a form of analysis is required that has the capacity to study political struggles under both aspects." Tully's aspectival approach offers such analytical complexity. It permits the view that both distribution and recognition may be present, and it allows us to see that "citizens engaged in political struggles may place more emphasis on one aspect than another at specific times and political scientists and theorists may do the same" (Tully 2000: 469–70).[9]

By abandoning the post-materialist thesis and its analytical limitations and by adopting a richer aspectival form of analysis that surveys the particular details of events, a complex picture of this protest movement and its distributive principles come to light. Few would deny that the participants of this movement felt a powerful sense of belonging. This and other forms of recognition were important aspects of this struggle. But to characterize the January 25 movement exclusively in such post-materialist terms would be to simply ignore certain facts of the matter. The January 25, 1995, National Day of Strike and Action was a self-described movement against debt and poverty, against privatization, deregulation and deficit reduction. The issues of distribution must therefore be seen as critically central aspects of this protest. All along the way the participants of this mobilization emphasized their aims in very clear redistributive terms as a movement in opposition to neoliberalism. In any case, January 25, 1995, constitutes a highly significant protest movement in Canadian history, worthy of further study. As a social movement, the student movement behind the January 25 protest would inspire a new generation of activists, many of whom continue today to defend and promote a broad progressive agenda of equity and social justice.

PRIMARY SOURCES AND NEWSPAPER ARTICLES

Audet, Brigitte. 1995. "Students' plight raised in house." *Whitehorse Star*. January 25.

Brandon Sun. 1995. "On the March" January 26.

Canada, Human Resources Development (HRD). 1994a. *Improving Social Security in Canada: A Discussion Paper*. Ottawa: Minister of Supply and Services Canada. October.

_____. 1994b. *Improving Social Security in Canada — Federal Support to Post-Secondary Education: A Supplementary Paper*. Ottawa: Minister of Supply and Services Canada. October.

Canada. 1994. "Lloyd Axworthy announces strategy for Social Security reform" *News Release*, with Backgrounder #1, "Why Social Security Reform" and Backgrounder #2 "The Process and Timetable" Ottawa: January 31.

Canada, Standing Committee on Human Resources Development (HRD). 1994c. "Consultation Process." Ottawa: October.

Canadian Federation of Students (CFS). 1994a. "Lobby Report. March 29."

_____. 1994b. Minutes: Semi-Annual General Meeting. May.

_____. 1994c. "Lifelong Learning, or Lifelong Debt?" *A Brief Submitted to the House of Commons Standing Committee on Human Resources Development*. November 4.

_____. 1994d. Minutes: Annual General Meeting. November.

_____. 1994e. "The Canadian Federation of Students Sets a Date for a National Day of Strike and Action." *Press Advisory*. November 14.

_____. 1994f. "Taking it to the Streets: Students Vote to Strike." *News Release*. November 15.

_____. 1994g. "CFS Member Locals Meet with Axworthy." *Membership Advisory*. November 21.

_____. 1994h. "Countdown." *The Strike and Action Update* No. 1, November 30.

_____. 1995. "Lobbying Report #16 (November 16, 1994)." Report of the National Chairperson — National Executive Meeting. Ottawa: Jan. 6–8.

Carlisle, Derek. 1994. "Government Relations Coordinator Report." Canadian Federation of Students. September.

Caron, Guy. 1994. "Speech Given at the Press Conference on October 12 (re: Strike)." Report of the National Chairperson — Canadian Federation of Students Annual General Meeting. November 9–14, 1994, Ottawa: 12–13.

Caron, Régys. 1995. "Grève d'un jour dans deux cégeps." *Le journal de Québec* (Quebec City). January 26.

Carrière, Louise. 1994. "The Social Security Review." *The Student Advocate*. Ottawa: Canadian Federation of Students, 3, 1 (Fall).

Clairmont, Susan. 1995. "400 Trent students march." *Peterborough Examiner*. January 26.

Council of Ontario Universities (COU), Ontario Ministry of Education and Training, Association of Colleges of Applied Arts and Technology of Ontario, Association of Universities and Colleges of Canada, and Government of Canada. 1995. *Final Report of the Income-Contingent Repayment Plan Symposium.* Toronto: Queen's Printer for Ontario.

Duncan, Caryn. 1992. *Compromising Access: A Critical Analysis of Income-contingent Loan and Post-secondary Education Funding Schemes.* Ottawa: Canadian Federation of Students.

_____. 1994. "The Income Contingent Loan and University Funding Scheme: Why This Is not the Solution for Canada." A speech given at McMaster University. Hamilton, ON: Canadian Federation of Students, February 11.

Ferguson, Derek. 1994. "40,000 students urged to 'strike.'" *Toronto Star.* October 13.

Fisher, D. et al. 2005. "Canadian Federal Policy and Post-Secondary Education." *Alliance for International Higher Education Policy Studies.* August. Available at <http://www.nyu.edu/iesp/aiheps/research.html> (accessed on July 18, 2007).

Fong, Petti. 1995. "Education Cutbacks: Students rally to teach Axworthy a lesson." *Vancouver Sun.* January 26.

Francis, Dave. 1995. "Moncton students protest proposed funding reforms." *Times-Transcript.* January 26.

Globe and Mail. 1994. "Protest." November 17.

_____. 1995. "As Mr. Axworthy fades away." May 17.

_____. 1995. "Equity and Education." Editorial. January 25.

Graefe, Peter. 1994. "12,000 students march on Parliament." *McGill Daily.* November 21.

Greenspon, Edward. 1994. "Elites ought to pay, Axworthy says." *Globe and Mail.* November 16.

_____. 1995a. "Axworthy tries to raise social debate's tone." *Globe and Mail.* January 13.

_____. 1995b. "Social reforms take a back seat." *Globe and Mail.* January 31.

Handschuh, Darren. 1995. "Students take to the streets: More than 100 college students gather to protest proposed tuition hikes, cutbacks." *Vernon Daily News.* January 26.

Helm, Denise. 1995. "Sea of Students in Victoria: Rally Day 'just the beginning.'" *Times Colonist* (Victoria, B.C.). January 26.

Ivens, Andy. 1995. "Angry students fight cuts: Thousands rally against Ottawa's looming axe." *The Province.* January 26.

Konschuk, Tracy. 1995. "Students walk out in protest of federal cuts." *Nelson Daily.* January 26.

L'Acadie Nouvelle. 1995. "1500 étudiants de l'U de M manifestent leur inquiétude." January 26.

La Presse. 1994. "Une pluie d'oeufs accueille le ministre." November 17.

Le Devoir. 1995. "La résistance étudiante." January 26.

Lévesque, Lia. 1995. "Contre la réforme Axworthy: Universitaires et Cégépiens descendent dans las rue." *Le Journal de Montréal.* January 26.

Liberal Party of Canada. 1993. *Creating Opportunity: The Liberal Plan for Canada.* Ottawa.

Marshall, Andy. 1995. "Proposal fuels student ire." *Calgary Herald.* January 26.

Martin, Paul. 1995. "The Canadian Experience in Reducing Budget Deficits and Debt." Budget Deficits and Debt: Issues and Options: A symposium sponsored by the Federal Reserve Bank of Kansas City, Jackson Hole, Wyoming, August 31–September 2, 203-225. Available at <http://www.kc.frb.org/PUBLICAT/

SYMPOS/1995/Sym95prg.htm> (accessed July 18, 2007).

McMartin, Pete. 1994. "Angry protesters take over hearing on social services as MPs give way." *Vancouver Sun*. November 17.

McRae, Allan. 1995. "UCC students, staff battle planned cuts." *Kamloops Daily News*. January 26.

Milloy, M.J., and Jessica Low. 1995. "Eclectic marchers unite: Unions and community groups demonstrate with students." With Aubrey Cohen and Kabir Ravindra. "Commentaries." *McGill Daily Culture*. January 26–February 11.

Montpetit, Caroline. 1995b. "Devoir de résistance." *Le Devoir*. January 26.

_____. 1995a. "Les étudiants manifestent dans vingt villes canadiennes." *Le Devoir*. January 25.

Moore, Lynn. 1995. "Students crowd streets to oppose funding plan." *The Gazette* (Montreal). January 26.

Murray, Caroline. 1995. "Students join nation-wide strike." *Star Daily* (Whitehorse, Yukon). January 25.

Nielsen, Jens. 1995. "Ottawa gets blasted for education plans." *Star Phoenix* (Saskatoon, Sask.). January 26.

O'Brien, Mike. 1995. "U of R hit by strike." *Leader Post* (Regina, Sask.). January 26.

Ohler, Shawn. 1995. "250 Students protest cuts: Rowdy crowd slams federal Liberals, appeals for provincial support." *Edmonton Journal*. January 26.

Ontario, Ministry of Colleges and Universities. 1984. *Ontario Universities: Options and Futures* (Bovey Commission). The Commission on the Future Development of the Universities of Ontario. Toronto, December 12.

Philp, Margaret.1994. "Consensus growing for social-policy reform." *Globe and Mail*. January 25.

Roy, Paul.1995. "Des milliers d'étudiants manifestent à Montréal contre la réforme Axworthy." *La Presse*. January 26.

Smith, Stuart L. 1991. *Report: Commission of Inquiry on Canadian University Education* Ottawa: Association of Universities and Colleges of Canada.

Stager, D.A.A. 1989. *Focus on Fees: Alternative Policies for University Tuition Fees*, Toronto: Council of Ontario Universities, July.

The Province. 1994. "Protesters throw food." November 17.

_____. 1995. "Students in Revolt." January 26.

Tye, Dana. 1995. "Federal proposal for loan program raises fears." *Nanaimo Daily Free Press*. January 26.

Vancouver Sun. 1995. "Education Cutbacks: Students Rally to teach Axworthy a lesson." January 26.

Vila, Christine. 1994. "Student federation votes for national student strike." *McGill Daily*. November 23.

Voir. 1995. January 26–February 1.

Ward, Doug. 1994. "Campus boycott to protest reforms." *Vancouver Sun* and *Canadian Press*. October 13.

Westley, Dawn. 1994. "Parliament Hill faces student protest." *McGill Tribune*. November 22.

Wilton, Katherine.1995. "Traffic tied up tight." *The Gazette* (Montreal). January 26.

NOTES

1. For example, Caron rejected "these unjustified cuts... in the direction of less public involvement and to privatization." He also argued that with skyrocket-

ing debt-loads and employment uncertainties the proposals would undermine accessibility to education because "students from low-income backgrounds or even middle-class families... will think twice... before accepting such a heavy debt burden..." (Caron 1994).

2. Some reports estimated "twelve to fifteen thousand students from 45 universities and colleges." (Westley 1994: 1; Graefe 1994: 1) Photographs of the event were published in the *Globe and Mail* (November 17, 1994: A4) and on the cover page of *La Presse* (November 17, 1994: A1).

3. For example, there were guest appearances on such CBC radio programs as "The House" with Jason Moscovitz on October 15, 1994, and "Cross Country Check-Up," with Rex Murphy on November 20, 1994.

4. Four bilingual flyers were produced. A handbill entitled "ICLRPs and Student Debt Load" explained how income contingent loans would lead to higher debt. The handbill "ICLRP: A Bad Acronym, A Bad Program" outlined key criticisms of the plan. Another entitled "Schools are put on the market" critically examined vouchers. And "CSLP: Making a good thing better" addressed ways to improve the Canada Student Loans Program.

5. They included the following: step 1: create a strike committee; step 2: hold regular and open meetings; step 3: establish volunteer list for leafleting, and to staff information tables on campus; step 4: speak to classes to explain the social security review and its impact on students "to get reaction from them and to find out how they would like to be involved." Furthermore, "Find ways to motivate them to take action, spread the word..." (CFS 1994h).

6. For example, *Brandon Sun*, January 26, 1995: A1; *Francis* 1995; Handschuh 1995; *The Province*, January 26, 1995: A5; *L'Acadie Nouvelle*, January 26, 1995; Marshall 1995: A1; *McRae* 1995: A3; *Leader Post*, January 26, 1995: A1; O'Brien 1995: A1; *Vancouver Sun*, January 26, 1995: A1–A2.

7. Another chant demanded: "Des sous pour l'école, pas pour les monopoles!" (money for schools, not for corporations!) (Monpetit 1995: A1, A3). One of the songs satirically adapted "Oh Canada," as "Ô Axworthy. Videur de portefeuilles. Mauvaises réforme. Tu en feras ton deuil...." (Oh Axworthy, you clean out our wallets, your reforms are bad, and you're going to be sorry..." (Levesque 1995).

8. On January 13, 1995, the *Globe and Mail* reported that the Prime Minister's Office was "concerned about rocking the boat in Quebec... in the run up to the referendum on sovereignty." It noted: "What PMO officials especially want to avoid is a situation in which Quebec can itself build alliances with other provinces and interest groups to oppose Mr. Axworthy" (Greenspon 1995b: A4). And in a subsequent editorial the newspaper revealed that in February Axworthy "was talking less about real reform and more about the debt and national unity" suggesting that the government wanted to present "a deficit-cutting budget and fight the referendum before introducing social reform" (*Globe and Mail*, May 17, 1995: A20).

9. Tully sketched out this aspectival approach in a number of publications beginning with James Tully, *Strange Multiplicity: Constitutionalism in an Age of Diversity*, Cambridge: Cambridge University Press, 1995.

REFERENCES

Adams, Christopher. 1991. "The COR and Reform Parties: Locations of Canadian Protest Party Support." Paper presented to the Annual Canadian Political Science Association conference.

Agre, Philip E. 2002. "Real-Time Politics: The Internet and the Political Process." *The Information Society* 18, 5.

Allman, Paula. 2001a. *Critical Education Against Global Capitalism*. Westport, CT: Bergin and Garvey.

_____. 2001b. *Revolutionary Social Transformation: Democratic Hopes, Political Possibilities, and Critical Education*. Westport, CT: Bergin and Garvey.

Allyn, David. 2001. *Make Love, Not War: The Sexual Revolution, An Unfettered History*. New York: Routledge.

Anderson, James. 2002. "Questions of Democracy, Territoriality and Globalisation." In James Anderson (ed.), *Transnational Democracy: Political Spaces and Border Crossings*. Routledge: New York.

Angus, Ian. 1981. *Canadian Bolsheviks: The Early Years of the Communist Party of Canada*. Montreal: Vanguard Publications.

Ashcroft, Bill, Gareth Grifiths and Helen Tiffin. 2000. *Post-Colonial Studies: The Key Concepts*. London: Routledge Taylor and Francis Group.

Assembly of First Nations. 2005. "First Nations Education Action Plan." Assembly of First Nations (May 31).

Association of Canadian Community Colleges. 2005. *Meeting the Needs of Aboriginal Learners: Overview of Current Programs and Services, Challenges, Opportunities, and Lessons Learned, Final Report*. Ottawa, June.

Aunger, Edmund A. 1981. *In Search of Political Stability: A Comparative Study of New Brunswick and Northern Ireland*. Montreal: McGill University Press.

Avakumovic, Ian. 1975. *The Communist Party of Canada: A History*. Toronto: McClelland and Stewart.

Ayres, Jeffrey M. 1999. "From the Streets to the Internet: The Cyber-Diffusion of Contention." *The Annals of the American Academy of Political and Social Science*, 566 (November).

_____. 2001. "Transnational Activism in the Americas: The Internet and Mobilizing Against the FTAA." Paper presented to the annual meetings of the American Political Science Association, San Francisco, August 29–September 2.

_____. 2004. "Framing Collective Action Against Neoliberalism: The Case of the 'Anti-Globalization' Movement." *Journal of World-Systems Research* 10, 1.

Backhouse, Constance, and David H. Flaherty (eds.). 1992. *Challenging Times: The Women's Movement in Canada and the United States*. Montreal: McGill-Queen's University Press.

Bailey, Beth. 1998. "From Panty Raids to Revolution: Youth and Authority, 1950–1970." In Joe Austin and Michael Nevin Willard (eds.), *Generations of Youth: Youth Cultures and History in Twentieth-Century America*. New York: New York University Press.

Barnes, Samuel H., and Max Kaase. 1979. *Political Action: Mass Participation in Five Western Democracies*. London: Sage.

Barney, Darin. 2005. *Communication Technology*. Vancouver: UBC Press.

Barnsley, Paul. 2004. "Community Escapes Third Party." *Windspeaker* 21, 12 (March).

Bashevkin, Sylvia. 1998. *Women on the Defensive: Living through Conservative Times*. Toronto: University of Toronto Press.

Basque, Jean-Claude. 1992. "Une structure syndicale méconnue: les conseils de travail." *Égalité: revue acadienne d'analyse politique* 31 (Printemps).

Baum, Gregory, and Duncan Cameron. 1984. *Ethics and Economics: Canada's Catholic Bishops on the Economic Crisis*. Toronto: James Lorimer.

Beaudin, Michel. 1994. "They Persevered as Though They Saw the One Who Is Invisible." In Christopher Lind and Joseph Mihevc (eds.), *Coalitions for Justice*. Ottawa: Novalis, St. Paul University.

Behiels, Michael. 2004. *Canada's Francophone Minority Communities. Constitutional Renewal and the Winning of School Governance*. Montreal and Kingston: McGill-Queen's University Press.

Berkowitz, Sandra J. 2003. "Can We Stand with You? Lessons from Women in Black for Global Feminist Activism." *Women and Language* 26, 1.

Betcherman, Lita-Rose. 1982. *The Little Band: The Clashes Between the Communists and the Canadian Establishment, 1928–1932*. Ottawa: Deneau .

Beyerlein, Kraig, and John R. Hipp. 2006. "A Two-Stage Model for a Two-Stage Process: How Biographical Availability Matters for Social Movement Mobilization." *Mobilization: An International Journal* 11, 3.

Bibby, Reginald W. 1982. *The Precarious Mosaic: Intergroup Relations in the Canadian 80s*. Lethbridge, AB: University of Lethbridge Press.

Bissell, Claude. 1974. *Halfway Up Parnassus: A Personal Account of the University of Toronto, 1932–1971*. Toronto: University of Toronto Press.

Bleiker, Roland. 2002. "Activism after Seattle: Dilemmas of the Anti-globalization Movement." *Pacifica Review* 14, 3.

_____. 2005. "Seattle and the Struggle for a Global Democratic Ethos." In Catherine Eschle and Bice Maiguashca (eds.), *Critical Theories, International Relations and "The Anti-Globalisation Movement": The Politics of Global Resistance*. London: Routledge.

Blumer, Herbert. 1939. "Collective Behavior." In Robert E. Park (ed.), *Principles of Sociology*. New York: Barnes and Noble.

Boldt, Menno, and J. Anthony Long. 1988. "Native Indian Self-Government: Instrument of Autonomy or Assimilation?" In J. Anthony Long and Menno Boldt (eds.), *Governments in Conflict?* Toronto: University of Toronto Press.

Bonnet, Laura. 1996. "Building Brides and Expanding Expectations: The Work of the Canadian Institute for the Advancement of Women, 1976–1996." *Feminist Voices/Voix féministes* 1.

Bouzek, Donald (producer). 2005. *Building a Nation, the Back Row: Labour's Cold War*. Athabasca University/Access Television Network.

Breitkreuz, Rhonda S. 2005. "Engendering Citizenship? A Critical Feminist Analysis of Canadian Welfare-to-Work Policies and the Employment Experiences of Lone Mothers." *Journal of Sociology and Social Welfare* 32, 2.

British Columbia Ministry of Advanced Education. 2006. "Proposed Aboriginal Post-Secondary Education Strategy: Discussion Draft." Ministry of Advanced Education: Colleges and University Colleges Branch (March).

Brodie, Janine. 1995. *Politics on the Margins: Restructuring and the Canadian Women's Movement.* Halifax: Fernwood Publishing.

_____. 1998. "Restructuring and the Politics of Marginalization." In Caroline Andrew and Manon Tremblay (eds.), *Women and Political Representation in Canada.* Ottawa: University of Ottawa Press.

_____. 2002. "The Great Undoing: State Formation, Gender Politics, and Social Policy in Canada." In Catherine Kingfisher (ed.), *Western Welfare in Decline: Globalization and Women's Poverty.* Philadelphia, PA: University of Pennsylvania Press.

Brookfield, Stephen D. 2005. *The Power of Critical Theory: Liberating Adult Learning and Teaching.* San Francisco, CA: Jossey-Bass.

Browne, Craig. 2006. "Democratic Paradigms and the Horizons of Democratization." *Contretemps* 6.

Brownsey, Keith, and Michael Howlett. 1992. *The Provincial State: Politics in Canada's Provinces and Territories.* Toronto: University of Toronto Press.

Brunelle, Dorvalle, and Christian Deblock. 2000. *Les mouvements d'opposition à l'intégration par les marchés dans les Amériques: vers la constitution d'une Alliance sociale continentale.* Montréal: Groupe de recherche sur l'intégration continentale, Université du Québec à Montréal.

Brym, Robert J. 2001. *Society in Question: Sociological Readings for the 21st Century.* Third Edition. Scarborough, ON: Nelson Thompson Learning.

Burt, Sandra. 1997. "The Status of Women: Learning to Live Without the State." In Andrew Johnson and Andrew Stritch (eds.), *Canadian Public Policy: Globalization and Political Parties.* Toronto: Copp Clark.

Bush, Susannah. 2001. "Contradictions: The New Consultative Relationship between the Federal Government and National Women's Advocacy Organizations Operating in English-Canada." M.A. thesis, Carleton University.

Cairns, Alan C. 2000. *Citizens Plus.* Vancouver, BC: UBC Press.

Cañadell, Rosa M. 1993. "Chilean Women's Organizations: Their Potential for Change." *Latin American Perspectives* 20, 4.

Canadian Association of University Teachers, Commission on University Government in Canada. 1966. *Report.* Toronto: University of Toronto Press.

Canadian Taxpayer's Federation. 2003. "Increasing Accountability for Natives and Taxpayers." Available at: <www.taxpayer.com/main/news.php?news_id=337> (accessed November 30, 2003).

Carroll, William K., and R.S. Ratner. 1995. "Old Unions and New Social Movements." *Labour/Le Travail* 35 (Spring).

Carty, Victoria, and Jake Onyett. 2006. "Protest, Cyberactivism and New Social Movements: The Reemergence of the Peace Movement Post 9/11." *Social Movement Studies* 5, 3.

Cavanagh, John, Sarah Anderson and Karen Hansen-Kuhn. 2001. "Crossborder Organizing around Alternatives to Free Trade: Lessons from the NAFTA/ FTAA Experience." In Michael Edwards and John Gaventa (eds.), *Global Citizen Action.* Boulder, CO: Lynne Rienner .

Cavanagh, John, and Jerry Mander (eds.). 2004. *Alternatives to Economic Globalization:*

A Better World is Possible. Second Edition. San Franscico, CA: Berrett-Koehler .

Chovanec, Donna M. 1994. "The Experience of Consciousness-raising in Abused Women." MA thesis, University of Alberta, Edmonton, AB.

_____. 2004a. "Between Hope and Despair: Social and Political Learning in the Women's Movement in Chile." Doctoral thesis, University of Alberta, Edmonton.

_____. 2004b. "Learning Power from the Margins: Analyzing Action and Reflection in a Social Movement." Proceedings of the Joint International Conference of the Adult Education Research Conference and the Canadian Association for the Study of Adult Education, University of Victoria, Victoria, BC.

_____. 2006. "Between Finding Ourselves and Losing Ourselves: The Consequences of Social Movement Participation." Proceedings of the Annual Conference of the Canadian Association for the Study of Adult Education, York University, Toronto, ON.

Chuchryk, Patricia M. 1989. "Feminist Anti-Authoritarian Politics: The Role of Women's Organizations in the Chilean Transition to Democracy." In Jane S. Jaquette (ed.), *The Women's Movement in Latin America: Feminism and the Transition to Democracy*. Boston: Unwin Hyman.

Clark, Ian. 2003. "Legitimacy in a Global Order." In David Armstrong, Theo Farrell and Bice Maiguashca (eds.), *Governance and Resistance in World Politics*. Cambridge: Cambridge University Press.

Clarke, Harold D., et al. 1996. *Absent Mandate: Canadian Electoral Politics in an Era of Restructuring*. Third Edition. Toronto: Gage Educational Publishing.

Comeau, Pauline, and Aldo Santin. 1990. *The First Canadians: A Profile of Canada's Native People Today*. Toronto, ON: James Lorimer.

Commission on the Government of the University of Toronto. 1970. *Toward Community in University Government: Report of the Commission on the Government of the University of Toronto*. Toronto: University of Toronto Press.

Connolly, William E. 1995. *The Ethos of Pluralization*. Minneapolis, MN: University of Minnesota Press.

Conway, Janet M. 2004. *Identity, Place, Knowledge: Social Movements Contesting Globalization*. Halifax: Fernwood.

Cormier, Michel, and Achille Michaud. 1992. *Richard Hatfield: Power and Disobedience*. Fredericton: Goose Lane.

Corry, J.A. 1969. "University Government." *Queen's Quarterly* 76, 4.

Cortez Díaz, Aylen, and Milka Villagra Parra. 1999. "Imaginario y Prácticas Socio-Políticas delLas Mujeres Opositoras a la Dictadura Militar en Chile." Unpublished manuscript, Arica, Chile.

Crozier, M., S.H. Huntington and J. Watanuki. 1975. *The Crisis of Democracy*. New York: New York University Press.

Dalton, Russell. 2005. *Citizen Politics: Public Opinion and Political Parties in Advanced Industrial Democracies*. Fourth edition. New York: Seven Bridges Press.

Davidson, D.J., and W.R. Freudenburg. 1996. "Gender and Environmental Concerns: A Review and Analysis of Available Research." *Environmental Behaviour* 28.

Dawson, Michael, and John Bellamy Foster. 1998. "Virtual Capitalism: Monopoly Capital, Marketing, and the Information Highway." In Robert W. McChesney, Ellen Meiskins Wood and John Bellamy Foster (eds.), *Capitalism and the Information Age: The Political Economy of the Global Communication Revolution*. New York: Monthly Review Press.

de Sousa Santos, Boaventura. 2006. *The Rise of the Global Left: The World Social Forum and Beyond*. London: Zed Books.

de Vaney, Ann. 2000. "Technology in Old Democratic Discourses and Current Resistance Narrative: What is Borrowed? What is Abandoned? What is New?" In Ann de Vaney, Stephen Gance and Yan Ma (eds.), *Technology and Resistance: Digital Communications and New Coalitions Around the World*. New York: Peter Lang.

de Vaney, Ann, and Stephen Gance. 2000. "Introduction." In Ann de Vaney, Stephen Gance and Yan Ma (eds.), *Technology and Resistance: Digital Communications and New Coalitions Around the World*. New York: Peter Lang.

Dean, Mitchell. 1995. "Governing the Unemployed Self in Active Society." *Economy and Society* 24, 4.

_____. 2002. "Liberal Government and Authoritariansim." *Economy and Society* 31, 1.

della Porta, Donatella. 1992. "Political Socialization in Left Wing Underground Organizations." *International Social Movement Research* 4.

_____. 1999. "Protest, Protestors, and Protest Policing." In M. Guini, D. McAdam and Charles Tilly (eds.), *How Social Movements Matter*. Minneapolis, MN: Minnesota University Press.

della Porta, Donatella, Massimiliano Andretta, Lorenzo Mosca and Herbert Reiter. 2006. *Globalization from Below: Transnational Activists and Protest Networks*. Minneapolis, MN: Minnesota University Press.

deVries, Marten W. 1996. "Trauma in Cultural Perspective." In Bessel A. van der Kolk, Alexander C. McFarlane and Lars Weisaeth (eds.), *Traumatic Stress: The Effects of Overwhelming Experience on Mind, Body, and Society*. New York: Guilford Press.

Diefenbaker, John G. 1976. *One Canada: Memoirs of the Rt. Honourable John G. Diefenbaker, Volume II, Years of Achievement, 1957–1962*. Toronto: MacMillan of Canada.

Doucet, Marc G. 1999. "Standing Nowhere(?): Navigating the Third Route on the Question of Foundation in International Theory." *Millennium: Journal of International Studies* 28, 2.

_____. 2005a. "The Democratic Paradox and Cosmopolitan Democracy." *Millennium: Journal of International Studies* 34, 1.

_____. 2005b. "Territoriality and the Democratic Paradox: The Hemispheric Social Alliance and Its Alternatives for the Americas." *Contemporary Political Theory* 4, 3.

Drache, Daniel, and Duncan Cameron (eds.). 1985. *The Other Macdonald Report: The Consensus on Canada's Future that the Macdonald Commission Left Out* Toronto: James Lorimer.

Dryzek, John S. 2006. "Transnational Democracy in an Insecure World." *International Political Science Review* 27, 2.

Dyck, Noel. 1991. *What is the Indian "Problem"? Tutelage and Resistance in Canadian Indian Administration*. St. Johns, NF: ISER.

Dyck, Rand. 1996. *Provincial Politics in Canada*. Scarborough: Prentice-Hall.

Earl, Jennifer. 2007. "Where have all the protests gone? Online." *Washington Post*, February 4.

Edkins, Jenny. 1999. *Poststructuralism and International Relations*. Boulder, CO: Lynne Rienner.

Ellis, Lee C. 2002. "Ten Days for Global Justice: A Study of a Non-formal Approach to

Global Education in Alberta." PhD thesis, University of Alberta, Edmonton.

_____. 2006. "Adult education and social responsibility in a social movement: Ten Days for Global Justice." Proceedings of the Annual Conference of the Canadian Association for the Study of Adult Education. York University, Toronto ON.

Ericson, Richard, and Aaron Doyle. 1999. "Globalization and the Policing of Protest: The Case of APEC 1997." *British Journal of Sociology* 50, 4 (December).

Eschle, Catherine, and Bice Maiguashca (eds.). 2005. *Critical Theories, International Relations, and the "Anti-Globalization Movement": The Politics of Global Resistance.* London: Routledge.

Findlay, Sue. 1987. "Facing the State: The Politics of the Women's Movement Reconsidered." In Heather Jon Maroney and Meg Luxton (eds.), *Feminism and Political Economy.* Toronto: Methuen.

First Nations Education Steering Committee. 2005. *First Nations Post-Secondary Education Handbook for the BC Region With Reference to the National Post-Secondary Education Program Guidelines.* Vancouver, BC: First Nations Education Steering Committee.

Fiske, Jo-Anne. 1993. "Child of the State, Mother of the Nation: Aboriginal Women and the Ideology of Motherhood." *Culture* 10, 2/3.

Fitzpatrick, P.J. 1972. "New Brunswick: The Politics of Pragmatism." In Martin Robin (ed.), *Canadian Provincial Politics: The Party Systems of the Ten Provinces.* Scarborough: Prentice-Hall.

Flanagan, Tom. 2000. *First Nations? Second Thoughts.* Quebec: McGill-Queen's University Press.

Fleming, Berkeley, and Margaret Whitla (eds.). 1990. *So You Want Your Child to Learn French!* Second Revised Edition. Ottawa: Canadian Parents for French.

Fleras, Augie, and Jean Leonard Elliott. 1992. *The Nations Within: Aboriginal-State Relations in Canada, the United States, and New Zealand.* Toronto, ON: Oxford University Press.

Foley, Griff. 1999. *Learning in Social Action: A Contribution to Understanding Informal Education.* London: Zed Books.

Forbes, H.D. 1990. "Absent Mandate '88? Parties and Voters in Canada." *Journal of Canadian Studies* 25, 2 (Summer).

Foucault, Michel. 1978. *The History of Sexuality: An Introduction.* Volume 1. New York, NY: Vintage Books.

Fox, Jonathan A., and David L. Brown (eds.). 2000. *The Struggle for Accountability: The World Bank, NGOs, and Grassroots Movements.* Cambridge, MA: The MIT Press.

Frank, David. 2006. "Re-Connecting with History: A Community-University Research Alliance on the History of Labour in New Brunswick." *Labour: Studies in Working-Class History of the Americas* 3, 1 (Spring).

Fraser, Graham. 2006. *Sorry, I Don't Speak French: Confronting the Canadian Crisis that Won't Go Away.* Toronto: Douglas Gibson.

Freire, Paulo. 1970/1990. *Pedagogy of the Oppressed.* Myra Bergman Ramos, Trans. New York: Continuum.

_____. 1984. "Education, Liberation and the Church." *Religious Education* 79, 4.

Frideres, James S. 1998. *Aboriginal Peoples in Canada: Contemporary Conflicts.* Fifth Edition. Scarborough, ON: Prentice Hall Allyn and Bacon Canada.

Friedland, Martin L. 2002. *The University of Toronto: A History.* Toronto: University of Toronto Press.

Friedman, Milton. 1955 [1982]. "The Role of Government in Education." In Robert A.

Solo (ed.), *Economics and the Public Interest*. Westport, CT: Greenwood Press.

Gabriel, Ellen, and Beverly Jacobs. 2005. "Loss of Indian Status: A Foremost Aboriginal Issue." *Canadian Dimension* 39, 4.

Garland, David. 1997. "'Governmentality' and the Problem of Crime: Foucault, Criminology, Sociology." *Theoretical Criminology* 1, 2.

Gauchet, Marcel, Pierre Manent and Alain Finkielkraut. 2003. *La démocratie de notre temps*. Genève: Éditions du Tricorne.

Gehl, Lynn. 2004. "The Rebuilding of a Nation: A Grassroots Analysis of the Aboriginal Nation-Building Process." *Canadian Journal of Native Studies* 23, 1.

Gidengil, Elisabeth, Andre Blais, Neil Nevitte, Richard Nadeau. 2004. *Citizens*. Vancouver: UBC Press.

Gidney, Catherine. 2004. *A Long Eclipse: The Liberal Protestant Establishment and the Canadian University 1920–1970*. Montreal and Kingston: McGill-Queen's University Press.

Gitlin, Todd. 1987. *The Sixties: Years of Hope, Days of Rage*. New York: Bantam Books.

Gonick, Cy. 1975. *Inflation or Depression: The Continuing Crisis of the Canadian Economy*. Toronto: James Lorimer.

Goodwin, Jeff, James M. Jasper and Francesca Polletta. 2001. "Introduction: Why Emotions Matter." In Jeff Goodwin, James M. Jasper and Francesca Polletta (eds.), *Passionate Politics: Emotions and Social Movements*. Chicago: University of Chicago Press.

Goodwin, Jeff, and Steven Pfaff. 2001. "Emotion Work in High-risk Social Movements: Managing Fear in the U.S. and East German Civil Rights Movement." In Jeff Goodwin, James M. Jasper and Francesca Polletta (eds.), *Passionate Politics: Emotions and Social Movements*. Chicago: University of Chicago Press.

Gosse, Van. 2005. *Rethinking the New Left: An Interpretative History*. New York: Palgrave Macmillan.

Graham, John. 2000. "Getting the Incentives Right: Improving Financial Management of Canada's First Nations, Policy Brief No.8 — May 2000." Ottawa, ON: Institute on Governance.

Gramsci, Antonio. 1971. *Selections From the Prison Notebooks* (Quinton Hoare and Geoffrey Nowell Smith, Trans.). New York: International .

Green, Joyce. 2001. "Canaries in the Mines of Citizenship: Indian Women in Canada." *Canadian Journal of Political Science/Revue Canadienne de Science Politique* 34, 4.

Griffith, N.E.S. 1993. *The Splendid Vision*. Ottawa: Carleton University Press.

Guigni Marco, Marko Bandler and Nina Eggert. 2006. "The Global Justice Movement: How Far does the Classic Social Movement Agenda Go in Explaining Transnational Contention?" Geneva, Switzerland: United Nations Research Institute for Social Development, Civil Society and Social Movements Program.

Guno, Marcia. 1996. "In the Spirit of Sharing: Honouring First Nations Educational Experiences." MA dissertation, Department of Sociology and Anthropology. Simon Fraser University, Vancouver, B.C.

Gurr, Ted Robert. 1970. *Why Men Rebel*. Princeton: Princeton University Press.

Hacking, Ian. 1986. "Making Up People." In Thomas C. Heller, Morton Sosna and David E. Wellbery (eds), *Reconstructing Individualism: Autonomy, Individuality, and the Self in Western Thought*. Stanford, California: Stanford University Press.

Hall, Budd L. 2006. "Social Movement Learning: Theorizing a Canadian Tradition." In

Tara Fenwick, Tom Nesbit and Bruce Spencer (eds.), *Contexts of Adult Education: Canadian Perspectives*. Toronto: Thompson Educational Publishing.

Hall, Budd L., and Darlene Clover. 2005. "Social Movement Learning." In Leona M. English (ed.), *International Encyclopaedia of Adult Education*. New York: Palgrave.

Hall, Budd L., and Thomas Turay. 2006. *State of the Field Report: Social Movement Learning*. Vancouver, BC: University of British Columbia.

Hall, Michael H. 2001. "Measurement Issues in Surveys of Giving and Volunteering and Strategies Applied in the Design in Canada's National Survey of Giving, Volunteering, and Participating." *Nonprofit and Voluntary Sector Quarterly* 30, 3.

Hammerly, Hector. 1989. *French Immersion: Myths and Reality. A Better Classroom Road to Bilingualism*. Calgary: Detselig Enterprises.

Hannigan, John A. 1991. "Social Movement Theory and the Sociology of Religion: Toward a New Synthesis." *Sociological Analysis* 52, 4.

Harding, Jim. 2005. *Student Radicalism and National Liberation: Essays from the New Left Revolt in Canada — 1964–74. Vol.1: In the Throes of Change: Writings of Jim Harding*. Fort Qu'Appelle, SK: Crows Nest Publishing.

Hardt, Michael, and Antonio Negri. 2003. "Foreword." In William F. Fisher and Thomas Ponniah (eds.). *Another World is Possible: Popular Alternatives to Globalization at the World Social Forum*. Black Point, NS: Fernwood Publishing.

Harrison, Trevor. 2000. "The Changing Face of Prairie Politics: Populism in Alberta." *Prairie Forum* 25, 1 (Spring).

Hart, Mechtild. 1992. *Working and Educating for Life: Feminist and International Perspectives on Adult Education*. London: Routledge.

Hayday, Matthew. 2001. "Confusing and Conflicting Agendas: Federalism, Official Languages and the Development of the Bilingualism in Education Program in Ontario, 1970–1983." *Journal of Canadian Studies* 36, 1 (June).

_____. 2005. *Bilingual Today, United Tomorrow: Official Languages in Education and Canadian Federalism*. Montreal and Kingston: McGill-Queen's University Press.

Hébert, Karine. 2003. "Between the Future and the Present: Montreal University Student Youth and the Postwar Years, 1945–1960." In Michael Gauvreau and Nancy Christie (eds.), *Cultures of Citizenship in Post-War Canada, 1940–1955*. Montreal and Kingston: McGill-Queen's University Press.

_____. 2004. "Carabines, poutchinettes, co-eds ou freshettes sont-elles des étudiantes? Les filles à l'Université McGill et à l'Université de Montréal (1900–1960)." *Revue d'histoire de l'Amérique française* 57, 3 (hiver).

_____. 2005. "From Tomorrow's Elite to Young Intellectual Workers: The Search for Identity among Montreal Students, 1900–1958." In Bettina Bradbury and Tamara Myers (eds.), *Between Public and Private: Identity, Nation and Governance in Quebec*. Vancouver: UBC Press.

Hemispheric Social Alliance (HSA). 2002. *Alternatives for the Americas*. Available at <http://www.cptech.org/ip/ftaa/FTAAAlternative2003E.pdf> (accessed April 18, 2007).

Heron, Craig, (ed.). 1998. *The Workers' Revolt in Canada, 1917–1925*. Toronto: University of Toronto Press.

High, Steven. 2003. *Industrial Sunset: The Making of North America's Rust Belt, 1969–1984*. Toronto: University of Toronto Press.

Hiller, Harry H. 2006. *Canadian Society: A Macro Analysis*. Toronto, ON: Pearson Prentice Hall.

Holford, John. 1995. "Why Social Movements Matter: Adult Education Theory, Cognitive Praxis, and the Creation of Knowledge." *Adult Education Quarterly* 45, 2.

Holst, John D. 2002. *Social Movements, Civil Society, and Radical Adult Education*. Westport, CT: Bergin and Garvey.

hooks, bell. 1990. *Yearning: Race, Gender, and Cultural Politics*. Toronto: Between the Lines.

Horn, Michiel. 1999. "Students and Academic Freedom in Canada." *Historical Studies in Education* 11, 1.

Howard, Dick. 2002. *The Specter of Democracy*. New York: Columbia University Press.

Howlett, Dennis (ed.). 1996. *There ARE Alternatives: Education and Action Guide, Ten Days for World Development, February 9–19, 1996*. Toronto: Our Times.

Hudson, H., and T. Keefer, L. Rabkin and A. Thompson (eds.). 1997. *When Campus Resists: The Politics of Space, Power, and the Culture of Resistance in the Guelph Occupation Movement*. Guelph. ON: Occupation Press.

Hull, Jeremy. 2005. "Post-Secondary Education and Labour Market Outcomes Canada, 2001." Ministry of Indian and Northern Development. Ottawa, ON: Minister of Public Works and Government Services Canada. Available at <http://www.ainc-inac.gc.ca/pr/ra/pse/01/01_e.pdf> (accessed October 2007).

Igartua, José. 2006. *The Other Quiet Revolution: National Identities in English Canada, 1945-1971*. Vancouver: UBC Press.

INAC (Indian and Northern Affairs Canada). 2003. "Post-Secondary Education National Program Guidelines." November.

_____. 2005. "Evaluation of the Post-Secondary Education Program." Indian and Northern Affairs Canada Corporate Services: Department Audit and Evaluation Branch. Assisted by Hanson/McLeod Institute. June.

Inglehart, Ronald. 1990. *Culture Shift in Advanced Industrial Society*. New Jersey: Princeton University Press.

Inglehart, Ronald, and Pippa Norris. 2003. *Rising Tide: Gender Equality and Cultural Change Around the World*. New York: Cambridge University Press.

Inglehart, Ronald, and Christian Welzel. 2005. *Modernization, Cultural Change, and Democracy: The Human Development Sequence*. New York: Cambridge University Press.

International Forum on Globalization (IFG). 2002. *Alternatives to Economic Globalization: A Better World is Possible*. San Franscico, CA: Berrett-Koehler .

Jasper, James. 1997. *The Art of Moral Protest*. Chicago: University of Chicago Press.

Jenkins, J Craig. 1983. "Resource Mobilization Theory and the Study of Social Movements." *Annual Review of Sociology* 9.

Jenson, Jane, and Susan D. Phillips. 1996. "Regime Shift: New Citizenship Practices in Canada." *International Journal of Canadian Studies* 14.

Johnston, Hugh. 2005. *Radical Campus: Making Simon Fraser University*. Vancouver: Douglas and McIntyre.

Kahn, Richard, and Douglas Kellner. 2004. "Virtually Democratic: Online Communities and Internet Activism." In Andrew Feenberg and Darrin Barney (eds.), *Community in the Digital Age: Philosophy and Practice*. Toronto: Rowman and Littlefield.

Kastner, Andrea. 1994. "Social Theory and Epistemology in New Social Movements:

Implications for Adult Education." Proceedings of the 13th Annual Conference for the Canadian Association for the Study of Adult Education. Vancouver, BC: Simon Fraser University.

Kealey, Gregory. 1995. *Workers and Canadian History*. Montreal: Queen's-McGill University Press.

Keeter, Scott, Cliff Zukin, Molly Andolina and Krista Jenkins. 2002. *The Civic and Political Health of the Nation: A Generational Portrait*. College Park, MD: Center for Informational and Research on Civic Learning and Engagement.

Kniss, Fred, and Gene Burns. 2004. "Religious Movements." In David A. Snow, Sarah A. Soule and Hanspeter Kriesi (ed.), *The Blackwell Companion to Social Movements*. Oxford: Blackwell Publishing Limited.

Kostash, Myrna. 1980. *Long Way From Home: The Story of the Sixties Generation in Canada*. Toronto: James Lorimer.

Krause, Audrey. 1997. "The Online Activist: Tools for Organizing in Cyberspace." *Mother Jones* April 28.

Kriesi, Hanspeter, R. Koopmans, J.W. Duyvendak and M.G. Giugni. 1995. *The Politics of New Social Movements in Western Europe*. Minneapolis: University of Minnesota Press.

Kurlansky, Mark. 2004. *1968: The Year That Rocked the World*. New York: Ballantine Books.

Kutner, Laurie A. "Environmental Activism and the Internet." *Electronic Green Journal* 12. Available at <http://egj.lib.uidaho.edu/egj12/kutner1.html> (accessed March 17, 2005).

Kuumba, M. Bahati. 2001. *Gender and Social Movements*. Walnut Creek, CA: AltaMira Press.

Labelle, Gilles. 2003. "Maurice Merleau-Ponty et la genèse de la philosophie politique de Claude Lefort." *Politique et sociétés* 22, 3.

Laclau, Ernesto. 2001. "Democracy and the Question of Power." *Constellations* 8, 1.

Lambert, Wallace, and G.R. Tucker. 1972. *Bilingual Education of Children: The St. Lambert Experiment*. Rowley, MA: Newbury House.

Lanceley, Darlene. 1991. "The Post-Secondary Education Assistance Program for Indian Education: An Historical Overview, 1876 to 1977." In Terry Wotherspoon (ed.), *Hitting the Books: The Politics of Educational Retrenchment*. Toronto: Garamond Press.

_____. 1999. "Canadian Policy — First Nation Involvement in the Funding and the Politics of Post-Secondary Education: How Much is Enough?" In *Indigenous Education Around the World: Workshop Papers from the World Indigenous People's Conference: Education*. Available from Education Resources Information Centre (ERIC).

Lange, Elizabeth A. 2001. "Living Transformation: Beyond Midlife Crisis to Restoring Ethical Space." Doctoral thesis, University of Alberta, Edmonton, AB.

_____. 2004. "Transformative and Restorative Learning: A Vital Dialectic for Sustainable Societies." *Adult Education Quarterly* 54, 2.

Lansley, Renée N. 2004. "College Women or College Girls? Gender, Sexuality, and In Loco Parentis on Campus." PhD dissertation, Ohio State University.

Lather, Patti. 1991. *Getting Smart: Feminist Research and Pedagogy With/In the Postmodern*. New York: Routledge.

Lawrence, Bonita. 2003. "Gender, Race and the Regulation of Native Identity in Canada and the United States: An Overview." *Hypatia* 18:2.

_____. 2004. *"Real" Indians and Others: Mixed-Blood Urban Native Peoples and Indigenous Nationhood.* Vancouver: UBC Press.

Laycock, David. 1990. *Populism and Democratic Thought in the Canadian Prairies, 1910–1945.* Toronto: University of Toronto Press.

LeBon, Gustave. 1960 [1895]. *The Crowd.* New York: Viking Press.

Lefort, Claude.1989. *Democracy and Political Theory.* Trans. by D. Macey. Minneapolis, MN: University of Minnesota Press.

Lefort, Claude. 1999. *La complication: retour sur le communisme.* Paris: Fayard.

Lefort, Claude, and Marcel Gauchet. 1971. "Sur la démocratie: le politique et l'institution du social." *Textures* 3.

Levitt, Cyril. 1984. *Children of Privilege: Student Revolt in the Sixties, A Study of Student Movements in Canada, the United States, and West Germany.* Toronto: University of Toronto Press.

Lexier, Roberta. 2003. "Student Activism at the University of Saskatchewan, Regina Campus, 1961–1974." MA thesis, University of Regina.

Lind, Christopher, and Joseph Mihevc. 1994. *Coalitions for Justice.* Ottawa: Novalis, St. Paul University.

Lipsey, Richard G. 1977. "Wage-Price Controls: How To Do a Lot of Harm Trying to Do a Little Good." *Canadian Public Policy* III, 1 (Winter).

Long, J. Scott. 1997. *Regression Models for Categorical and Limited Dependent Variables.* Thousand Oaks, CA: Sage Publications.

Luke, Carmen, and Jennifer Gore (eds.). 1992. *Feminisms and Critical Pedagogy.* New York: Routledge.

Maaka, Rodger, and Augie Fleras. 2005. *The Politics of Indigeneity: Challenging the State in Canada and Aotearoa, New Zealand.* New Zealand: University of Otago Press.

Manley, John. 2002. "'Audacity, Audacity, Still More Audacity': Tim Buck, the Party, and the People." *Labour/Le Travail* 49.

Manuel, George, and Michael Poslums. 1974. *The Fourth World: An Indian Reality.* New York: Collier-Macmillan Canada.

Margolis, Michael, and David Resnick. 2000. *Politics as Usual: The Cyberspace "Revolution."* Thousand Oaks, CA: Sage.

Martel, Marcel. 2006. "'S'ils veulent faire la révolution, qu'ils aillent la faire chez eux à leurs risques et périls. Nos anarchistes maisons sont suffisants': occupation et répression à Sir George-William," *Bulletin d'Histoire Politique* 15, 1 (automne).

Martin, Geoffrey R. 1998. "We've Seen it All Before: The Rise and Fall of the New Brunswick Confederation of Regions Party, 1988–1995." *Journal of Canadian Studies* 33, 1 (Winter).

Marwick, Arthur. 1998. *The Sixties: Cultural Revolution in Britain, France, Italy, and the United States, c.1958–c.1974.* Oxford: Oxford University Press.

Marx, Gary T., and Douglas McAdam. 1994. *Collective Behavior and Social Movements: Process and Structure.* Englewood Cliffs, NJ: Prentice Hall.

Maslove, Allan M., and Gene Swimmer. 1980. *Wage Controls in Canada, 1975–78: A Study of Public Decision Making.* Montreal: Institute for Research on Public Policy.

Massicotte, Marie-Josée. 2004. "Forces d'émancipation et démocratie participative dans les amériques: un regard sur l'Alliance sociale continentale." *Politique et sociétés* 23, 2–3.

Massolin, Philip A. 2001. "Modernization and Reaction: Postwar Evolutions and the

Critique of Higher Learning in English-Speaking Canada, 1945–1970." *Journal of Canadian Studies* 36, 2 (Summer).

Matthew, Nathan. 2001. "First Nations Education Financing." First Nations Education Finance Paper: First Nations Education Steering Committee.

McAdam, Doug. 1982. *Political Process and the Development of Black Insurgency, 1930–1970*. Chicago: University of Chicago Press.

_____. 1986. "Recruitment to High-Risk Activism: The Case of Freedom Summer." *American Journal of Sociology* 92 (July).

_____. 1992. "Gender as a Mediator of the Activist Experience: The Case of Freedom Summer." *American Journal of Sociology* 97, 5 (March).

_____. 1999. *Political Process and the Generation of Black Insurgency, 1930–1970*. Chicago: University of Chicago Press.

McAdam, Doug, Sydney Tarrow and Charles Tilly. 2001. *Dynamics of Contention*. Cambridge: Cambridge University Press.

McBride, Stephen. 1983. "Public Policy as a Determinant of Interest Group Behaviour: The Canadian Labour Congress' Corporatist Initiative, 1976–1978." *Canadian Journal of Political Science* 16, 3 (Spring).

McChesney, Robert W. 1998. "The Political Economy of Global Communication." In Robert W. McChesney, Ellen Meiskins Wood and John Bellamy Foster (eds.), *Capitalism and the Information Age: The Political Economy of the Global Communication Revolution*. New York: Monthly Review Press.

McCormack, Ross A. 1977. *Reformers, Rebels, and Revolutionaries: The Western Canadian Radical Movement, 1899–1919*. Toronto: University of Toronto Press.

McFarlane, Peter. 1993. *Brotherhood to Nationhood: George Manuel and the Making of the Modern Indian Movement*. Toronto, ON: Between the Lines.

McGrew, Anthony 1997. "Globalization and Territorial Democracy." In Anthony McGrew (ed.), *The Transformation of Democracy? Globalization and Territorial Democracy*. Cambridge: Polity Press.

McKay, Ian. 2005. *Rebels, Reds, Radicals: Rethinking Canada's Left History*. Toronto: Between the Lines.

McLean, C. Amie. 2007. "Indigenous Education and the Post-Secondary Student Support System: Colonial Governance, Neo-Liberal Imperatives, and Gendered Outcomes." MA dissertation, Department of Sociology and Anthropology, Simon Fraser University, Vancouver, BC.

McPhail, Clark, David Schweingruber and John D. McCarthy. 1998. "Policing Protest in the United States: 1960–1995." In Donatella della Porta and Herbert Reiter (eds.), *Policing Protest*. Minneapolis, MN: University of Minnesota Press.

Menard, Scott. 1995. *Applied Logistic Regression Analysis*. Thousand Oaks, CA: Sage Publications.

Mertes, Tom (ed.). 2004. *A Movement of Movements: Is Another World Possible?* London: Verso.

Mezirow, Jack. 1991. *Transformative Dimensions of Adult Learning*. New York: Jossey-Bass.

Miller, James Rodger. 2000. *Skyscrapers Hide the Heavens: A History of Indian-White Relations in Canada*. Toronto: University of Toronto Press.

Milne, William J. 1996. *The McKenna Miracle: Myth or Reality*. Toronto: University of Toronto Press.

Milner, J.B., Alwyn Berland and J. Percy Smith. 1968. "Report on Simon Fraser University by the Special Investigating Committee of the Canadian Association of University Teachers, February 9, 1968." *CAUT Bulletin* 16, 4 (April).

Mitchinson, Wendy. 1987. "Early Women's Organizations and Social Reform: Prelude to the Welfare State." In Allan Moscovitch and Jim Albert (eds.), *The Benevolent State: The Growth of Welfare in Canada.* Toronto: Garamond Press.

Mlacak, Beth, and Elaine Isabelle (eds.). 1979. *So You Want Your Child to Learn French! A Handbook for Parents.* Ottawa: Canadian Parents for French.

Moffat, Jeanne. 1994. "Ten Days for World Development." In Christopher Lind and Joseph Mihevc (eds.), *Coalitions for Justice.* Ottawa: Novalis, St. Paul University.

Morris, Aldon, and Naomi Braine. 2001. "Social Movements and Oppositional Consciousness." In Jane Mansbridge and Aldon Morris (eds.), *Oppositional Consciousness: The Subjective Roots of Protest.* Chicago: University of Chicago Press.

Morris, Marika. 1999. *The Other Side of the Story: A Feminist Critique of Canada's National Response to the UN Questionnaire on the Implementation of the Beijing Platform for Action.* Ottawa: Canadian Feminist Alliance for International Action.

Morrison, Joan, and Robert K. Morrison. 1987. *From Camelot to Kent State: The Sixties in the Words of Those Who Lived It.* New York: Times Books.

Mouffe, Chantal. 2000. *The Democratic Paradox.* London: Verso.

Moyano, Maria Jose. 1992. "Going Underground in Argentina: A Look at the Founders of a Guerilla Movement." *International Social Movement Research* 4.

Mudge, Stephanie L. 2003. "Are Education and Training the New Welfare State? The Content and Consequences of Changing Social Morality in the European Union and the United States." Paper submitted to The International Sociological Association Annual Meeting of the Research Committee on Poverty, Social Welfare and Social Policy, August 21–24 2003, University of Toronto.

Murdocca, Carmella. 2001. "Her Home is .ca: Feminist Post-ings On-line." In Lara Karaian, Lisa Bryn Rundle and Allyson Mitchell (eds.), *Turbo Chicks: Talking Young Feminisms.* Toronto: Sumach.

Napolean, Val. 2001. "Extinction by Number: Colonialism Made Easy." *Canadian Journal of Law and Society* 16, 1.

Näsström, Sofia 2003. "What Globalization Overshadows." *Political Theory* 31, 6.

National Indian Brotherhood. 1972. *Indian Control of Indian Education: Policy Paper.* Ottawa: National Indian Brotherhood.

Neatby, Nicole. 1997. *Carabins ou Activistes? L'idéalisme et la radicalisation de la pensée étudiante à l'Université de Montréal au temps du duplessisme.* Montreal and Kingston: McGill-Queen's University Press.

Nepstad, Sharon Erickson, and Christian Smith. 1999. "Rethinking Recruitment to High-Risk/Cost Activism: The Case of the Nicaragua Exchange." *Mobilization* 4, 1.

Neu, Dean, and Richard Therrien. 2003. *Accounting for Genocide: Canada's Bureaucratic Assault on Aboriginal People.* Black Point, NS: Fernwood Publishing.

Nevitte, Neil.1996. *The Decline of Deference* Peterborough, ON: Broadview Press.

Newman, Peter C. 1963. *Renegade in Power: The Diefenbaker Years.* Toronto and Montreal: McClelland and Stewart.

Nie, Norman H., Jane Junn and Kenneth Stehlik-Barry. 1996. *Education and Democratic Citizenship in American.* Chicago: University of Chicago Press.

Norrie, Kenneth, Douglas Owram and J.C. Herbert Emery. 2002. *A History of the Canadian Economy*. Third edition. Scarborough, ON: Nelson Thomson Learning.

Norris, Pippa. 2002. *The Democratic Phoenix: Reinventing Political Activism*. New York: Cambridge University Press.

Norris, Pippa, and Ronald Inglehart. 2004. *Sacred and Secular: Religion and Politics Worldwide*. New York: Cambridge University Press.

Norris, Pippa, Stefaan Walgrave and Peter Van Aelst. 2005. "Who Demonstrates?" *Comparative Politics* 37, 2.

Norton, Wayne, and Tom Langford. 2002. *A World Apart: The Crowsnest Communities of Alberta and British Columbia*. Kamloops, BC: Plateau Press.

Nunes Rodrigo 2005. "Nothing Is what Democracy Looks Like." In David Harvie, Keir Milburn, Ben Trott and David Watts (eds.), *Shut Them Down! The G8, Gleneagles 2005 and the Movement of Movements*. Leeds: Dissent! and Autonomedia.

Nye, Joseph, Philip Zelikow and David King. 1997. *Why People Don't Trust Government*. Cambridge, MA: Harvard University Press.

O'Brien, Robert, Anne Marie Goetz, Jan Aart Scholte and Marc Williams. 2000. *Contesting Global Governance: Multilateral Institutions and Global Social Movements*. Cambridge: Cambridge University Press.

OCAP (Ontario Coalition Against Poverty). 2004. "Article About Third World Conditions in Pikangikum First Nation." April 15. Available at <http://ocap.ca/node/128> (accessed December 2007).

Office of the Auditor General of Canada. 2003. "Report of the Auditor General of Canada to the House of Commons: Chapter 10; Other Audit Observations." Ottawa (November)

_____. 2004. "Report of the Auditor General to the House of Commons: Chapter 5; Indian and Northern Affairs Canada: Education Program and Post-Secondary Student Support." Ottawa (November).

_____. 2006. "Report of the Auditor General of Canada to the House of Commons: Chapter 5; Management of Programs for First Nations." Ottawa (November).

Olavarría, Margot. 2003. "Protected Neoliberalism: Perverse Institutionalization and the Crisis of Representation in Postdictatorship Chile." *Latin American Perspectives* 30, 6.

Oliver, Pamela E., and Daniel J. Myers. 2003. "Networks, Diffusion, and Cycles of Collective Action." In Mario Diani and Doug McAdam (eds.), *Social Movements and Networks: Relational Approaches to Collective Action*. Oxford: Oxford University Press.

Ollivier, Michèle, and Wendy Robbins. 1997. "Speaking of PAR-L." In Scarlet Pollock and Jo Sutton (eds.), *Virtual Organizing, Real Change: Women's Groups Using the Internet*. Available at <www.womenspace.ca> (accessed 25 September 2007).

_____. 1999. "Electronic Communications and Feminist Activism: The Experience of PAR-L." *Atlantis* 24, 1.

Ollivier, Michèle, Wendy Robbins, Diane Beauregard, Jennifer Brayton and Geneviève Sauvé. 2006. "Feminist Activists Online. Observations from Canada: A Study of the PAR-L Research Network." *Canadian Review of Sociology and Anthropology* 43, 4.

Ollivier, Michèle, Wendy Robbins, Jennifer Brayton and Genevieve Sauve. 2002. "The PAR-L Research Network: A Study of On-line Activism." Available at <www.unb.ca/par-l/strategies/no3> (accessed August 7, 2003).

Orloff, Ann. 1993. "Gender and the Social Rights of Citizenship: The Comparative

Analysis of Gender Relations and Welfare States." *American Sociological Review* 58, 3.

Ormiston, Alice. 2002. "Educating "Indians": Practices of Becoming Canadian." *Canadian Journal of Native Studies* 22, 1.

Owram, Doug. 1996. *Born at the Right Time: A History of the Baby Boom Generation.* Toronto: University of Toronto Press.

Pal, Leslie. 1993. *Interests of State. The Politics of Language, Multiculturalism and Feminism in Canada.* Montreal and Kingston: McGill-Queen's University Press.

Pampel, Fred C. 2000. *Logistic Regression: A Primer.* Thousand Oaks, CA: Sage Publications.

Panitch, Leo, and Donald Swartz. 2003. *From Consent to Coercion: The Assault on Trade Union Freedoms.* Third edition. Aurora, ON: Garamond Press.

Paquet, Gilles, and Robert Shepherd. 1996. "The Program Review Process: A Deconstruction." In Gene Swimmer (ed.), *How Ottawa Spends 1996–7: Life Under the Knife.* Ottawa: Carleton University Press.

Passy, Florence. 2003. "Social Networks Matter. But How?" In Mario Diani and Doug McAdam (eds.), *Social Movements and Networks: Relational Approaches to Collective Action.* Oxford: Oxford University Press.

Petrie, Michelle. 2004. "A Research Note on the Determinants of Protest Participation: Examining Socialization and Biographical Availability." *Sociological Spectrum* 24.

Phillips, Susan D. 1990. "Projects, Pressure and Perceptions of Effectiveness: An Organizational Analysis of National Canadian Women's Groups." Ph.D. thesis, Carleton University.

Pinard, Maurice. 1971. *The Rise of A Third Party: A Study in Crisis Politics.* Englewood Cliffs, NJ: Prentice-Hall.

Pitsula, James M. 2006. *As One Who Serves: The Making of the University of Regina.* Montreal and Kingston: McGill-Queen's University Press.

Pollock, Scarlett, and Jo Sutton. 1998. "Women Click: Feminism and the Internet." In Susan Hawthorne and Renate Klein (eds.), *CyberFeminism: Connectivity, Critique and Creativity.* Melbourne: Spinifex Press.

Pompana, Yvonne E. 1997. "Devolution to Indigenization: The Final Path to Assimilation of First Nations." MSW, Faculty of Social Work, University of Manitoba, Winnipeg.

Poyen, Janet McCrae. 1989. "Canadian Parents for French: A National Pressure Group in Canadian Education." MA dissertation, University of Calgary.

Pross, A. Paul. 1992. *Group Politics and Public Policy.* Second edition. Toronto: Oxford University Press.

Prozorov Sergei. 2005. "X/Xs: Toward a General Theory of the Exception." *Alternatives: Global, Local, Political* 30, 1.

Putnam, Robert D. 2001. *Bowling Alone.* New York: Simon and Schuster.

Putnam, Robert, Susan J. Pharr and Russell J. Dalton. 2000. "What's Troubling the Trilateral Democracies?" In Susan J. Pharr and Robert Putnam (ed.), *Disaffected Democracies: What's Troubling the Trilateral Countries?* Princeton, NJ: Princeton University Press.

R.A. Malatest and Associates Ltd. 2004. "Aboriginal Peoples and Post-Secondary Education: What Educators Have Learned." Montreal, QC: Canadian Millennium Scholarship Foundation.

Rainie, Lee, and John Horrigan. 2007. *Election 2006 Online.* Washington: The Pew

Research Center.

Ramsey, Bruce. 1990. *The Noble Cause: The Story of the United Mine Workers of America in Western Canada.* Calgary: District 18, United Mine Workers of America.

Rancière, Jacques. 1995. *On the Shores of Politics.* London: Verso.

_____. 2006. "Democracy, Republic, Representation." *Constellations* 13, 3.

Reed, Paul, and Kevin Selbee. 2000. "Distinguishing Characteristics of Active Volunteers in Canada." *Nonprofit and Voluntary Sector Quarterly* 29, 4.

_____. 2001. "The Civic Core in Canada: Disproportionality in Charitable Giving, Volunteering, and Civic Participation." *Nonprofit and Voluntary Sector Quarterly* 30, 4.

_____. 2002a. "Volunteers Are Not All the Same: Heterogeneity in the Voluntary Sector." Paper presented at the 31st ARNOVA Annual Conference, Montreal, QC, November 14–16.

_____. 2002b. "Is There a Distinctive Pattern of Values Associated with Giving and Volunteering? The Canadian Case." Paper presented at the 31st ARNOVA Annual Conference, Montreal, QC, November 14–16.

Regan Shade, Leslie. 2002. *Gender and Community in the Social Construction of the Internet.* New York: Peter Lang.

_____. 2004. "Gender and the Commodification of Community: Women.com and gurl. com." In Andrew Feenberg and Darin Barney (eds.), *Community in the Digital Age: Philosophy and Practice.* Toronto: Rowman and Littlefield.

Reitz, Jeffery, and Rupa Banerjee. 2007. "Racial Inequality, Social Cohesion and Policy Issues in Canada." Available at Institute for Research on Public Policy <http://www.irpp.org/indexe.htm> (accessed March 25, 2007).

Report of the Royal Commission on Aboriginal Peoples. 1996. "Chapter 9: The Indian Act." In "Part 2: False Assumptions and a Failed Relationship." In *Volume 1: Looking Forward, Looking Back.* Ottawa, ON: Ministry of Supply Services Canada. Available at <http://www.ainc-inac.gc.ca/ch/rcap/sg/cg9_e.pdf> (accessed October 2007).

Ricard, François. 1994. *The Lyric Generation: The Life and Times of the Baby Boomers.* Toronto: Stoddart Publishing.

Rosanvallon, Pierre. 2000. *La démocratie inachevée: Histoire de la souveraineté du peuple en France.* Paris: Édition Gallimard.

Rose, Nikolas. 1998. "Governing Risky Individuals: The Role of Psychiatry in New Regimes of Control." *Psychiatry, Psychology, and Law* 5, 2.

Ross, Robin. 1984. *The Short Road Down: A University Changes.* Toronto: University of Toronto Press.

Rossi, Dionysios. 2003. "Mountaintop Mayhem: Simon Fraser University 1965–1971." MA thesis, Simon Fraser University.

Rounce, Andrea. 2004. "Access to Post-Secondary Education: Does Class Still Matter?" Ottawa, ON: Canada: Canadian Centre for Policy Alternatives.

Ruhl, Lealle. 1999. "Liberal Governance and Prenatal Care: Risk and Regulation in Pregnancy." *Economy and Society* 28, 1.

Russell, Peter H. 1977. "The Anti-Inflation Case: The Anatomy of a Constitutional Decision." *Canadian Public Administration* 20, 4 (Winter).

Samuel, Alexandra. 2004. *Hacktivism and the Future of Political Participation.* Doctoral dissertation, Harvard University.

Sandberg, Don. 2005. "Accountability and Self-Rule: Expiry of an old Agreement Opens the Door to Accountability." *Winnipeg Free Press*, April 7.

Saskatchewan Indian. 1989. "Ottawa's Assault on First Nations Education." April

1989. Available at <www.sicc.sk.ca/saskindian/a89apr06.htm> (accessed October 2007).

Satzewich, Vic, and Terry Wotherspoon. 2000. *First Nations: Race, Class, and Gender Relations*. Regina, SK: Canadian Plains Research Centre.

Savage, Larry. 2001. "Disorganized Labour: Canadian Unions and Constitutional Reform." M.A. thesis, Brock University.

Sawer, Marian. 1996. *Femocrats and Ecorats: Women's Policy Machinery in Australia, Canada and New Zealand*. Geneva: UNDP.

Schissel, Bernard, and Terry Wotherspoon. 2003. *The Legacy of School for Aboriginal People: Education, Oppression, and Emancipation*. Don Mills, ON: Oxford University Press.

Schmitt-Boshnick, Margo. 1996. "Spaces for Democracy: Social Learning Within a Women's Collective." MA thesis, University of Alberta, Edmonton.

Scholte, Jan Aart. 2002a. "Civil Society and Democracy in Global Governance." *Global Governance* 8, 3.

_____. 2002b. "Civil Society Voices and the International Monetary Fund." Report Prepared for the North South Institute, Ottawa.

_____. 2004. "Democratizing the Global Economy: The Role of Civil Society." Centre for the Study of Globalisation and Regionalisation, University of Warwick.

Schuetze, Hans G., and William L. Day. 2001. "Post-Secondary Education in BC 1989–1998: The Impact of Policy and Finance On Access, Participation, and Outcomes." Vancouver, BC: University of British Columbia and the Centre for Policy Studies in Higher Education and Training.

Schussman, Alan, and Sarah Soule. 2005. "Process and Protest: Accounting for Individual Protest Participation." *Social Forces* 84, 2.

Schwartz, Midred A. 2006. *Party Movements in the United States and Canada: Strategies of Persistence*. Lanham, MD: Rowman and Littlefield.

Schweingruber, David. 2000. "Mob Sociology and Escalated Force: Sociology's Contribution to Repressive Police Tactics." *The Sociological Quarterly* 41, 3.

Scott, Anne. 2001. "(In)forming Politics: Processes of Feminist Activism in the Information Age." *Women's Studies International Forum* 24, 3/4.

Scott, Duncan Campbell. 1898. "The Onondaga Madonna." In Thomas Friedman (ed.), *Canadian Literature: Genre and History (2002)*. Kamloops, BC: UCC Print Services.

Scott, Sue M. 1992. "Personal Change Through Participation in Social Action: A Case Study of Ten Social Activists." *The Canadian Journal for the Study of Adult Education* 6, 2.

Scott-Dixon, Krista. 2001. "Girls Need E-Zines: Young Feminists Get On-line." In Lara Karaian, Lisa Bryn Rundle and Allyson Mitchell (eds.), *Turbo Chicks: Talking Young Feminisms*. Toronto: Sumach.

Seager, Allen. "Socialists and Workers: The Western Canadian Miners, 1900–1921." *Labour/Le Travail* 21.

Sen, Jai, Anita Anaud, Arturo Escobar and Peter Waterman (eds.). 2004. *The World Social Forum: Challenging Empires*. New Delhi: Viveka Foundation.

Shapiro, Andrew L. 1999. *The Control Revolution: How the Internet is Putting Individuals in Charge and Changing the World We Know*. New York: PublicAffairs.

Sharpe, Sydney, and Don Braid. 1992. *Storming Babylon: Preston Manning and the Rise of the Reform Party*. Toronto: Key Porter.

Simeon, Richard. 1972. *Federal-Provincial Diplomacy: The Making of Recent Policy in*

Canada. Toronto: University of Toronto Press.

Skocpol, Theda. 1985. "Bringing the State Back In: Strategies of Analysis in Current Research." In Peter B. Evans, Dietrich Rueschmeyer and Theda Skocpol (eds.), *Bringing the State Back In*. Cambridge: Cambridge University Press.

Slowey, Gabrielle A. 2001. "Globalization and Self-Government: Impacts and Implications for First Nations in Canada." *The American Review of Canadian Studies* 31, 1/2 (Spring/Summer).

Smith, Dennis. 1995. *Rogue Tory: The Life and Legend of John G. Diefenbaker*. Toronto: MacFarlane, Walter and Ross.

Smith, J. Percy. 1968. "Developments at Simon Fraser University." *CAUT Bulletin* 17, 1 (October).

Smith, Jackie. 2002. "Globalizing Resistance: The Battle of Seattle and the Future of Social Movements." In Jackie Smith and Hank Johnston (eds.), *Globalization and Resistance: Transnational Dimensions of Social Movements*. Lanham, MD: Rowman and Littlefield .

Smith, Linda Tuhiwai. 1999. *Decolonizing Methodologies: Research and Indigenous Peoples*. London: Zed Books.

Smith, Michel. 2000. "Looking Out for Our Indigenous People: The Canadian Experience." *Australian Journal of Public Administration* 59, 3 (Fall).

Smith, Miriam. 2005. *A Civil Society? Collective Actors in Canadian Political Life*. Peterborough, ON: Broadview Press.

Smith, Peter Jay, and Elizabeth Smythe. 2003. "This Is What Democracy Looks Like: Globalization, New Information Technology and the Trade Policy Process: Some Comparative Observations. *Perspectives on Global Development and Technology* 2, 2.

Snow, David, E. Burke Rochford, Steven Worden and Robert Benford. 1986. "Frame Alignment Processes, Micromobilization, and Movement Participation." *American Sociological Review* 51.

Spencer, Bruce. 1998. *The Purposes of Adult Education: A Guide for Students*. Toronto: Thompson Educational.

Stackhouse, John G. 1993. *Canadian Evangelicalism in the Twentieth Century*. Toronto: University of Toronto Press.

Staggenborg, Suzanne. 2001. "Beyond Culture versus Politics: A Case Study of a Local Women's Movement." *Gender and Society* 15, 4 (August).

Staggenborg, Suzanne, and Verta Taylor. 2005. "Whatever Happened to the Women's Movement?" *Mobilization: An International Journal* 10, 1.

Starr. Amory. 2005. *Global Revolt: A Guide to the Movements against Globalization*. London: Zed Books.

Statistics Canada. 1991. *Results of the 1991 National Census*. Ottawa: Government of Canada.

_____. 2006a. *Canadian Internet Use Survey*. Available at <www.statcan.ca/Daily/English/060815/d060815b.htm> (accessed August 18, 2006).

_____. 2006b. *Women in Canada, Fifth Edition: A Gender-Based Statistical Report*. Statistics Canada: Social and Aboriginal Statistics Division. Ottawa, ON: Ministry of Industry.

Stevenson, Winona. 1999. "Colonialism and First Nations Women in Canada." In Enakshi Dua and Angela Robertson (eds.), *Scratching the Surface: Canadian Anti-Racist Feminist Thought*. Toronto: Women's Press.

Stewart-Miller, Melanie. 1998. *Cracking the Gender Code: Who Rules the Wired World?*

Toronto: Second Story Press.

Stonechild, Blair. 2006. *The New Buffalo: The Struggle for First Nations Higher Education*. Winnipeg: University of Manitoba Press.

Suri, Jeremi. 2003. *Power and Protest: Global Revolution and the Rise of Détente*. Cambridge, MA: Harvard University Press.

_____ (ed.). 2007. *The Global Revolutions of 1968: A Norton Casebook in History*. New York: W.W. Norton.

Surman, Mark, and Darren Wershler-Henry. 2001. *Commonspace Beyond Virtual Community*. Toronto: FT.Com.

Sutton, Jo, Scarlett Pollock and Lynn Hauka. 2002. "Women, Communication Rights and the Internet." Report prepared for the United Nations expert meeting, Information and Communication Technologies and Their Impact on and Use as an Instrument for the Advancement and Empowerment of Women, Seoul, Republic of Korea, November 11–14.

Swain, Merrill. 1978. "French Immersion: Early, Late or Partial?" *Canadian Modern Language Review* 34, 3.

Tarrow, Sidney. 2005a. *Power in Movement: Social Movements and Contentious Politics*. Second edition. New York: Cambridge University Press.

_____. 2005b. *The New Transnational Activism*. Cambridge: Cambridge University Press.

Taylor, Verta. 1989. "Social Movement Continuity: The Women's Movement in Abeyance." *American Sociological Review* 54 (October).

Taylor, Verta, and Nancy Whittier. 1998. "Guest Editor's Introduction: Special Issue on Gender and Social Movements: Part I." *Gender and Society* 12, 6.

Teivainen, Teivo. 2002. "The World Social Forum and Global Democratisation: Learning from Porto Alegre." *Third World Quarterly* 23, 4.

_____. Forthcoming. *Democracy in Movement: The World Social Forum as a Process of Political Learning*. London: Routledge.

Thompson, John Herd, and Allen Seager. 1985. *Canada 1922–1939: Decades of Discord*. Toronto: McClelland and Stewart.

Thorburn, Hugh. 1985. *Interest Groups in the Canadian Federal System*. Toronto: University of Toronto Press.

Tilly, Charles. 1977. *From Mobilization to Revolution*. Reading, MA: Addison-Wesley.

_____. 2004. *Social Movements, 1768–2004*. Boulder, CO: Paradigm .

Tindall, D.B., Scott Davies and Celine Mauboules. 2003. "Activism and Conservation Behavior in an Environmental Movement: The Contradictory Effects of Gender." *Society and Natural Resources* 16, 10 (November).

Tossutti, L.S., and Mark Wang. 2006. "Family and Religious Networks: Stimulants or Barriers to Civic Participation and the Integration of Newcomers?" Paper presented to the 78th Annual Meeting of the Canadian Political Science Association, Toronto, Ontario, June 1–3.

Trudeau, Pierre Elliott. 1974 [1956]. *The Asbestos Strike*. James Boake, Trans. Toronto: James Lewis and Samuel.

Tully, James. 2000. "Struggles over Recognition and Distribution." *Constellations: An International Journal of Critical and Democratic Theory* 7, 4 (Fall).

Ullman, Stephen H. 1990. "Political Disaffection in the Province of New Brunswick: Manifestations and Sources." *American Review of Canadian Studies* 20, 2 (Summer).

Vahabzadeh, Peyman. 2007. "Globalization and the New Modes of Activism." *Labour/Le Travail* 59 (Spring).

Vair, George. 2006. *The Struggle against Wage Controls: The Saint John Story, 1975–1976.* St. John's, NF: Canadian Committee on Labour History.

Valdés, Teresa, and Marisa Weinstein. 1993. *Mujeres que Sueñan: Las Organizaciones de Pobladoras en Chile, 1973–1999.* Santiago, Chile: FLACSO-Chile.

Valenzuela, María Elena. 1991. "The Evolving Roles of Women Under Military Rule." In Paul W. Drake and Iván Jaksic (eds.), *The Struggle for Democracy in Chile, 1982–1990.* Lincoln, NE: University of Nebraska Press.

Van Aelst, Peter, and Stefaan Walgrave. 2001. "Who is that (wo)man in the street? From the normalisation of protest to the normalisation of the protester." *European Journal of Political Research* 39.

Verba, Sidney, Kay Lehman Schlozman and Henry E. Brady. 1995. *Voice and Equality: Civic Voluntarism in American Politics.* Cambridge, MA: Harvard University Press.

Verjee, Begum. 2003. "Towards an Aboriginal Approach to Culturally Appropriate Assessment Methodologies." Kwantlen University College, Diversity and Educational Consulting BSZ, Holdings Inc. April.

Vickers, Jill, Pauline Rankin and Christine Appelle. 1993. *Politics as if Women Mattered: A Political Analysis of the National Action Committee on the Status of Women.* Toronto: University of Toronto Press.

Waiser, Bill. 2003. *All Hell Can't Stop Us: The On-to-Ottawa Trek and Regina Riot.* Calgary: Fifth House.

Warkentin Craig. 2001. *Reshaping World Politics: NGOs, the Internet, and Global Civil Society.* Lanham, MD: Rowman and Littlefield.

Waylen, Georgina. 1993. "Women's Movements and Democratisation in Latin America." *Third World Quarterly* 14, 3.

Weldon, J.C. 1991. "Wage Controls and the Canadian Labour Movement." In Allen Fenichel and Sidney H. Ingerman (eds.), *On the Political Economy of Social Democracy: Selected Papers of J.C. Weldon.* Montreal: McGill-Queen's University Press.

Welton, Michael R. (ed.). 1995. *In Defense of the Lifeworld: Critical Perspectives on Adult Learning.* Albany, NY: SUNY Press.

Welzel, Christian, Ronald Inglehart and Franziska Deutsch. 2005. "Social Capital, Voluntary Associations and Collective Action: Which Aspects of Social Capital Have the Greatest 'Civic' Payoff?" *Journal of Civil Society* 1, 2.

Whalley, George (ed.). 1964. *A Place of Liberty: Essays on the Government of Canadian Universities.* Toronto: Clarke Irwin.

Whitaker, Chico. 2004. "The WSF as an Open Space." In, Jai Sen, Anita Anaud, Arturo Escobar and Peter Waterman (eds.), *The World Social Forum: Challenging Empires.* New Delhi: Viveka Foundation.

Wilson-Smith, Anthony, and Edward Greenspon. 1996. *Double Vision: The Inside Story of the Liberals in Power.* Toronto: Doubleday.

Wright, Brandon. 2002. "Internet Organizing." In Mike Prokosch and Laura Raymond (eds.), *The Global Activist's Manual: Local Ways to Change the World.* New York: Nation Books.

Young, Lisa, and Joanna Everitt. 2004. *Advocacy Groups.* Vancouver: UBC Press.